# THE TEXTUAL DEVELOPMENT OF
# THE QUMRAN COMMUNITY RULE

BY

SARIANNA METSO

BRILL
LEIDEN · NEW YORK · KÖLN
1997

This book is printed on acid-free paper.

**Library of Congress Cataloging-in-Publication Data**

Metso, Sarianna.
    The textual development of the Qumran Community rule / by Sarinna
Metso.
        p.    cm. — (Studies on the texts of the desert of Judah, ISSN
0169-9962 ; v. 21)
    Includes bibliographical references and index.
    SBN 9004106839 (cloth : alk. paper)
    1. Manual of discipline—Criticism, Textual.    2. Qumran community.
I. Title.    II. Series.
BM488.M3M48      1996
296.1'55—dc20                                                    96–17974
                                                                      CIP


**Die Deutsche Bibliothek - CIP- Einheitsaufnahme**

**Metso, Sarianna:**
The textual development of the Qumran community rule / by
Sarinna Metso.  - Leiden ; New York ; Köln : Brill, 1997
    (Studies on the texts of the desert of Judah ; Vol. 21)
    ISBN 90-04-10683-9
NE: GT

ISSN   0169-9962
ISBN   90 04 10683 9

PRINTED IN THE NETHERLANDS

THE TEXTUAL DEVELOPMENT OF
THE QUMRAN COMMUNITY RULE

# STUDIES ON THE TEXTS OF THE DESERT OF JUDAH

EDITED BY

F. GARCÍA MARTÍNEZ
A. S. VAN DER WOUDE

VOLUME XXI

CONTENTS

CHAPTER II

THE LINES OF TEXTUAL TRADITION

IN THE COMMUNITY RULE

CHAPTER III
THE LITERARY DEVELOPMENT
OF THE COMMUNITY RULE

## PREFACE

In 1988-90 it was my privilege to be one of a group of undergraduate students who under the direction of Associate Professor Raija Sollamo produced a Finnish translation of the major non-biblical Dead Sea Scrolls for publication by the Helsinki University Press. Her insight and willingness to devote her time and energies to guiding her students to a greater comprehension of the principles and methods of scholarship have made an indelible impression on me, and her constant encouragement and caring support have also sustained me during my studies abroad. In this connection I should also like to thank Professor Timo Veijola for his active interest in my particular field and for the opportunity to present my work for discussion in his Old Testament postgraduate seminar in Helsinki.

I owe a great debt of gratitude to Professor Hartmut Stegemann of the University of Göttingen who made it possible for me to commence working on the then as yet unpublished material of the Community Rule in 1992. His expertise in the method of manuscript reconstruction and his instructive criticism, which in the various stages of the work compelled me to revise some of my views and argue others more carefully, induced me to extend my three months' stay in Göttingen to almost three years.

The enthusiastic atmosphere among the group of young Qumran scholars working in Göttingen has been a great pleasure to me. I should like to express my warmest thanks to Dr. Annette Steudel, who proved herself a proficient and inspiring tutor and a true friend. I am deeply grateful for the time we spent together discussing themes and questions both in and outside the field of Qumran studies.

As a member of the Göttingen team I had the opportunity to participate in three study trips to Jerusalem in the summers of 1992-94 and to meet the international community of Qumran scholars working at the École Biblique et Archéologique Française and the Rockefeller Museum. The weeks spent there were invaluable, since some parts of my work could not be undertaken anywhere else. My special thanks are due to the scholars and staff of the École Biblique and the Rockefeller Museum.

Under the terms of the Erasmus Programme I was able to benefit from the learned guidance of Professor Michael A. Knibb at King's College, London. My studies in London took place in February-July 1993 when I was still at the very beginning of the process of writing and the outline of the work was still in a state of continuous flux. Professor Knibb's acumen in the field of Qumran studies, and his critical and enlightening comments on the first drafts of this work were of great help in defining and delineating its scope and limits. He acted as my academic opponent at my doctoral disputation in Helsinki in April 1996, and he was so kind as to offer still further constructive suggestions for improvements. This volume is a slightly revised version of my doctoral dissertation. I should also like to thank Professor Geza Vermes who during my stay in England provided me with the opportunity of attending the Oxford Qumran Forum. Professor Vermes is preparing the edition of the 4QS fragments together with Professor Philip Alexander for the DJD series.

My warm thanks are due to Mr. Michael Cox, M.A., Lic.Theol., for accepting the task of revising and correcting my English. Very rarely does one have the luxury of having one's English revised by a native Englishman, who is also familiar with the Dead Sea Scrolls as well as being fluent in Finnish. His competence has been of great significance in the completion of this work.

I am very grateful to Professor Florentino García Martínez for accepting my work for publication in this series under his editorship. My thanks also go to the staff at E.J. Brill, in particular to Mr. Hans van der Meij.

I wish to express my gratitude to the Foundation of the 350th Anniversary of the University of Helsinki, Deutscher Akademischer Austauschdienst and the Finnish Academy for making this work financially possible.

I dedicate this book to my parents Leila and Aarno Metso thanking them for their loving support at every stage of this work.


Helsinki, October 1996

Sarianna Metso

# ABBREVIATIONS AND SIGLA

The abbreviations for journals, series and ancient literature follow the style recommended in the *Society of Biblical Literature Membership Directory and Handbook* 1994, 226-240. The following conventions and sigla are used in the transcription of the Hebrew texts:

| | |
|---|---|
| [  ] | Lacuna caused by physical damage to the leather |
| [כול] | Supplements to the text |
| ̊ | Undecipherable letter |
| א̊ | Letter seriously damaged; reading uncertain |
| א̇ | Letter damaged; reading substantially certain |
| <א> | Deletion by scribe |
| כֹל | Correction by scribe; insertion of interlinear letter |
| *vacat* | Uninscribed leather |

# INTRODUCTION

Along with the Damascus Document, the Community Rule (Serekh ha-yaḥad) has perhaps exercised the strongest influence on our views with regard to the Essenes. The Community Rule has been seen as a foundational document expressing the main characteristics of the teachings and practices of the Qumran community. Qumranic Hebrew has also been thought to display its most typical features in the Community Rule. Reconstructions of the history of the life of the community have been largely based on the Community Rule, but before it is possible to pose the question as to the historical reality behind the text, one needs to be acquainted with the literary process which produced the document. Only thereafter is it possible (critically) to use the text as an aid for historical reconstruction.

Redaction criticism of the Community Rule has so far been almost entirely based on the manuscript 1QS. Due to its small size the fragment of the Community Rule found in Cave 5 was of very little use for analysis of the text, and the material from Cave 4 remained inaccessible until recent years. The availability of the material of the Community Rule found in Qumran Cave 4 has now opened up a new perspective on the development of the text and makes it possible for us to test earlier theories. The purpose of this investigation is to present a literary- and redaction-critical analysis of the Community Rule on the basis of the complete material found in Qumran Caves 1, 4 and 5, and to describe the textual and redactional development of the document.

The heading סרך היחד has been preserved in two copies of the Community Rule (1QS and 4QSᵃ), and in the *verso* of the handle-sheet of the scroll containing 1QS, 1QSa and 1QSb. Although the title 'Community Rule' has established itself in the field of Qumran studies, in discussing the group of manuscripts designated with the letter S we are actually dealing with a varied collection of texts representing several literary genres, originating at different times and deriving from different sources. When discussing the Community Rule, the manuscript 1QS has generally been used as a point of reference. It must be emphasized, however, that the Community Rule is not to be identified with the manuscript 1QS, for we cannot presume that there ever existed a standardized text. For practical purposes, I have nevertheless used the manuscript 1QS as a basis for the comparison of the different copies of the Community Rule.

Because the manuscript 1QS has been published several times since its *editio princeps* by M. Burrows (1951), I consider it unnecessary to provide any new transcription of the Hebrew text of this manuscript in my thesis.

The physical characteristics of the manuscript and the latest edition of this manuscript by E. Qimron (1994) will nevertheless be dealt with and scrutinized critically. As to the material from Cave 5, I have considered it useful to provide transcriptions when discussing the variants. I have included not only fragment 5Q11, which presumably represents a genuine copy of the Community Rule, but also fragment 4 of manuscript 5Q13, a copy of a different text citing a phrase (1QS III,4-5) from the Community Rule. The transcriptions are based on the edition published by J.T. Milik in 1962, but the latest edition of 5Q11 by J.H. Charlesworth (1994), and that of 5Q13 by L.H. Schiffman (1994), have been taken into consideration.

At the time I commenced this investigation, no edition of the Cave 4 fragments was available. The transcriptions of the 4QS fragments included in this work have been prepared from the photographs distributed by the Israel Antiquities Authority and with the aid of the original fragments preserved in the Jerusalem Rockefeller Museum.[1] The work has been carried out independently from that of Qimron; only at the final stage of work have I included a discussion concerning Qimron's edition. The extremely fragmentary state of the preserved text from Cave 4 might make it very difficult for the reader to follow the text without having the lacunae filled in, so I have filled them in whenever possible, using the parallel text of 1QS. These textual reconstructions cannot very often offer more than a rough estimate; the orthographical and other peculiarities of each manuscript have not been thoroughly considered when filling in the lacunae. It is generally known that the scribes retained a certain freedom when using *plene* and *defective* forms, and the same scribe may have been very inconsistent in his use of different orthographical forms, even within a single manuscript.[2] Therefore, an accurate reconstruction is seldom possible. In the remarks attached to the transcriptions I have pointed out apparent variants included in the fragments in comparison with 1QS.

I have decided not to provide translations in connection with the transcriptions of the 4QS material. The fragments have been translated into Spanish by F. García Martínez (1992), into English by W.G.E.

---

[1] I have attempted to maintain the sigla and numeration provided by Milik 1960, 410-416. In some cases, however, this has not been possible. Some sigla have been changed by the editorial team of the Dead Sea Scrolls project, and it is the present names and sigla listed in the inventory list of the Companion Volume (Tov and Pfann 1993, 38) that are followed here. Concerning the numeration of individual fragments, there will be no standardized system as long as the DJD edition of the 4QS fragments is still awaited.

[2] See e.g. Tov 1986, 31-57 (esp. p. 36).

Watson (1994) and into German by J. Maier (1995).[3] In the later analysis of the text, however, I have deemed it useful to provide an English translation of certain Hebrew passages. In the case of 1QS, I have made use of the translations by M.A. Knibb (1QS I-IX) and A.R.C. Leaney (1QS X-XI).[4] These translations have also functioned as the basis for the translated passages of the material from Caves 4 and 5.

On the basis of the scattered fragments alone, little can be said with regard to the total composition of a manuscript or to the lacking passages. Therefore, a necessary requirement for the textual analysis is the material reconstruction of the manuscripts. I have carried it out using a method developed by H. Stegemann. The method has been described in detail in his article of 1990,[5] and it has been successfully used in the study by C. Newsom on the Songs of the Sabbath Sacrifice (11QShirShabb) and in that by A. Steudel on Midrash on Eschatology (4QMidrEschat).[6] With the aid of this method, the order of the fragments and the distance between them in the original scroll can be determined by comparing shapes and places where the fragments are damaged. All the information derived from column dividers, *vacat* lines, marks of stitching, darkened areas or even worm-holes needs to be be made use of.[7] In addition to descriptions of the physical characteristics of the fragments and of the reconstructions of the

---

[3] García Martínez 1992, 66-79 and 1994, 20-32 (English). The English translation by Watson is an adaptation of the Spanish one by García Martínez. Maier 1995, 203-214.

[4] Since English is not my mother tongue and there are several good translations available, it did not seem sensible to produce a translation of my own. Personally I prefer the translation by M. Knibb (1987, 77-144), but he has not provided any translation of columns 1QS X-XI. Therefore, in the case of the translation of columns X-XI I have made use of that by A.R.C. Leaney (1966, 233-262).

[5] Stegemann 1990, 189-220.

[6] Newsom 1985, Steudel 1994. A short summary of this method is also available in my article of 1993. The mathematical aspects of the reconstruction method have been thoroughly considered by D. Stoll 1996, 205-224.

[7] Stegemann 1990, 189-220. The method is based on the fact that "the distance between corresponding gaps or between fragments corresponding in shape increases as one moves form the inner layers of the scroll outward, and decreases as one moves inward from the exterior layers. As the circumference of the circle is $2\pi r$, the rate of this increase or decrease is arithmetic: when one shortens the radius, 'r', of a layer at a constant rate, i.e. according to the thickness of the leather or papyrus mof the scroll and the tightness of the wrap, the following layers will always be shorter, by double this rate times $\pi$ (=3.1415)" (1990, 194-195). The way the scroll was deposited in the cave - with the beginning of its text in its outer layers or in its innermost layers - can be established by observing whether the distances between the corresponding points of damage increase or decrease as one moves from right to left or vice versa. "Since there was no standard length in the scrolls, one can only state how much text has been lost between preserved fragments of a scroll and the scroll's innermost column; calculations in the other direction are not possible (1990, 201)." However, "in about half of the cases... the remains of the badly damaged scrolls come only from their middle section. Therefore, it is theoretically possible to make some estimate as to the length of the original scroll in these specific cases (1990, 201)."

scrolls, charts of the reconstructed manuscripts appear in the appendices to this thesis.

Whereas the first part of my thesis involves the description of the material of the Community Rule found in Caves 1, 4 and 5, the second and third parts present a literary- and redaction-critical analysis of the text. On the basis of the evidence presented in chapter I, an analysis of the differences between the manuscripts is to be undertaken. This analysis involves both the linguistic variants and the variants in content, and aims at distinguishing the signs of redactional activity observable in the manuscripts. The mutual relationships between the manuscript copies as well as the question as to the possible presence of more than a single textual family within the manuscript tradition will be considered in greater depth.

The third and final section of this work deals with the thematically parallel passages within the textual corpus of the Community Rule. Thus, in the evaluation of the material from Caves 1, 4 and 5 both the internal and the external evidence of the manuscripts will be discussed. The contribution of the 4QS material to our understanding of the redaction of the text will be considered against the background of earlier research based solely on the manuscript 1QS.

From the very beginning of research on the Community Rule the manuscript 1QS has been acknowledged as a collection of different texts.[8] Columns I-IV, containing a liturgical section and the doctrine of the two spirits, are very different from the regulations of columns V-VII, or from the text of columns VIII-IX, which some scholars have asserted to be the manifesto of the community. The last two columns of 1QS contain a calendrical section and a final psalm (X-XI). Detailed surveys of the history of research on the Community Rule have been provided by H. Bardtke (1974), M. Delcor (1978) and J. Murphy-O'Connor (1986).[9] Therefore, in what follows only the broad lines of discussion and the latest investigations will be dealt with. Since the complete material from Cave 4 was not available for earlier scholars studying the redaction of the Community Rule, their conclusions cannot be anything but tentative. One of the goals of the present study is to determine whether and which of the earlier studies stand the test of the evidence from Cave 4.

[8] Burrows (1950, 162) made such a remark even before the publication of his *editio princeps* of 1QS. P. Guilbert (1961, 11-12) was one scholar who suggested that the Community Rule originated from one writer, but his suggestion has not met with a favourable response.

[9] Bardtke 1974, 257-291, Delcor 1979, 851-857, 860, Murphy-O'Connor 1986, 128-129.

For a protracted period of time, the manuscript 1QS being our only source for the study of the Community Rule, the situation in Qumran scholarship was very similar to that in Old Testament studies, where the scholar is largely dependent on the internal evidence of the text. The material of the Community Rule from Cave 4 provides a unique opportunity to obtain concrete evidence of the stages of the development of a text, and thus to test more conventional methods of literary and redaction criticism.

We may now devote our attention to outlining the history of research on this subject. The manuscript 1QS, which is the best preserved copy of the Community Rule, was found in 1947 in Cave 1 among the first scrolls to be discovered and it was published four years later by Burrows.[10] Subsequently Bardtke, A.M. Habermann, J. Licht and F.M. Cross published the text of the same manuscript,[11] but Burrows' edition remained until recently the one mainly consulted, although when deciding on a suitable edition for the graphic concordance of the Qumran texts issued in 1991 by the Princeton Dead Sea Scrolls Project (ed. J.H. Charlesworth) a new transcription, prepared by Qimron in 1979, was selected.[12] In 1994 Qimron's transcription was re-published with a critical apparatus in an edition issued by the Princeton Dead Sea Scrolls Project.[13] This volume also includes a new transcription by Charlesworth of the fragment of the Community Rule found in Cave 5 (5Q11);[14] this was first published in 1962 by Milik in the series *Discoveries in the Judaean Desert of Jordan.*[15]

As early as 1956 Milik issued a brief report on the fragments of the Rule of the Community found in Cave 4.[16] More information concerning the contents of the fragments was given four years later when Milik listed variants of the 4QS manuscripts in a book-review of the monograph by P. Wernberg-Moeller.[17] Milik identified ten fragmentary manuscripts of the Community Rule using the sigla 4QSa-j. In an article published in 1972 Milik stated as his preliminary view that the oldest form of the Community Rule comprised more or less the material of 1QS V,1-IX,11, and that it was composed perhaps by the Teacher of Righteousness himself

---

[10] Burrows 1951.
[11] Bardtke 1954, 37-48, Habermann 1959, 51-70, Licht 1965, Cross et al. 1972, 127-147. The vocalized edition by E. Lohse (1986, 1-43) may also be mentioned in this connection.
[12] Qimron 1979, 112-132, Charlesworth 1991.
[13] Qimron-Charlesworth-Cross 1994, 53-104.
[14] Charlesworth 1994.
[15] Milik 1962, 180-181. The fragment gives parallels to 1QS II,4-7 and II,12-14.
[16] Milik 1956, 60-61.
[17] Milik 1960, 410-416.

at the beginning of his ministry in 150-145 B.C. Later redactors inserted extensive passages at the beginning and end of the document. The second stage of the redaction, he argued, consisted of 1QS I,16-III,12.[18]

For a long time Milik's list of variants was the main source for scholars studying the 4QS fragments. In 1977 he published a transcription of one 4QSᵇ fragment with a tabular reconstruction of the same manuscript (the present siglum is 4QSᵈ),[19] but since 1977 Milik has published nothing relating to 4QS fragments. Now the preparation of the edition of 4QSᵃ⁻ʲ for the series *Discoveries in the Judaean Desert of Jordan* has been entrusted to G. Vermes and P.S. Alexander. At the beginning of 1991 Vermes published an article about the 4QSᵇ,ᵈ-parallels to 1QS V.[20] In the same year Qimron published two columns of the manuscript 4QSᵈ providing parallels to 1QS VIII,24-IX,10 and IX,15-X,2.[21] In the Princeton Dead Sea Scrolls volume published in 1994 Qimron provided transcriptions of almost all the fragments of the Community Rule found in Cave 4.[22] Since the publication of the Brill microfiche edition edited by E. Tov (1992), study of the as yet unpublished material has been possible for some four years now. The Israel Antiquities Authority has also facilitated free access to the scrolls for all scholars.

Apart from the daring attempt of H.E. Del Medico (1951) to demonstrate the existence of five distinct sources within the material of 1QS broken up into thirty fragments, and to restore their original order without any proper analysis of the text,[23] very little attention was paid in the 1950s to the literary-critical problems of the Community Rule. Although several scholars made vague remarks concerning the composite character of the manuscript, there was no attempt at a thoroughgoing literary-critical analysis of the text.[24] Studies of isolated sections appeared, however. J. Licht suggested in 1958 that 1QS III,13-IV,26 (the doctrine of

---

[18] Milik 1972, 135.

[19] Milik 1977, 75-81.

[20] Vermes 1991, 250-255.

[21] Qimron 1991, 434-443.

[22] Qimron-Charlesworth-Cross 1994, 53-103. In the same edition, F.M. Cross presents a list of paleographical dates of the 4QS manuscripts (p. 57). See the important review of Qimron's edition by F. García Martínez (1996, 47-56). García Martínez correctly points out that some fragments belonging to the 4QS material are not included in Qimron's edition. He also discusses some readings which he considers problematical in Qimron's edition. I should also like to mention the recent edition by C. Martone, *La "Regola della Comunità" : Edizione critica* (1995) based on all manuscripts of the Community Rule from Caves 1, 4 and 5. Unfortunately it came to my hands too late to be commented upon further here.

[23] Del Medico 1951, 27-30. See also 1957, 160.

[24] Dupont-Sommer 1953, 90, Wernberg-Moeller 1957, 56 n. 49, K.G. Kuhn 1960, 652, Maier 1960 I, 21.

the two spirits) had been created following a chiastic pattern,[25] and this view remained unchallenged for more than ten years.[26] E.F. Sutcliffe (1959) studied 1QS VIII-IX and claimed that in these columns the words בהיות אלה בישראל "When these exist in Israel" (VIII,4,12; IX,3) refer to the future, to a community which was soon to be established, and they reflect a viewpoint which does not occur elsewhere in the Rule. Sutcliffe argued that the columns 1QS VIII-IX represent the oldest material in the Community Rule.[27] This idea of Sutcliffe was of major importance for some of the later theories concerning the redaction of the document.

In the late 1950, two significant studies on the scribal character of 1QS were also published. Independently from each other, M. Martin (1958) and P. Guilbert (1958) distinguished the typical features of the two hands occurring in 1QS VII-VIII and separated the work of scribe A from that of scribe B.[28] Martin argued that scribe B had used a revisor exemplar while revising the text.[29] Guilbert suggested that most of the additions and corrections made by scribe B were made without the aid of another manuscript, which was perhaps better preserved than the *Vorlage* used by scribe A. According to Guilbert, scribe B had interpreted the text in a rather personal way, since it seemed to him in some places difficult to decipher and insufficiently intelligible. The work of two scribes has been further analysed by E. Puech (1979). As was not the case with Martin and Guilbert, Puech was able to make use of the list of 4QS variants which had meanwhile been published by Milik (1960). Puech came to a conclusion very similar to that of Martin: at least some of the corrections in column VII were based on another manuscript, which, in Puech's view, was perhaps 4QSe. Although he admits that some of the additions made by B are not included in 4QSe, he argues that they may have been present in some other manuscript more contemporary with 1QS.[30]

In publications that appeared in 1964, the approach of A.-M. Denis and H. Becker in discerning interpolations within the Community Rule was far more cautious than that of Del Medico. Denis saw the text as divided into three sections by the insertion of two passages before the final psalm: the

---

[25] Licht 1958, 88-99. The theory of the chiastic structure of 1QS III,13-IV,26 and thus of the literary unity of the section was accepted by e.g. Guilbert 1959, 328 and Leaney 1966, 145-146.

[26] Licht's theory was rejected by von der Osten-Sacken (1969, 17-18) who demonstrated the existence of three literary levels in 1QS III,13-IV,26.

[27] Sutcliffe 1959, 134-138.

[28] Guilbert 1958, 199-212, Martin 1958, 439-442.

[29] Martin (1958, 447-448) claimed moreover that after the revision made by scribe B, scribe A returned to the text and further corrected it.

[30] Puech 1979, 35-43.

doctrine of the two spirits (III,13-IV,26) and the penal code (VI,24-VII,25).
Within the remaining sections (general introduction and ritual of entry I-
III,12, rules for entry and for organisation V-VI, plan of the community
and rule for the Maskil VIII-IX) he separated sections V,13-20 (the law of
impurity), V,23-VI,13 (rules for internal organisation), VIII,10b-12 (the
law of silence) and VIII,16-IX,2 (the small code) as interpolations.[31] As
distinct from Denis, Becker argued that VIII,4-19 formed an insertion (he
saw VIII,20-IX,2 as a unity), and because of the discrepancy between IX,7
ff. and VI,24 he considered IX,7 ff. to be an addition. He regarded V,20-25
and VI,13-23 as parallel passages representing two different stages in the
development of the community.[32]

Questions regarding the cult of the community were the subject of
studies by M. Weise (1961), H.-W. Kuhn (1966) and G. Klinzing (1971).
Weise provided a thorough investigation of the festival calendar (1QS
IX,26-X,8) and the covenant ceremony (1QS I,18-II,18).[33] Linking the
columns at the beginning and at the end of the manuscript raised the issue
as to whether the *Sitz im Leben* of the final psalm could have been that of
the renewal of the covenant.[34] Kuhn, although admitting the connection
between the sections, argued that the context of the final psalm might not
necessarily have been the renewal of the covenant, for the covenant songs
may have become part of the community's daily times of prayer.[35]
Klinzing carried out a detailed investigation of 1QS VIII,1-IX,11 (die
Gemeinde als Tempel) which, in his opinion, is the most incoherent section
within the Community Rule and forms a closing passage for the
regulations of the community of 1QS V-VII.[36]

---

[31] Denis 1964, 34-47.

[32] Becker 1964, 39-42.

[33] Weise 1961.

[34] Weise pointed out terminological connections between the covenant ceremony and the
final psalm (e.g. pp. 79 n. 2, 85, 89 n. 2). His observations were utilized by e.g. Murphy-
O'Connor (1969, 544) and Pouilly (1976, 81) who maintained that the Sitz im Leben of the
final psalm was the same as 1QS I,16-II,25a.

[35] H.-W. Kuhn 1966, 31-32: "Andererseits ist nun aber doch mit der Möglichkeit zu
rechnen, dass die gegenüber den atl. Psalmen neue Form der essenischen Bekenntnislieder, die
die Gemeinde wahrscheinlich im Zusammenhang ihres Bundesfestes fand, auch in die
täglichen Gebetszeiten übernommen wurde, so dass man von einer Erweiterung des "Sitzes im
Leben" zu sprechen hätte" (p. 32). The studies of both Weise and Kuhn were influenced by the
analysis of G. Jeremias (1963) on 'the songs of the Teacher' and 'songs of the community'. In
discussing the covenant ceremony, the study of K. Baltzer (1960, 105-115) also calls for
mention.

[36] Klinzing (1971, 50-66) also referred to the evidence of Cave 4 (Milik's list of 4QS
variants) in giving the reasons for his view. Interestingly, Klinzing saw connections between
some sections of columns V and VIII-IX. See Murphy-O'Connor's recension of Klinzing
(1972, 215-244).

The view of Sutcliffe, that 1QS VIII-IX represented the oldest material in the Community Rule, was adopted by Leaney in his commentary (1966),[37] and Leaney dated the material to the period c. 130 B.C. He also suggested that the section V,1-VI,23 (though composite) may originate from the time before the withdrawal into the desert. Leaney attributed the final section X,1-XI,22 to the Teacher of Righteousness and dated it to about 110 BC. Sutcliffe's idea gained more support in the theory of Murphy-O'Connor which, to his mind, was "the first attempt to construct a comprehensive hypothesis to explain the composition of 1QS." He argued that it is "a three-stage development from the Manifesto (VIII,1-16; IX,3-X,8), in which the Teacher of Righteousness proposed to move to Qumran. Penal legislation for a small community (VIII,16-IX,2) was later added. Subsequently, the community redefined itself (V,1-13) and enacted more elaborate legislation (V,15-VII,25). Finally, material from various sources was combined to form an exhortation to authentic observance (I,1-IV,26; X,9-XI,22)." Murphy-O'Connor also suggested that the literary stages of the text correspond with the archaeological phases of the site of Khirbet Qumran.[38] The theory of Murphy-O'Connor was evaluated and further developed by J. Pouilly. He agrees substantially with Murphy-O'Connor, but assigns VIII,10-12 to stage two, and V,13-VI,8 to stage four.[39]

Many of the scholars who acknowledge the existence of the Manifesto doubt the possibility of dividing the textual process into four precise stages and assigning to them phases of occupation of the Qumran site.[40] Puech (1979 and 1993), for example, suggests that the text evolved in three stages instead of four, the first one being constituted by parts of columns VIII-IX (le noyau de fondation), the second by columns V-VII (motivations d'entrée dans la communauté et le code penitentiel) with the exception of some additions, and the third stage by columns I-IV (composition liturgique et doctrinale) and IX-XI (considérations pour l'instructeur et hymnes).[41] P. Arata Mantovani (1983) also presupposes three stages in the development of the text, but he divides them somewhat differently: VIII,1-IX,26 (tradizione A), V,1-13a. 15b-VII,25 (tradizione B), I-IV; V,13b-15a;

---

[37] Leaney 1966, 112, 115, 211, and subsequently Murphy-O'Connor 1969, 529, Pouilly 1976, 15, Puech 1979, 106-107, Dohmen 1982, 81-86, Knibb 1987, 129.

[38] Murphy-O'Connor 1969, 528-549 and 1986, 129.

[39] Pouilly 1976.

[40] See e.g. Delcor 1979, 852-854 and Knibb 1987, 77-78.

[41] Puech 1979, 103-111 and 1993, 421-422, "Cette troisième étape n'est pas nécessairement de rédaction postérieure à la deuxième, mais son adjonction au rouleau est postérieure; cela est clair pour les col. i-iv, plus difficilement démontrable pour les col. ix 12 - xi" (p. 422).

X,4b.6a.9-XI,22 (tradizione C).[42] C. Dohmen (1982), on the other hand, found three different stages of development in columns VIII-IX alone: 1) VIII,1-7a+12b-15a+IX,16b-21a (das Manifest), 2) VIII,7b-12a/IX,12-16a+IX,21b-26 (die Erweiterung des Manifestes), 3) IX,3-11+VIII,15b-19/VIII,20-IX,2 (die "erste Regel" und ihre Erweiterung).[43]

D. Dimant rejects the idea of textual stages reflecting the different life-situations in the community. She points to the "apparent doublets" within the composition and proposes that the redactor(s) followed a chiastic pattern in arranging the material.

*Introduction - general aims, 1:1-15*
Entrance into the covenant, 1:16-3:12
Ideology - to the *Maskil*, 3:13-4:26
The life of the community, 5:1-6:23
The penal code, 6:24-7:25
The model community, 8:1-9:11
Instructions - to the *Maskil*, 9:12-26
Hymns, 10:1-11:22

"In the context of chiasm," she says, "the parallelisms appear to have a literary-ideological significance."[44] Dimant's theory has been commented upon by Puech, who sees the chiastic pattern as not so apparent in all parts of the text, especially in III,13-IV,26 and IX,12-26. He points out that 4QS$^d$ has preserved what remains of 1QS I-II, V-VI and IX-XI, and addresses the text in the parallel of 1QS V,1 to the *maskil* (4QS$^d$ 2 I) and not to the men of the community.[45]

Stegemann argues in his recent monograph (1993) that the scroll of 1QS, 1QSa and 1QSb consists of *four* different community rules (Gemeindeordnungen), the first being 1QS I,1-III,12 (die Gemeinschafts-ordnung), the second 1QS V,1-XI,22 (die Disziplinarordnung), the third 1QSa (die älteste Gemeindeordnung der Essener), and the fourth 1QSb (die Segensordnung).[46] He considers the doctrine of the two spirits to be an appendix to 1QS I,1-III,12 (Gemeinschaftsordnung), which in his opinion is agenda-like in the strictest sense. 'Die Disziplinarordnung,'[47] he thinks,

---

[42] Arata Mantovani 1983, 69-91.

[43] Dohmen 1982, 81-96.

[44] Dimant 1984, 501-502. See also her criticism of Murphy-O'Connor in n. 92, p. 502.

[45] Puech 1993, 422 n. 3.

[46] Stegemann 1993, 152-164.

[47] Stegemann (1993, 156) argues that during the time of 'Disziplinarordnung', the older legal corpora of the pre-Essene communities were still recognised as unchanged and legal. Stegemann refers to 1QS IX,10 ff. and says that to these older legal corpora belonged, for example, Sabbath regulations and a festival calendar, regulations for cultic purity, marriage, inheritance, land-ownership and tithes. Stegemann asserts that all this was already satisfactorily regulated in pre-Essene communities and needed no re-enacting. He sees this as

is a collection of organizational regulations developed successively in the first decades of the Essenes' *yaḥad*. Stegemann refers to the earlier versions of the text found in Cave 4 and maintains that the text in 1QS V,1-XI,22 represents the latest phase of the development of this rule.[48]

The relevance of the fragments found in Cave 4 for the redaction criticism of the Community Rule has so far been touched upon only in occasional comments. No comprehensive or detailed study of the entire document has yet been provided. In this work the present writer intends to take this step and to investigate the complete material of the Community Rule found in Caves 1, 4 and 5 in order to create an overall picture of the textual and redactional development of the Community Rule.

---

the reason why all these items are missing in 1QS V,1-XI,22, which in his view is essentially limited to new regulations concerning organization and discipline.

[48] Stegemann (1993, 157,159) explicitly mentions 4QS[e] as a version which still lacks passages present in the later versions of the 'Disziplinarordnung'. On p. 156 he is apparently referring to 4QS[b,d]: "Schon der Textbeginn in 1QS V,1 ist gegenüber der ursprünglichen Fassung abgewandelt..."

CHAPTER ONE

MATERIAL OF THE COMMUNITY RULE
FROM QUMRAN CAVES 1, 4 AND 5

*1. Manuscript 1QS*

*1.1. The Scroll of 1QS, 1QSa and 1QSb (1Q28, 1Q28a and 1Q28b)*

Manuscript 1QS is the best preserved of all the copies of the Community
Rule, and it provides the most important parallel text for analyzing the
4QS fragments.[1] Manuscript 1QS consists of five leather sheets stitched
together, and they contain eleven columns, each of which has
approximately 26 lines. The first sheet contains columns I-III, the second
columns IV-V, the third sheet columns VI-VII, the fourth columns VIII-X,
and the fifth column XI alone (the following text of 1QSa begins with a
new sheet). The length of manuscript 1QS is approximately 187 cm. The
manuscript has only a few gaps, and they are located in the lower edges of
columns, but there are many textual errors, corrections, glosses and marks
in the margins, especially in columns VII and VIII.

Two other documents, the Rule of the Congregation (1QSa) and Words
of Blessing (1QSb), were copied on the same scroll by the same scribe.
These manuscripts have been preserved only fragmentarily, for they were
written on the outer layers of the scroll. Since the scroll was rolled with the
beginning of the text in the inner layers, it is impossible to say from the
point of view of the material evidence whether the scroll consisted of more
than the eighteen columns which have been preserved.[2] The length of the
preserved parts of the scroll is about three metres. The scroll of 1QS, 1QSa

---

[1] Material comparable to the Community Rule can be found in the Damascus Document
and fragments of it from Caves 4, 5 and 6, in 4QOrdinances[a-c] (4Q159, 4Q513, 4Q514),
4QSerek Dameseq (4Q265), 4QDecrees (4Q477) and also in as yet unpublished fragments of
4QLeqet (4Q284a), 4QCommunal Ceremony (4Q275; formerly 4QS[x]) and 4QOrder of the
Community (4Q279; formerly 4QS[y]). The 4QD fragments are being edited by J.M.
Baumgarten in the DJD series. See the preliminary publication of 4QD, 5QD and 6QD by
Baumgarten and M.T.Davis in the series of the Princeton Theological Seminary Dead Sea
Scrolls Project (1995, 59-79). The fragments of 4QOrd[a-c] are included in DJD V and VII. Part
of 4QSD has been published by Baumgarten in his article of 1994 (pp. 3-10), and 4QDecrees
has also been published in a separate article by E. Eshel (1994, 111-122).
[2] The contents of the text of 1QSb indicate, however, that at least one further column must
have followed column V of 1QSb.

and 1QSb has been dated on palaeographical grounds to 100-75 B.C., and recent radio-carbon tests confirm this dating.[3]

On the *verso* of the handle sheet belonging to the beginning of 1QS, there is a line written vertically across the scroll. This line contained the title of the scroll. Eight letters are preserved, and the first word can easily be completed: סר]ך היחד ומן|. The words סרך היחד presumably refer to the text of 1QS I-XI, whereas ומן should probably be understood as commencing that part of the title which referred to 1QSa and 1QSb. Manuscripts 4QSª and 4QSᶜ have partly preserved the same title as 1QS, and they also indicate that the word ומן did not belong to the title of this document.[4]

## 1.2. The Scribal Structure of 1QS

The scribe(s) of 1QS used two basic techniques for indicating sections within the text: unwritten spaces (*vacats*) and marks in the margin. A *vacat* very often appears in connection with an introductory formula: 1QS II,19, III,13, IV,2,15, V,1, VI,8,24, VIII,12,20, IX,3,12,21.[5] But a *vacat* can also precede a smaller break in the text: I,21, II,4,11,19, IV,6,9, V,13,25, VI,10, VIII,16.

A *vacat* does not always signify the beginning of a new section. Presumably the *Vorlage* which the copyist of 1QS was using was in some places so poorly preserved that he was unable to read it properly. *Vacat*s

---

[3] On the palaeographical dating of 1QS, see Cross 1958, 58 and Avigad 1965, 71. The radio-carbon tests are reported in Bonani et al. 1991, 27-32 and Jull et al. 1995, 11-19.

[4] Milik 1955, 107 and plate XXII. Stegemann (1993, 152-159) is of the opinion that סרך היחד refers to 1QS I,1-III,12 only, and that 1QS I,1-III,12 (die Gemeinschaftsordnung), 1QS III,13-IV,26 (die Zwei-Geister-Lehre) and 1QS V,1-XI,22 (die Disziplinarordnung) form three independent works and can be compared with 1QSa and 1QSb. Stegemann points out that 1QS should be seen as a collection of different texts (Schriftensammlung, see 1988, 98). Now, although it is clear that sections 1QS I,1-III,12, III,13-IV,26 and V,1-XI,22 originally existed independently (see below the evidence of the material from Cave 4), it seems to me that in manuscript 1QS they were meant to belong together, for the text of 1QSa has been clearly separated from 1QS by leaving the rest of column 1QS XI empty. Also, the rest of column 1QSa II preceding the manuscript 1QSb has been left unwritten. If the scribe had intended to start a new text after 1QS I,1-III,12, he would have commenced the doctrine of the two spirits (1QS III,13-IV,26) with a new column and not continued writing in the same column. Since the text of 1QS I-XI appears to form a unit separable from 1QSa and 1QSb in the scroll, I consider it more likely that the words סרך היחד refer to the whole of the text of 1QS I-XI, and ומן commences the part of the title which refers to the texts of 1QSa and 1QSb. It can also be noted that no manuscript containing only the text parallel to 1QS I,1-III,12 has been found at Qumran, while 4QSᵇ is another example of a manuscript including the same sections as 1QS. For the use of the preposition מן in a title, cf. 4QMidrEschat III,14.

[5] 1QS II,19 ...כה, III,13 למשכיל, IV,2 ואלה דרכיהן בתבל, IV,15 ...באלה, V,1 וזה הסרך לאנשי, ובהיות אלה VIII,12 ואל⁻ המשפטים אשר ישפטו בם במדרש יחד VI,24, הזה הסרך למושב הרבים VI,8, היחד, אלה החוקים למשכיל IX,12, ובהיות אלה בישראל IX,3, ואלה המשפטים אשר ילכו בם VIII,20, ⁻ליחד בישראל, ואלה תכוני הדרך למשכיל IX,21.

due to the poor condition of the *Vorlage* occur especially in columns VII and VIII. Some of these *vacat*s were later filled in by the second scribe, but by omitting some of the words written by the first scribe he also created further *vacat*s in the text. In column VII (after line 7) there is an unusually large *vacat* of nearly three lines, but it was caused by a defect in the leather,[6] as also in the case of VI,10, IX,9,14 and 16.

The manuscript has two kinds of marks in the margin.[7] Small hooks similar to cryptic *ayin*[8] appear most frequently beside *vacat*s (I,20, II,10,18, III,12, IV,1,8,14, V,13,25, VI,8,23, VIII,12,19, IX,11,22) and elsewhere too to mark the end of a section or of an important sentence (1QS III,18, VIII,4,10, IX,5,19, XI,15).[9] Unusually large signs, which are composed of palaeo-Hebrew letters,[10] were drawn in the margins in V,1, VII,25 and IX,3 to mark sections of particular importance.[11]

## 1.3. The Recent Edition of 1QS

In comparison with the *editio princeps* of 1QS published by Burrows in 1951, the new transcription published by Qimron in 1994 clearly provides

---

[6] The break in the leather is due to a bone. The hole it caused in the leather can be seen in the margin at the level of lines 10-11. A similar kind of defect can also be seen in 1QIsa[a] XV,21-24.

[7] It is unclear whether the marks in the margin were written by the first scribe or by another scribe later.

[8] I should like to thank Stephen Pfann for sharing this information in a personal communication.

[9] The small hooks are never at the beginning of a new section, but always at the end, see e.g. the last lines of 1QS (XI,22) and 1QSa (II,22). They are marked below the line, even when a new section starts on the same line, see e.g. 1QS III,18, V,13,25.

[10] According to Tov (1995, 330-339), the sign in 1QS V,1 is a paleo-Hebrew *waw*, that in 1QS VII,25 is "composed of a paleo-Hebrew *zayin* with an ornamental line on top (similar to 1QIsa[a] XXII,10 [fig. 2.1]) and a triangular form below" (p. 336). In n. 14 Tov refers to E.Puech ("Une Apocalypse Messianique (4Q521)", RevQ 60 (1992), pp. 475-519) who "explains the triangular forms as *ayin* and the two signs together as (זה/ה(עו/ד)." The sign in 1QS IX,3 is a combination of *paragraphos* sign, paleo-Hebrew *zayin* and paleo-Hebrew *samekh* (Tov 1995, 336).

[11] The signs in V,1 point to the beginning of the set of regulations for community life, and the sign at the end of column VII presumably marks the end of this section, for the next column begins a unit very different from the one of the two preceding columns. Tov (see the bibl. ref. in the previous note) finds it likely, as well, that the sign in 1QS VII,25 signifies the end of a section. An alternative view has been proposed by H. Stegemann (in a personal consultation). He is of the opinion that the sign of VII,25 marks the beginning of a new unit like those in 1QS V,1 and IX,3. He presumes that this unit started with the word ויהי at the end of col. VII (the word is not preserved, but Stegemann reconstructs it as the last word of the lacuna at the end of the column). There is no doubt that the sign in IX,3 marks the beginning of the third of the sections starting with the formula בהיות אלה בישראל .

the reader with more information about the manuscript.[12] For instance, whereas Burrows makes no difference between more and less certain readings, Qimron has indicated the degree of probability in his transcriptions.[13] Qimron has also taken into consideration the specific palaeographical features due to the scribe, such as using medial letters in final positions.[14] Erasures of letters and words made by the scribe(s) are marked in Qimron's transcription, and in some places Qimron has been able to identify the erased letters.[15] Close to lacunae, especially, Qimron has often been able to retrace a greater amount of text than has Burrows, and Qimron has also made suggestions as to reconstructing the text.[16] In footnotes Qimron has pointed out corrections and additions made by the scribe(s).[17]

Because there is no visible difference between *waw* and *yod* in the manuscript,[18] most of the differences between the editions involve these letters. Different readings of any other type are far less numerous.[19] For some readings Qimron has given a reference to a parallel manuscript in footnotes, and some of the readings appear to have been commented upon in Qimron's Qumran Hebrew grammar.[20] Some of the differences, however,

---

[12] F.García Martinéz (1996, 47-50) also provides a comparison with the edition of Licht (1965) in his recently published recension of Qimron's edition. García Martínez writes: "Par rapport à l'édition de Licht, il y a donc des progrès dans l'édition de Qimron, mais un progrès assez limité en fin de compte" (p. 50).

[13] Using points and rings to indicate the certainty of a reading is a common usage in the Dead Sea Scrolls editions, but in addition to these marks Qimron also uses vertical strokes above letters. The meaning of these strokes is explained nowhere in Qimron's edition.

[14] Especially in cases of *kaph* it is often difficult to judge between medial and final letters. Compare, for instance, the following transcriptions of *kaph* in Qimron's edition with the original manuscript: II,17 בדך, but II,13 יתברכ; III,21 ובמלאך, but חושכ two words earlier; VI,6 להברכ, but VI,5 להברך; VI,22 בסרך, but בדכ in the same line.

[15] In most cases Qimron agrees with Martin 1958, 431-448. See, however, VII,20 Qimron (במהרה) in agreement with Milik 1951, 148, n. 2, Martin במשב, Wernberg-Moeller 1957, 42 בבאיר; X,8 Qimron (אושא), Martin אני, and X,19 Qimron (א(טוֹֿ פֿאֿףֿ לֿשֿבֿֿי; Martin refers to Wernberg-Moeller אפיא באף לשבי. Qimron has two readings which to my understanding have not been listed before: VIII,5 (ל) at the beginning of the *vacat*, and VIII,10 (בֿהֿמֿֿה הֿלֿך).

[16] Contrary to Burrows, Qimron has of course been able to use the parallel material found in Cave 4.

[17] Qimron does not often state, however, whether he thinks the corrections and additions were made by the first or by the second scribe.

[18] Despite Wernberg-Moeller 1960, 223-236.

[19] IV,1 (B: עדי, Q: מו|עדי), IV,12 (B: נקמה, Q: נקמה see footnote), V,20 (B: הונם, Q: הֿוֿנֿֿם), VII,8 (B: יטי, Q: () יֿטֿי), VII,19 (B: ולוא, Q: ()לוא), VII,23 (B: לפני, Q: מלפי), X,4 (B: הם, Q: יֿוֿֿם), XI,21 (B: סרורו, Q: מדורו see footnote), XI,21 (B: מצור רק, Q: מצידוק see footnote).

[20] For למשב (B: למשב) in III,1, במהר (B: במהיר) in III,3, and נגעיהם (B: נגיעיהם) in III,14,23 and IV,12 see Qimron 1986, 111; for מלאה (B: מילאה) in VI,17,21 and VIII,26 see ibid., pp. 110 and 117; for רנליהו (B: רנליהו) in VI,13 and לפיהו (B: לפיהו) in VI,26 see ibid., p. 61; for במרם (B: במרים) in VII,5 see ibid., p. 110. See also Qimron's article of 1990, 128-131.

remain difficult to explain and might have deserved a comment in the edition.[21]

Although Qimron's edition is more accurate than Burrows' in reading not only the text but also other marks made by the scribes, it sometimes lacks consistency: Qimron has marked only some of the separating marks supplied by scribes in the margin, the small hooks, but ignored the larger marks in the margin in V,1, VII,25 and IX,3. The word and line distances as well as *vacat*s do not always correspond to the manuscript,[22] and the placing of some of the supralinear corrections is not quite accurate.[23] The transcription prepared by Qimron and the translation by Charlesworth do not always match.[24]

---

[21] At least the following readings can be questioned: (1) Qimron reads הפקד instead of הפקיד in VI,14 although the latter form appears as a similar kind of *terminus technicus* in the Old Testament (Jer 20:1; 29:26; 2 Chr 31:13; Neh 11:14,22; 12:42; 2 Chr 24:11) and in other Qumranic writings (4QBer[d] !,4; 4QMyst 57,2; 4QSap.Work A b 5,1, readings from the 'Preliminary Concordance'). (2) In I,8, V,20 and IX,6 Qimron has להיהד instead of להדר (Burrows). Qimron states in his Grammar (1986, 55) that the form represents a hithpa'el form which has assimilated its *taw* to *yod*. I find the assimilation less probable here and I prefer to read reflexive niph'al. In V,14, on the other hand, Qimron reads Qal ייחד instead of niph'al יחד (Burrows). In Qumran Hebrew, however, *primae yod* verbs do not occur with a double *yod* in the Qal imperfect, whereas cases with one *yod* are very common. (3) Qimron prefers Qal perfect ודבק to jussive ידבק (Burrows) in II,15. In the context of the curse in II,15-16, there are three sentences expressing a wish (jussive forms יבערו...ידבק...ויבדילהו), whereas the fourth sentence reveals the outcome of the curse (consecutive perfect ונכרת) and, therefore, uses a consecutive perfect form. Use of the consecutive perfect form in connection with the verb נכרה is prominent in the Old Testament, see e.g. Exod 30:33,38; Lev 17:4,9; Ex 12:15,19; Lev 7:20,21,27; Num 15:30. (4) Qimron suggests Aramaic suffixes in VI,13 רגלוהי and VI,26 לפנוהי (Burrows רגליהו and לפניה), although the use of *-éhu* beside *-âw* is by no means exceptional in Hebrew, cf. נבוליהו in Nah 2:4 instead of the more common נבוליו.

[22] Contrary to Burrows' opinion, Qimron also recognizes *vacat*s in VI,10, VII,2,3,13,14, VIII,16,18, X,2. In some of these cases the difference as to normal word space is so minute that it is difficult to judge whether the scribe really intended to leave a *vacat* in the manuscript. For example, I can see no difference in word space between אל and היחד in VI,10 in comparison with the word spaces between the words איש אשר יש in VI,12, but in the first case Qimron sees a *vacat*. On the other hand, there is no difference in size between the *vacat*s in VIII,16 and 18 in the manuscript, but in Qimron's transcription the *vacat* in VIII,16 is hardly recognizable (the *vacat* in VIII,18 has been marked clearly in the transcription). In X,7 Qimron reads a normal word space between לקץ and ומעד, while Burrows has a *vacat* there. Qimron ignores the unusually wide line spaces in VII,7-8 and IX,11-12. He also leaves a normal word space even when one is missing in the manuscript, see, e.g. מאחריאל in II,17, לפירחותם in II.20, רעהוילון in VII,17, עלדבריו in VII,21.

[23] Compare the manuscript and the transcription of the supralinear words and letters in II,13, III,2, VI,17, VII,22, VIII,5,11,13.

[24] See, for example, VII,11 where Qimron transcribes ותם, but Charlesworth translates 'falls asleep' according to Burrows' transcription והנם, and XI,3 where Qimron transcribes אורי, but Charlesworth translates 'his light' following Burrows' transcription אורו.

## 2. Manuscripts 4QS<sup>a-j</sup>

### 2.1. 4QS<sup>a</sup> (4Q255)

#### 2.1.1. Description of the Fragments

The papyrus manuscript 4QS<sup>a</sup>, which was written on the *recto* of the text of 4Qpseudo-Hodayot,[25] has been preserved in four fragments. The hand of 4QS<sup>a</sup> is very irregular and the distance between lines varies greatly. In fragment 1 the distance is 0.8 - 1.1 cm. At its shortest the distance between lines is 0.5 cm in the middle of fragment 2 between lines 6 and 7.

Fragment 1 (7.6 cm x 6.8 cm) has preserved parts of six lines from the upper left-hand corner of column I. These lines are parallel to 1QS I,1-5 and partly fill the gap at the beginning of 1QS.

Fragment 2 is the largest (11.5 cm x 9.2 cm) with nine almost complete lines from the upper right-hand corner of a column. There were about seven words per line and from the ends of the lines only about a word and a half are missing. The fragment provides a parallel to 1QS III,7-12.

Fragment 3 (6.9 cm x 7.6 cm) is a piece from a lower left-hand corner.[26] There is no direct parallel in 1QS to the five lines of this fragment, but the vocabulary is similar to the doctrine of the two spirits (1QS III,13-IV,26). There is a slight possibility that fragment 3 forms a loose parallel to 1QS III,20-25.[27]

Fragment 4 (2.6 cm x 4.3 cm) has preserved only a few letters from the right edge of a column, but no recognizable word or part of a word which could help to identify the fragment.[28]

Compared to 4QS<sup>a</sup>, the copyist of 1QS uses *plene* writing more frequently, especially in presenting *holem*. An even more striking orthographical feature is that the copyist of 4QS<sup>a</sup> does not use final *kaph* but writes כ in the final position, too (frg. 1 l. 1 and frg. 3 l. 5). According to Cross, this manuscript, written in a crude cursive script, dates from the

---

[25] The text of 4QpseudoHodayot (4Q433a) is as yet unpublished. It is to be edited by E.Schuller.

[26] In Rockefeller Museum plate 177 the fragment has broken into two pieces, but in PAM 43.254 one can still see the fibre connecting them.

[27] Cf. esp. דרכי אור 1QS III,20, בני אור l. 24, בני אור and אור וחושך l. 25.

[28] Fragments 3 and 4 are missing in Charlesworth's list of Cave 4 fragments (1994, 55), and Qimron has not provided any transcriptions regarding these fragments. There is no doubt, however, that these fragments belong to the same manuscript as fragments 1 and 2.

second half of the second century B.C., probably from the end of the century.[29]

## 2.1.2. The Problem of Reconstruction

Although the preserved fragments of 4QSa are relatively large, they are unfortunately not numerous enough to enable us to determine the original measurements of the scroll. The fragments are also very different in shape, which makes it difficult to recognize any places where the fragments show signs of similar damage, indicating that they were located one on top of the other in the original scroll. A special problem regarding the reconstruction of papyri is caused by the fact that when papyrus deteriorates, the humidity usually splits the material instead of gradually eroding it as it does in the case of leather. The patterns in fragments which were situated over one another in a leather scroll are often almost identical, whereas the fragments which were placed one over another in a papyrus scroll usually show much greater variation in shape.

In the case of 4QSa, the physical characteristics of the fragments only provide a little information for the reconstruction, and the parallel text of 1QS does not take us very much further. The text on the other side (PseudoHodayot), which in principle could be used as an aid in the reconstruction, does not solve the problems here, either. Only a few aspects can be considered here: each of fragments 1,2 and 3 most likely belonged in separate columns. Fragments 1 and 2 could not have been very close to each other in the scroll, since both of them have preserved upper margins, and whereas the former provides a parallel to 1QS I,1-5, the latter is a parallel to 1QS III,7-12. In the case of fragments 2 and 3, the text of 1QS does not help us to determine the distance between the fragments, because there is no direct parallel to fragment 3. It seems, however, that fragment 3 did not belong to the same column along with fragment 2. Fragment 3 has preserved a column divider on the left-hand side; the shape of the edge corresponds with the left-hand-side edge of fragment 2. This left-hand-side edge of fragment 2 does not reach the margin, however, but breaks down in the middle of lines, which indicates that the fragments could not have belonged in the same column. If fragment 3 really forms a loose parallel to 1QS III,20-25, it probably belonged to the column on the left-hand side of fragment 2.

---

[29] Cross 1994, 57. The dating is consistent with the tentative palaeographical dating given by A.Steudel and myself in the Jerusalem Rockefeller Museum in summer 1993. For the palaeography of the Dead Sea Scrolls, see Birnbaum 1952, Avigad 1958, 56-87 and Cross 1961, 170-264.

Determining the number of lines per column appears to be very difficult. Presuming that fragment 3 provides a loose parallel to 1QS III,20-25 and the length of the text of the two spirits in 4QSa was about the same as in 1QS - which is not at all certain - there were about eleven lines between fragments 2 and 3. This would give twelve as the total number of lines per column. In this case there were six columns between fragments 1 and 2.[30] Since the fragments give no indication as to the direction the scroll was rolled in, the number of columns in the original scroll cannot be estimated.[31]

### *2.1.3. Transcription and Variants*

Frg. 1 (1QS I,1-5)

1 [ ]ם̊ ל̊[ח]יו̊ ספר סרכ היחד
2 [לדרוש אל בכול לב ובכ]ול נפש לעשות
3 [הטוב והישר לפניו כאשר] צוה ביד̇ מ̇ושה
4 [וביד כול עבדיו הנביאים ולא]ה̇וב כ[ו]ל̊[ אשר]
5 [בחר ולשנוא את כול אשר מא]ס̊ לר[חוק מכול]
6 [רע ולדבוק בכול מעשי טוב ]ולע̊ש̇[ות אמת]

Remarks:
1. Note an ordinary *kaph* in the final position in סרכ.
4-6. Qimron places the word בחר at the end of line 4 and not at the beginning of line 5. Accordingly, he reads the word רע at the end of line 5, and suggests that the last word in line 6 was וצדקה. In Qimron's transcription the position of the preserved letters in lines 4-6 do not correspond to the original fragment and, therefore, I consider his word division less probable here.

Frg. 2 (1QS III,7-12)

1 וברוח קודשו ליחד בא̊מ̊ת̊[ו] יטה[ר מכול]
2 עונתו וברוח̇ ישר וע̊נוה [תכופ]ר חט[תו ובענות]
3 נפשו לכול חוקי אל יטהר בש[רו להזות]
4 מי נדה ולהתקדש במי דוכי יכ̈[ן פעמיו]
5 להלכתמים בכול דרכ[י] אל כאש̊[ר צוה]
6 למועדי תעדתו ול[א] לס̊ו̊ר̊ ימין

[30] Between the last preserved word of frg.1 and the first preserved word of frg. 2 there were 531 words (compared to 1QS). Presuming seven words per line in 4QS[a], there were 76 lines in between these fragments. In the column of frg. 1, where six lines are partly preserved, one has to count six more lines there to reach the total of twelve lines per column. This leaves 70 lines which divided by twelve lines per column makes about six columns.

[31] It would have been very interesting to know, for example, whether the scroll included the text parallel to 1QS V-XI, as well, or whether 4QS[a] is a copy with only the text of 1QS I-IV.

7 ושמֹאוֹל ואין לצעוֹ]ן [על אחד [מכול דבריו]

8 אז ירצה בכפורי ניח]וֹ[ה והיֹתה [לו לברית]

9 [יחד] עולמי]ם                           [

Remarks:
1. Instead of the genitive attribute קודשו with 3rd. masc. sg.suffix 1QS has the adjective attribute וברוח קדושה.
2. Cf. the orthography of 1QS: עונותו and יושר. Qimron reads עונתֹוֹ at the beginning of the line.
4. 1QS adds a preposition to במי: מי. Qimron may be correct in assuming (with a question mark, though) that the end of line 3 reads בכול in 4QSᵃ. After הכי 4QSᵃ presumably had יכ]ן instead of ויהכין (1QS). Qimron reads [ יֹ]ֹ which I find less probable.
5. A normal word space has been dropped out in להלכתמים and the form להלכ is incorrect (read ללכת תמים). The word להלכתמים may also have functioned as a kind of abbreviation or *terminus technicus* like אפהו (= אף הו) in 1QH X,3,12; XII,31.
6. 1QS reads תעודתי. The variant תעדתו is an example of the non-standard Qumranic spelling, where we find ו- instead of יו- (see Qimron 1986, 59).
7. Qimron reads לצעו]ד[, but this reading leaves too small a word space before על.
8. לפני אל (1QS) is missing between the words ניחוח and והיתה. This has not been noted by Qimron, who reads instead [עֹולמֹים בכֹפֹרֹי נֹיֹחֹוֹח לֹפֹנֹי    [ (9) [והיתה לו אֹל.

## Frg. 3 (a loose parallel to 1QS III,20-25?)

]וֹ בֹ[ °°°°                                1 [

]ֹדרכי איש                                 2 [

]רת להשכיל                                 3 [

]תֹ לנֹ ]ֹ[ °°°° בֹיאיש                      4 [

]אורֹ הֹ          ]הֹ חושכ °ֹ[               5 [

Remarks:
5. Note an ordinary *kaph* in the final position in חושכ.

## Frg. 4

1  לֹ °[

2  בֹ °[

3  לם °[

4  רפֹ]ד

5  הֹ

Remarks:
1. Only the lower stroke of the second letter has been preserved. The letters *bet*, *kaph*, and medial *mem* and *pe* are possible.
2. The second letter is either *nun* or *zayin*.
3. The third letter might be *sin/shin* or *pe*.
4. The third letter is *dalet* or *resh*.

## 2.2. 4QS^b (4Q256)

### 2.2.1. Description of the Fragments

Twelve fragments of 4QS^b have been preserved, and they provide parallel passages for all the main sections of 1QS except for the doctrine of the two spirits (1QS III,13-IV,26). The manuscript has been written very carefully on well-prepared skins. According to Milik, the manuscript belongs to the transitional period between the Hasmonean and Herodian script, and is to be dated to 50-25 B.C.[32] Cross is of the opinion that the manuscript represents the typical early Herodian Formal script of c. 30-1 B.C.[33]

Fragment 1 (4.1 cm x 2.2 cm) contains three partly preserved lines from the middle of a column and provides a parallel to 1QS I,16-19.

Fragment 2 (1.7 cm x 1.3 cm) with only one wholly preserved and two partly preserved words in two lines also comes from the middle of a column. The words correspond to 1QS I,21-23.

Fragment 3 (1.6 cm x 1.6 cm) belongs to the same column as fragment 2. With its two preserved words in two lines fragment 3 provides a parallel to 1QS II,4-5.

Fragment 4 (8.3 cm x 5.3 cm) comes from the upper left-hand side of a column. At the edge of the margin of 1.2 cm, marks of stitching are visible. On the right-hand side of the fragment, the surface of the leather has broken off. A small fragment (frg. 6), which can be seen beside fragment 4 in PAM 43.250, actually belongs on the right-hand edge of this fragment, over lines 1 and 2. The four partly preserved lines of fragments 4 and 6 provide a parallel to 1QS II,7-11.

Fragment 5 has preserved both the upper and lower margin of a column; the height of each column in this manuscript was 12.6 cm, and there were thirteen lines per column. The right-hand margin is also preserved, whereas the left-hand edge of the fragment, the length of which is 9.5 cm, breaks down in the middle of lines. Between lines 5 and 9, the surface of the leather is broken off. In the right-hand margin the ledger lines drawn by the scribe are noticeable. The fragment has the letter *gimel* in its upper right-hand corner, which is probably the reason why the fragment has been published twice already. Milik included with the reconstruction a photograph and a transcription. In his opinion the *gimel* signifies sheet number three of the scroll.[34] Vermes has published a photograph of the

---

[32] Milik 1977, 76-78.

[33] Cross 1994, 57.

[34] Milik 1977, 78: "Dans l'angle supérieur droit du fragment... le fragment qui se situe certainement à la première colonne de la feuille 3, de 4QS^d, se lit facilement la lettre hébraïque ghimel. On n'hésitera guère à lui attribuer la valeur numérique de "3", bien que les lettres-nombres ne fussent jusqu'ici connues que sur les monnaies juives anciennes et, d'autre

fragment as well, and a transcription with notes of the first three lines.[35] The fragment provides a loose, shorter parallel to 1QS V,1-20.

[Fragment 6 (1.6 cm x 1.6 cm) belongs together with fragment 4, as stated above.]

Fragment 7 (2.9 cm x 2.9 cm) comes from the middle of a column and provides a loose parallel to 1QS VI,10-13. However, the text of 1QS here is twice as long as in 4QS[b].

Fragment 8 (3.6 cm x 3.0 cm) belongs to the lower edge of a column. Three lines of the text correspond to 1QS VI,16-18.

Fragment 9 (2.7 cm x 2.0 cm) from the upper edge of a column contains only one word, but the fragment is identifiable: most probably the fragment is parallel to 1QS VII,7. The preserved left-hand margin of this fragment has a width of 1.5 cm.

Fragment 10 (20.0 cm x 6.1 cm) has preserved half of the upper edge of one column and the whole of the upper part of another column. The width of the column whose upper part is preserved in full is 10.7 cm plus the margins measuring 1.5 cm (right) and 1.2 cm (left). The preserved part of the right-hand column provides a parallel to 1QS IX,18-22, that of the left-hand side column a parallel to 1QS X,3-7.

Fragment 11 is in two pieces (2.8 cm x 2.6 cm; 4.5 cm x 3.3 cm). In PAM 43.240 they are in a fairly correct position in relation to one another. The fragment corresponds to 1QS X,14-18.

Fragment 12 (3.0 cm x 2.7 cm) comes from the upper left-hand corner of a column. Some of the upper margin as well as some of the left margin is preserved. The fragment contains a parallel to 1QS XI,22 and it has preserved a parallel to the last word of 1QS: יבין. This is not, however, the last word in the fragment. In line 2 the word ככול is clearly visible and it presumably belongs to the beginning of another work. In my opinion, one possibility is that the word belongs to 1QSa and presents a variant preposition, for the third word of 1QSa is לכול (cf. the change of preposition between 1QS VIII,14 and IX,20: במדבר/למדבר). But it is even more likely that the words are a part of a final formula, such as we have in 1QSa II,21: וכחוק הזה יעשו (According to this statute they shall do...). Whenever the words ככול appear in 1QS (6x), they are connected with either the law of God (4x) or the regulations of the community (2x). This supports the view that the sentence where the words ככול belong referred to the preceding regulations and stated something like "According to all these regulations they shall do...". The third possibility is that the words ככול commence a new work which is something other than 1QSa. According to

part, les textes de Qumran utilisent normalement des signes spéciaux pour les chiffres."

[35] Unfortunately Vermes' transcription is not entirely correct (see my remarks). Possibly Vermes (1991, 250-255) was not aware of Milik's transcription. See the review of Vermes' article by García Martínez (1992, 159).

the concordances of Kuhn and Charlesworth,[36] none of the manuscripts found at Qumran which preserved the beginning of a text have ככול in one of its first three lines. Manuscripts which in one of their first three lines have בכול, a less likely reading here, are five in number (1Q51 1 1.3, 1QH 1 1.3, 4Q508 1 1.3, 4Q520 1 1.2, CD I,2).

### 2.2.2. Material Reconstruction of the Manuscript

Milik published a reconstruction of this manuscript in tabular form in 1977. According to his reconstruction, the manuscript consisted of twenty columns in six leather sheets, and it had a total length of approximately 250 cm. The length of the lines per column varied between forty-six and sixty-eight letters. Each column had thirteen lines.[37]

Milik's reconstruction of 4QS$^b$ is based on a textual comparison with 1QS. Although a parallel text can admittedly provide some indication as to the original content of a defective manuscript, it cannot be relied on too much. Not a single fragment from the doctrine of the two spirits (1QS III,13-IV,26), for example, is preserved in 4QS$^b$. (How do we know whether it was included at all?) Nor is there any fragment from the text of 1QS VII,8-IX,17. There is no guarantee that the form of the text in 4QS$^b$ followed that of 1QS. In fact, Milik himself points out that the text of 4QS$^b$ in its parallel to 1QS V,1-20 is shorter than that of 1QS.[38]

Looking at the shapes of the preserved fragments of 4QS$^b$, it is obvious that they come from parts of the scroll that are very far apart. Each of the three larger fragments (4, 5 and 10), providing parallels to 1QS II,7-11, V,1-20 and IX,18-X,7, are very different in shape, which implies that there were several layers of leather between them. It seems impossible to recognize any places where the fragments show signs of similar damage. Fragment 11 (par. 1QS X,14-18) has a similar kind of lower edge as frg. 10 II, however, and they may have been situated one on top of the other in the scroll. If the column from which frg. 11 comes was of the same width of 12.2 cm (with a margin) as the column of frg. 10, the distance between their corresponding points of damage is 15.8 cm (there was a sewing seam, the traces of which are visible in frg. 10 II, between these columns; a double margin has to be counted there). Another pair of fixed points would be needed in order to determine whether this measurement of 15.8 cm

---

[36] K.-G. Kuhn 1960, Charlesworth et al. 1991.

[37] Milik 1977, 76-77. Milik mentions the possibility, however, that there might have been more than twenty columns in the scroll (p. 77). In his article Milik calls this manuscript 4QS$^d$, although he had earlier identified it as 4QS$^b$. In the present inventory lists of the Rockefeller Museum the siglum of this manuscript is 4QS$^b$, and it is this siglum that is used here.

[38] Ibid., p. 78.

included just one, or perhaps two or three, circumferences (i.e. layers of leather) in the scroll, and whether the scroll was rolled with the beginning of the text in the outer layers or *vice versa*. It is essential to find an answer to these questions in order to solve how far from each other fragments 4,5 and 10 were situated in the original scroll and how extensive a text can have followed the text of 1QS (cf. frg. 12). It does not seem possible to reconstruct this scroll on the basis of the physical characteristics of the fragments alone. The aid which the parallel text of 1QS might furnish must be considered next.

The presence of the section on the doctrine of the two spirits (1QS III,13-IV,26) can be tested by estimating the space required for the remaining unpreserved liturgical material (1QS II,7-III,12) and by considering the appearance of the first three leather sheets with and without the doctrine of the two spirits. In column III, where the last preserved fragments (frgs. 4 and 6; par. 1QS II,7-11) before the doctrine of the two spirits belong, there are approximately 13 words per line in a column of 13 lines. At the end of column III, the text presumably reached 1QS II,23. The rest of the liturgical material fitted the next column rather exactly (according to my calculation based on words per line 1QS II,23-III,13 takes thirteen lines and nine words). If there was no section on the doctrine of the two spirits, the text continued with 1QS V,1, which is preserved in a fragment from the upper right-hand corner of a column. This fragment has marks of stitching on its right-hand edge (frg. 5). The fragment parallel to 1QS II,7-11 from column III of 4QS$^b$ has also preserved a sewing seam. It is on the left-hand edge of the fragment. If the doctrine of the two spirits was not included, there was a leather sheet with only one column in the middle of a carefully prepared manuscript. The first sheet contained the first three columns, the second sheet only one column, the third presumably three. With the inclusion of the doctrine of the two spirits, the second sheet had four columns. The absence of the doctrine of the two spirits seems highly improbable.

The text of 4QS$^b$ in its parallel to 1QS V,1-20 is only half the length of the version of 1QS. This shorter version of 1QS V,1-20 has also been preserved in manuscript 4QS$^d$. Since the version of 4QS$^d$ is practically identical with that of 4QS$^b$, it is very probable that the text of 4QS$^b$ also followed that of 4QS$^d$ in its parallel to 1QS VI-VIII. The reconstruction of 4QS$^d$ (to be described later) shows that the text of 1QS VI-VIII was about one fifth shorter in 4QS$^d$ as compared to 1QS.[39] Taking into consideration the likelihood of the existence of a shorter text, it may be estimated that

---

[39] To be quite accurate, it is the text of 1QS VI,12-VIII,6 that is approx. 1/5 shorter in 4QS$^d$. See p. 40.

the unpreserved text parallel to 1QS V,20-IX,17 required six columns in the scroll of 4QS<sup>b</sup>. It is very surprising that in his tabular reconstruction Milik reached the same conclusion that there were six columns. In his article Milik gives no indication as to how he arrived at this result. If he based his calculation on 1QS, he should have included at least one more column in his reconstruction.

Milik's suggestion that the text corresponding to 1QS I,1-XI,22 needed twenty columns in 4QS<sup>b</sup> seems correct to me. Some details in his tabular reconstruction call for comment, however. In counting the letters per line Milik has not taken the word spaces into consideration, and therefore, numbers per line and the widths of columns do not match, and estimating the widths of the columns which have not preserved the whole of the upper margin, is practically impossible to do.[40] Including the word spaces corresponding to the numbers of letters per line, some indication as to the original width of the columns can be attained, since one centimetre in this manuscript comprises about six letters: Col. I (frg. 1, approx. 64 letters per line) 10.7 cm; col. III (frg.4, approx. 68 letters) 11,3 cm.; col. VIII (frg. 5, ca. 61 letters) 10.2 cm; col. XV (frg. 10 I; 58 letters) 9.7 cm; [col. XVI (frg. 10 II) has preserved the upper margin of 10.7 cm]; col. XVII (frg. 11, approx. 61 letters) 10,2 cm.

### 2.2.3. Transcription and Variants

Frg. 1 (1QS I,16-19)[41]

1  [ימין ושמאול וכול הבאים ]בסרך היחד יעבורו בבר]ית לפני אל לעשות ככול]

2  [אשר צוה ולוא לשוב מאחרו] מכול פֿ]חד וא]ימה ומצרף]ֿ נסיים בממשלת]

3  [בליעל ובעוברם בברית יהיו הכוהני]ֿם והל]ויים מברכים את אל ישועות ואת]

Remarks:
The orthography of the fragment, insofar as it is preserved, is identical with that of 1QS.

---

[40] According to Milik's table, column XVI (par. 1QS X,3-13) with the width of 10.5 cm contained 46 letters per line. But in 4QS<sup>b</sup> there were approximately six letters per centimetre, which makes a total of sixty-three letters in a column of 10.5 cm. Since the upper part of col. XVI is preserved, it can be calculated with certainty, that col. XVI really had 63 letters per line, but in columns which have preserved only a part of the line length, one can only trust that the estimated number of letters per line is correct. The numbers cannot be utilized if the word spaces have not been taken into consideration.

[41] Since neither the right-hand-side margin nor the left-hand-side margin is preserved in the fragment, and the original manuscript cannot fully be reconstructed, the accurate positioning of the fragment in column I is not known. Therefore, it is possible that the preserved part of three lines belongs either more to the right or more to the left. Nevertheless, there were approximately eleven words per line in this column.

## Frg. 2 (1QS I,21-23)

1 [מספרים את צדקות אל במעשי ]גבורת[ו]ם ומשמיעים כול חסדי רחמים על]

2 [ישראל והלויים מספרים את ע]ונות בנ[י] ישראל וכול פשעי אשמתם וחטאתם]

Remarks:
The orthography of the fragment, insofar as it is preserved, is identical with that of 1QS.

## Frg. 3 (1QS II,4-5)

1 [בדעת עולמים וישא פני חסדיו לכה לשלום עולמים ]והלויים[ מקללים את כול]

2 [אנשי גורל בליעל וענו ואמרו ארור אתה בכול מעשי רשע ]אשמתכה[ יתנכה אל זעוה ביד]

Remarks:
1. 1QS has the *plene* form והלויים.

## Frg. 4 (1QS II,7-11)

1 [כול נוקמי נקם ויפקוד אהריכה כל]ה ביד כול מ[ו]שלמי נמולים אר]ור אתה לאין רחמים כחושך

2 [מעשיכה וזעום אתה באפלת אש ]עולמים לוא[ יחונכה אל בקור]אכה ולוא יסלח לכפר עוונכה

3 [ישא פני אפו לנקמתכה ולוא יהיה לכה שלום בפי כול אוחזי אבות] וכול העוברים בברית

4 [אומרים אחר המברכים והמקללים אמן אמן והוסיפו הכוהנים והלויים ואמ]רו ארור

Remarks:
1. García Martínez (1996) suggests בחושך instead of כחושך. It seems to me, however, that in this manuscript the lower stroke of a *bet* is usually longer and acrosses the vertical stroke. Also the top of a *bet* has the form of a 'tick', which is not the case here.
2. 1QS reads *plene* עולמים. Note the 2nd sg. suffix in עוונכה. 1QS has -ך, and the noun is in the plural form.

## Frg. 5 (1QS V,1-20)[42]

1 מדרש למשכיל[ על אנשי התורה המתנדבים להשיב מכל רע ולהחזיק בכל]

2 אשר צוה ולהבדל מעדת[ אנשי העול ולהיות יחד בתורה ובהון ומשיבים]

3 על פי הרבים לכול דבר לתורה[ ול]הון ולעשות ענוה וצדקה ומשפט ואהבת]

4 חסד והצנע לכת בכול דרכיהמה אש̇ר [לא יל]ך[ איש בשרירות לבו לתעות]

5 כי אם ליסד מוסד אמת לישראל ליחד ל[כול] המתנדבים לקדש באהרן וביה]

6 אמת לישראל והלוים ע̇ל̇י̇ה̇ם̇ ליחד וכול הבא [לעצת היחד יקים על נפשו]

7 באס̇ר לשוב אל תורת משה בכול לב ו[בכול נפש כל הנגלה מן                    ]

[42] The textual reconstruction of this fragment is based on the parallel text of 4QS[d] 1 I.

8   עצה אנשי היחד ולהבדל מכׁוׁל [אנ]ׁשי העול [ואשר לא ינעו טהרת אנשי]

9   הקודש ואל יוכל אתו בׁיחד ואשר לׁוׁא ישיב איש מאנשי היחד על פׁיהם]

10  לכול תורה ומשפט וׁ[א]ׁשר לוא יבו עֹמֹ]            עבודה ואל יואכל]

11  [איש מא]ׁנשי הקודש ]                              ולא ישענו על כול]

12  [מעשי ההבל כי הבל כֹ]ׁל אשר לוא יׁ[דעו את בריתו וכול מנאצי דברו להשמיד]

13  [מחבל ומעשיהם לנׁ[ד]ׁרה לפנׁ[יׁו ]            [

**Remarks:**

1.  The title in 1QS is different. Instead of על אנשי התורה [למשכיל] 1QS reads מדרש
    וזה הסרך לאנשי היחד.

2.  4QS[b] lacks לרצונו (1QS). The infinitive להבדל has no conjunction ו in 1QS.
    Vermes' transcription (1991) lacks מעדה which can be read without difficulty.

3.  Instead of הדבים 1QS reads שומרי הברית על פי רוב אנשי היחד על פי בני צדוק הכוהנים
    המחזקים בברית. Vermes transcribed the word לכול erroneously יצא תכן הגורל על פיהם
    as *defective* לכל.

4.  Note the form of the suffix in דרכיהמה. 1QS has -הם. The words ועיניו אחר לבבו
    ומחשבת יצרו ואאם למול ביחד עורלת יצר ועורף קשה, included in 1QS after לתעות are
    lacking in 4QS[b].

5.  1QS lacks כי אם, but adds ברית עולם לכפר between the words ליחד and לכול.

6.  1QS has a definite form האמה and preposition ב instead of ל before ישראל. After
    ליחד more than a complete line of 1QS is missing: ולריב ולמשפט להרשיע כול עוברי
    חוק ואלה תכן דרכיהם על כול החוקים האלה בהאספם ליחד. Apparently the words
    יבוא בברית בעיני כול המתנדבים were not included in 4QS[b], either.

7.  Instead of באסר 1QS has בשבועת אסר. The proper name משה is in the *plene* form
    מושה in 1QS. Between the words משה and בכול the words ככול אשר צוה (1QS) are
    lacking in 4QS[b].

8.  Instead of עצה אנשי היחד 1QS has לבני צדוק הכוהנים שומרי הברית ודורשי רצונו ולריב
    מכול אנשי. After אנשי ברית המתנדבים יחד לאמתו והתלך ברצונו ואשר יקים בברית על נפשו
    1QS continues להבדל מכול העול ההולכים בדרך הרשעה כיא לוא החשבו בבריתו כיא לוא בקשו ולוא
    דרשהו בחוקיהו לדעת הנסתרות אשר תעו בם לאשמה והנגלות עשו ביד רמה לעלות אף למשפט
    Whereas 4QS[b] ולנקום נקם באלות ברית לעשות בם [מ]שפטים נדולים לכלת עולם לאין שרית
    has אל יבוא במים לנעת בטהרת אנשי הקודש, 1QS reads [ואשר לא ינעו לטהרת אנשי] הקודׁש.

9.  Whereas 4QS[b] reads כיא ואל יוכל אתו בׁיחד 1QS has ואל יוכל אתו בׁיחד כיא שבו מרעתם כיא
    טמא בכול עוברי דברו ואשר לוא יוחד עמו בעבודתו ובהונו פן ישיאנו עוון אשמה כיא ירחק ממנו
    בכול דבר כיא כן כתוב מכול דבר שקר תרחק.

10-11. Instead of ואשר לוא יוכל מהונם כול ולוא 1QS has ואל יואכל איש מא[נשי הקודש ]
    ישתה ולוא יקח מידם כול מאומה אשר לוא במחיר כאשר כתוב חדלו לכם מן האדם אשר נשמה
    באפו כיא במה נחשב הואה כיא כול אשר לוא נחשבו בבריתו להבדיל אותם ואת כול אשר להם.
    Instead of ולא ישענו על 1QS reads ולׁוׁא ישען איש הקודש על.

Frg. 6 (belongs together with fragment 4)

1   [ביד כול מׁ]

2   [עׁולמים לוׁא]

## Frg. 7 (1QS VI,10-13)

1          ] יֹדבר [
2     ה]רבים אל יֹ[דבר
3      [ איש אשר יש]
4   ] יֹדֹבֹר וכול הֹמתֹ]נדב

Remarks:
1.-4. Although all the preserved words in this fragment have their equivalent in
1QS, the fragment does not provide any direct parallel to 1QS VI,10-13; in 1QS
the text is about twice as long as in 4QS^b, especially in lines 3 and 4.
4. 1QS: וכולה מתנדב.

## Frg. 8 (1QS VI,16-18)

1       [ הכולֹ]
2   ב]טֹהרת הרבים עֹדֹ] אֹ]שֹ]ר
3    ]לֹ]וֹ] שנה תמימה ישֹא]לו

Remarks:
1-3. 4QS^b lacks וגם הואה אל יתערב בהון הרבים ובמילאת לו שנה בתוך היחד (line 3).
Comparing the number of letters per lines between 1QS and 4QS^b reveals that
the sentence וכאשר יצא הגורל על עצת הרבים יקרבו או ירחק is also missing in 4QS^b
(line 1).

## Frg. 9 (1QS VII,7)

1      ]ברוש]ו

## Frg. 10 I (1QS IX,18-22)

1   ]צדק לבחירי דרך איש כרוחו כת]כון העת להנחותם בדעה וכן לה]שכילם[
2   ]ברזי פלא ואמת בתוך אנשי היח]ד להלך תמים איש את רעהו בֹכוֹל
3   ]הנגלה להם היאה עת פנות הדרך למדבר ]ולהשכילם בכול הנמצא לעֹשוֹת
4   ]בעת הזואת והבדל מכול איש ולוא הסר דֹ]רֹכֹו מכול עול] ואלה תכוני[
5   ]הדרך למשכיל בעתים האלה לאהבתו עם שנ]אתו שנאת עֹ]ולם עם אנשי[
6   ]שחת ברוח הסתר לעזוב למו הון וע]מל כפֹים כעבד למושל בו[

Remarks:
3. 1QS lacks the preposition ב.

## Frg. 10 II (1QS X,3-7)

1   מאורות מזבול קודשו עם האספם למעון כבוד במבוא מועדים לימי^חדש יחד
2   תקופתיהמה עם מסר]ות]ם זה לזה בהתחדשם יום גדול לקודש קודשים ואות

למפתח ח[סדיו עו]ל[ם לר]אֹשי מועדים בכול קץ נהיה בר⁻אשית ירחים למועדיהם    3

[וי]םֹ[ן קודש בתכונם לז]כרון במועדיהם תרומת שפתים אברכנו כח[וק] חרות לעד    4

[בראשי שנים ובתקופה]ה מועדים בהשלם חוק תכונם יום מֹ[שפטו זה לזה]    5

[מועד קציר לקיץ ומועד זרע] מֹוֹעֹ דֹ דשא מוער⁻י [שנים לשבועיהם וברוש]    6

] °°°°[    7

**Remarks:**

1. 1QS lacks the suffix in the word קודש, and חדש is in the *plene* form חודש in 1QS.
2. Note the longer form of the suffix -המה in תקופתיהמה (1QS reads תקופתם). Instead of the noun יום 1QS reads the pronoun הם which is unsuitable in the context. The reading is a result of an orthographical error (י has been confused with ה).
3. 1QS reads ברשית without *aleph* which is added above the line in 4QSᵇ.
4. 1QS has an error in the laryngeal in הברכנו. 4QSᵇ gives the correct form אברכנו.
5. 1QS reads מועדיהם (with a suffix).
6. 1QS reads למוער, but there are no traces of *lamed* here in 4QSᵇ.

## Frg. 11 (1QS X,14-18)

[אברך שמו בראשית צאת ובוא לשבת וקום ועם משכב יצועי ]ארננה לו וא[ברכנו]    1

[תרומת מוצא שפתי ממערכת אנשים ובטרם אריס ידי ]להדשן בעדני תנובת    2

[הבל ברשית פחד ואימה ובמכון צרה עם בוקה אברכנו] בהפלא מודה בנבורתו    3

[אשוחח ועל חסדיו אשען כול היום וא[דעה] כיא ביד]ו משפט כול חי וא[מ]ת    4

[כול מעשיו ובהפתח צרה אהללנו ובישוע]תו [ארננה יחד לוא אשיב לאיש]    5

[נמול רע בטוב ארדף נבר כיא את אל מש]פט כול חי והוֹאֹה ישלם לאיש]    6

**Remarks:**

3. 1QS has the conjunction ו before בנבורתו.
5. Around [הו] the surface of the leather has broken off.

## Frg. 12 (1QS XI,22- )⁴³

[מֹה יבין    1

[ ° בכול [    2

]°[    3

**Remarks:**

1.-2. יבין is the last word of 1QS but in 4QSᵇ the text continues. See the discussion on pp. 23-24.

---

⁴³ This fragment is not included in Qimron's transcription.

A fragment of 4QS<sup>b</sup> difficult to identify:

On the right-hand-side edge of PAM 43.240 there is a fragment which has preserved a margin. Transcription:

אֹל 1
הֹן 2
  ° ] 3

Remarks:
Possible identifications: 1QS VI,10-11; 11-12; 17-18; 19-20; 24-25.

## 2.3. *4QS<sup>c</sup> (4Q257)*

### 2.3.1. *Description of the Fragments*

Like 4QS<sup>a</sup> manuscript 4QS<sup>c</sup> is written on papyrus with writing on both sides. The text of the Community Rule is on the *recto*. A couple of words are written on the *verso*, but the work cannot be identified. Also, the palaeography of 4QS<sup>c</sup> has the same features as 4QS<sup>a</sup>: in particular *lamed* and final *mem* show great resemblance to those of 4QS<sup>a</sup>. I have been able to date the manuscript to the first half of the first century B.C.,[44] but Cross is more accurate in his date of c. 100-75 B.C.[45] Except for the orthography, the text of 4QS<sup>c</sup> in the preserved parts is practically identical with that in 1QS.

The manuscript has preserved in eight pieces. Some of them cannot be seen in photographs PAM 42.374 and 43.256, but they have been placed correctly in the Rockefeller Museum plate no. 859.[46]

The largest piece of fragment 1 (22.3 cm x 7.3 cm) covers the upper part of three columns. In column I there are only a few letters preserved from the two last words of line 1, which correspond to 1QS I,2. In column II line 1 has been preserved relatively well, whereas only half of line 2 is left. In lines 3-5 only about two words at the end of each line are present. The preserved parts of column II provide a parallel to 1QS II,4-11. The right-hand side of six lines of column III belongs to the large piece of fragment 1, but the left-hand side of lines 1-6 of column III is in four pieces (1.2 cm

---

[44] This palaeographical dating is a result of my personal consultation with A. Steudel.

[45] Cross (1994, 57) states that the script is somewhat unusual, but he characterizes it as a Jewish Semiformal script.

[46] The four small pieces of fragment in question come from the middle of the upper part of column 4QS<sup>c</sup> 1 III and the left-hand margin of frg. 2. The transcriptions and reconstructions presented in this thesis were prepared by me in the Jerusalem Rockefeller Museum. With the aid of the Brill microfiche edition I later discovered that the whole of plate 859 is to be seen in PAM 43.262.

x 1.8 cm; 0.9 cm x 2.2 cm; 1.0 cm x 1.4 cm; 9.0 cm x 5.0 cm). The six more or less preserved lines of column III correspond to 1QS II,26-III,4. From the same column parts of lines 8-13 are in three pieces (1.5 cm x 1.9 cm; 3.2 cm x 3.3 cm; 2.0 cm x 2.0 cm). The lines provide a parallel to 1QS III,5-10.

Fragment 2 consists of three pieces, the largest of which (7.3 cm x 7.3 cm) comes from the upper left-hand corner and gives eight lines of text. In the second piece of this fragment a few words from the end of two lines as well as a part of the left-hand-side margin are preserved. Some marks of ink from the right-hand side of the next column can also be seen. A small piece of the fragment with only a few letters belongs to line two of this fragment, which as a whole provides a parallel to 1QS IV,4-10.

Fragment 3 (3,2 cm x 2.4 cm) belongs to the same column together with fragment two. Fragment 3 with its three lines and part of the left-hand margin comes from a lower part of the column, and corresponds to 1QS IV,13-15.

### 2.3.2. Material Reconstruction of the Manuscript

Because the way in which humidity and other deteriorative factors affect a papyrus manuscript is different from the way in which they affect a leather scroll, papyrus fragments do not usually contain as 'detailed' information for the reconstruction as do leather fragments. I neverthelesss find the following reconstruction of 4QS$^c$ very probable.

In the middle of the first line of column III, there is a rectangular section of the fragment with a width of approximately 4 cm and a height of approximately 1 cm. The upper right-hand corner of this part corresponds well with the upper right-hand corner of the 4 cm-wide 'block'[47] which has the margin in the middle between columns II and III. In the middle of the upper margin of column II there is again a section of the fragment with a width of roughly 4 cm. These corner-points provide a basis for the reconstruction. The distance of 9.5 cm between the latter two points is very accurate, for the points are preserved in a single fragment. The distance between the first and the second point is 9.3 cm. This distance is confirmed by three small fragments belonging in the middle and filling the broken lines 1-4 of III.

There are also three peak-like parts preserved in the upper margins of the fragments. These peaks were most likely situated on top of one another in the scroll. Two of these peaks are in fragment 1: at the beginning of column III and at the very beginning of the fragment, at the end of column

---

[47] The width of about 4 cm is clear in the upper margin and lines 1 and 2. The piece widens in the lower lines.

I. The distance between these peaks is 18.8 cm; they include two circumferences, one of 9.3 cm and one of 9.5, which have also been determined with the aid of the corner-points described above. The third peak is in the middle of fragment 2.

For determining the distance between the left-hand peak of fragment 1 and that of fragment 2 a rough comparison with the text of 1QS helps us to be assured that not too many or too few circumferences are counted in between. If the peak of fragment 2 is placed closer than five circumferences (9.1 - 8.9 - 8.7 - 8.5 - 8.3) from the left-hand peak of fragment 1, there is not enough space for one empty column between the third column of fragment 1 and column I of fragment 2. Since the last preserved line of fragment 1 corresponds to 1QS III,10 and the first preserved line of fragment 2 corresponds to 1QS IV,4, the fragments cannot possibly belong to two successive columns. One more column in between is needed. Originally each column of 4QS$^c$ had 20-21 lines and a width of approximately 14.4 cm (the width of a column plus margin was about 16 cm).

Placing fragment 3 in column II of fragment 2 is easy to do, for fragment 3 has preserved a part of the left-hand margin and corresponds well with the middle part of fragment 2. Fragment 3 belongs on the same horizontal level as the lowest piece of fragment 1 in column III.

As indicated above, the circumference in the outermost preserved layers is 9.5 cm, and in the innermost preserved layers it is 8.3 cm. The scroll was rolled from left to right, and each circumference decreases by 0.2 cm. A papyrus scroll could not have been wrapped as tightly as a leather one; the inner circumference of 4QS$^c$ was definitely not less than about 4 cm. In addition to the five columns which have been preserved, the length of the unpreserved layers of the scroll would have been at the most approx. 128 cm. With a width of about 16 cm per column, this makes seven columns and a handle sheet. The total number of columns in the scroll was thus twelve plus the handle sheets, and the total length approximately 225 cm.

We cannot be sure whether the text in the unpreserved parts of the scroll followed the form of 1QS or, for example, the form of 4QS$^e$, which lacks the section 1QS VIII,15b-IX,11.[48] The third option, which cannot be ruled out either, is that the text in 4QS$^c$ followed that of 4QS$^{b,d}$. This form is considerably shorter than 1QS in its parallel to 1QS V-VII, but it includes the section 1QS VIII,15b-IX,11.[49] If the text of 4QS$^c$ followed 1QS, the columns of 4QS$^c$ VI-XII had space for the text of 1QS IV,21-IX,2,

[48] See pp. 51-54.
[49] In the parallel to 1QS V manuscripts 4QS $^{b,d}$ are about 1/2 shorter and in the parallel to 1QS V-VI about 1/5 shorter than 1QS. See pp. 25 and 40.

according to our calculation.[50] In the case that 4QS$^c$ followed the form of 4QS$^e$, the text in the inner parts of the scroll may just about have reached the end of column 1QS IX.[51] If 4QS$^c$ followed the form of 4QS$^{b,d}$, the scroll ended with the text of 1QS IX,26 as well.[52] The question as to the type of the text in the unpreserved parts of the scroll cannot be solved conclusively. In any case the text parallel to 1QS X-XI (the final psalm) was likely to be absent in this scroll.

## 2.3.3. Transcription and Variants

Frg. 1 I (1QS I,2)[53]

1  בכול ל]בׄ ובכו̊ל
2                   ] °° [

Remarks:
1. The preserved letters partly fill the gap at the beginning of 1QS.

Frg. 1 II (1QS II,4-11)

1  והלויי̊ם מקללים את כול אנשי גורל] בלי[על וענו ואמרו אׄרׄור
2  [א]תׄהׄ [בכו]ל] מעשי רשע] אשׄמתכה יתנכה אל זעוה ביד כול נוקמ[י]
3  [נקם ויפקוד אחריכה כלה ביד כול משלמי גמו]ל[ים ארו]ר אתה
4  ] לאין רחמים כחושך מעשיכה וזעום אתה ]בׄאפלת
5  [אש עולמים לוא יחונכה אל בקוראכה ולוא יסלח לכפר עו]נכה
6  [ישא פני אפו לנקמתכה ולוא יהיה לכה ]שׄלׄוׄם [בפי אוחזי אבות]
7  [וכול העוברים בברית אומרים אחר] המברכים [והמקללים אמן אמן]
8  [והוסיפו הכוהנים והלויים ואמרו ארור בנ]ל[ו]לי לבו לעבור הבא]

Remarks:
4. The gap has been filled with the aid of 1QS. There may have been a *vacat* in the line, or the line had one or two more words which are not included in 1QS. The spaces between the words and letters may also have been unusually large.

---

[50] This calculation presupposes that there were eleven words per line and twenty-one lines per column in 4QS$^c$ (4QS$^c$ VI: 1QS IV,21b-V,9a; 4QS$^c$ VII: 1QS VI,9b-23a; 4QS$^c$ VIII: 1QS VI,23b-VI,11a; 4QS$^c$ IX: 1QS VI,11b-26a; 4QS$^c$ X: 1QS VI,26b-VII,16a; 4QS$^c$ XI: 1QS VII,16b-VIII,10; 4QS$^c$ XII: 1QS VIII,11-IX,2).

[51] According to this calculation, column 4QS$^c$ XII contained the text of 1QS VIII,12-15a + IX,12-26.

[52] This calculation is based on the estimation that columns 4QS$^c$ VI-XII contained approx. 1,617 words. The version of 4QS$^{b,d}$ in its (shorter) parallel to 1QS V-IX included approx. 1,550 words (see note 49).

[53] This text at the end of col. I of frg. 1 is not included in Qimron's transcription. Col. I of frg. 1 in Qimron's transcription is actually col. II of frg. 1.

5. Note the plural form of the noun and the different orthography of the suffix in the word עווניך in 1QS.

## Frg. 1 III (1QS II,26-III,10)

1 לוא י]עבור ביה[וׄ אמ]תו ]כׄ]יׄ]אׄ נׄעׄלׄהׄ נׄפׄשׄׄן ביסורי דעת[

2 משפטׄ]יׄ צדק לוא ]חזק [ל]משיב חיו ועם י]שרים לוא] יתח]שב[

3 ודעתׄן ו]כוחׄו והונו לוא] יביאׄו ]בעצת יחד כׄיׄא ב]כׄאׄון רשׄ]עׄ[

4 מחרש ונׄאׄ]לׄיׄ]ם בשׄ]וׄ]בתו [וׄ]לׄוׄאׄ יצדק במתׄׄו]ר ]שרירות

5 לבו וחושך י]בׄיׄט לדרכי] אור בעון תמימים לוׄאׄ יתח]שב[

6 לוא יזכה בכפוׄ]רׄים ולוׄ]אׄ יטהר במי נדה ולוא יתקדׄ]שׄ[

7 [בימים ונהרות ולוא יטהר בכול מי רחץ טמא טמא יהיה[

8 [כול יומי מואסו במ]שׄׄפׄטׄי אׄ]ל לבלתי התיסר ביחד[

9 [עצתו כיא בר]וׄח ע]צׄת] אׄמׄת אל ]דרכי איש יכופרו כול[

10 [עוונותו להבׄיׄ]טׄ בׄ]אׄור החיים וברוח קדושה ליחד באמתו יטהר[

11 [מכול עוונותו וברוח יושר וענוה תכופׄ]ר חׄטׄאׄׄתׄ]ו ובענות[

12 [נפשו לכול חוקי אל יטהר בש]רׄו להזות[ במי נדה ולהתקדש[

13 [במי דוכי ויכין פעמיו ללכת תׄׄ]מׄׄים בכׄׄול] דרכי אל[

14 [כאשר צוה צוה למועדי תעודתיו ולוא לסור יׄ]מׄׄיׄׄן [ושמאול ואין[

Remarks:
4. 1QS has ונאלים, but in 4QS^c the partly preserved letter before the first gap is more likely to be *aleph* than *waw* (ונׄאׄ]לׄיׄם).
11. Qimron suggests that what remains of the letters in this line is וענו]הׄ תׄכׄׄופׄׄ]ׄר.
14. Cf. Qimron's reading ולוא] לׄסׄוׄׄר] ימין. The reading [ושמאול יׄ]מׄׄיׄׄן, which is also the reading of the Preliminary Concordance, is also favoured by García Martínez (1996).

## Frg. 2 (1QS IV,4-10)

1 [ורוח דעת בכול מחשבת מעשה וקנאת משפטי צדק] ומחשבת קׄ]וׄ]רׄש

2 [ביצר סמוך ורוב הסדים על כול בני אמת וטהרׄ]ה כבוד מהעבת כול נלולי

3 [נדה והצנע לכת בערמת כול וחבא לאמת רזי] דעת אלה סודי רוח

4 לבני אמת תבל ופקודת כול הולכי בה למרפא ורוׄ]בׄ שלום באוׄ]רך ימים] וׄפׄׄרֹׄׄׄׄות זרע

5 [עם כול ברכות עד ושמחת עולמים בחיׄ]יׄׄ נֹׄׄׄׄצׄ[ח [וׄ]כׄליל כבוד עׄ]ם מדת הדר באור עולמים[

6 [ולרוח עולה רחוב נפש ושפול ידים בעבודת ]צׄדׄק *vacat*

7 [רשע ושקר נוה ורום לבב] כׄחש ורמיה אכזׄ]רׄי ורוב חנף קצור]

8 [אפים ורוב אולת וקנאת ז]רׄון מעשי תׄ]וׄעׄבה ברוח זנות ודרכי נדה[

Remarks:
2. The error in מתעב in 1QS should be corrected with 4QS^c to מהעבה.
7. Qimron suggests that line 6 had some words after the *vacat*, which is visible in the fragment, and that the words צדק] בעבודה were added above line 7 (the line space between this word and the word below is actually smaller than usual). In his transcription, these words should be read after נוה ורום לבב], however, and not

after ושפול ידים, as presupposed in 1QS. Thus, Qimron's transcription matches the marks in the fragment only if the word order is changed. On the other hand, my transcription does not fully match the position of the words in the fragment, either. I consider it possible that in 4QS[c] the text at the beginning of line 6 was a little shorter than in 1QS.

## Frg. 3 (1QS IV,13-15)[54]

1 [עד עם כלמה כלה באש מחשכים וכול קציהם לדורותם בא]בל ינון

2 [ורעת מרורים בהוות חושך עד כלותם לאין שרית ופליט]ה למו

3 [באלה תולדות כול בני איש ובמפלניהן ינחלו כול צבאותם ]ל[דורותם

Fragments of 4QS[c] which are difficult to identify:

A.  וכי]בוד לב [°

   [°ה טוב]

Remarks:
1. Corresponds to 1QS IV,11.
2. The closest parallels to this line are 1QS II,24 וענות טוב and 1QS IV,26 לדעת טוב.

C.  [קדש]

   [לוא °° ]

Remarks:
The fragment might be a parallel either to 1QS V,18-19 (cf. איש הקודש and אשר לוא ידעו) or to 1QS V,13-14 (cf. אנשי הקודש and לוא יוחד).

## 2.4. 4QS[d] (4Q258)

### 2.4.1. Description of the Fragments

The largest 4QS fragments belong to the manuscript known as 4QS[d]. The individual columns of this manuscript are remarkably small, however. The original size of a single column was not more than about 10.7 cm x 8.0 cm with only 13-14 lines. The script used in the manuscript is Herodian

---

[54] No transcription of this fragment has been included in Qimron's edition. On the other hand, I have been unable to read the beginnings of five lines of col. II of frg. 2 which are supplied by Charlesworth in Qimron's transcription.

and dates from the last third of the last century B.C.[55] The name of God (אל) is written in palaeo-Hebrew letters in frg. 2 III,9 and IV,8.

The beginning of column I of fragment 1 was most likely also the beginning of the whole manuscript. The margin of the right edge of the manuscript is unusually wide (2.1 cm) compared to the other margins (0.9 - 1.2 cm), and there are no marks of stitching at the right-hand edge of the leather sheet. The beginning of the text corresponds to 1QS V,1. At the beginning the introduction (1QS I,1-18a), a liturgical passage (I,18b-III,12) and the doctrine of the two spirits (III,13-IV,26) are lacking. The absence of 1QS I-IV is not surprising, for the contents of columns 1QS I-IV and V-XI are very different. The actual regulations for community life begin only with column V.

Fragment 1 (25.2 cm x 7.7 cm) contains the upper half of three columns and margins. Column I (width 9.7 cm not including margins) with its twelve partly preserved lines provides a loose parallel to 1QS V,1-19. Column II (width 9.7 cm) contains what remains of ten lines which provide a parallel to 1QS V,21-VI,7. Only the right-hand edge is left of column III. A few words from three lines provide a parallel to 1QS VI,9-12.

Fragment 2 has five columns. Column I is in two pieces, the first of which is 1.9 cm x 2.3 cm and the second 3.7 cm x 4.2 cm. Parts of twelve lines correspond to 1QS VIII,6-21. Columns II and III form one large fragment, the size of which is 21.4 cm x 8.7 cm. Column II (width 9.6 cm) has its upper half preserved in its entirety, and it provides a parallel to 1QS VIII,24-IX,10. The upper part of column III (9.7 cm) has also remained undamaged, and parts of other lines of the column have been preserved as well. The column provides a parallel to 1QS IX,15-X,3.[56] Columns IV and V belong to a fragment (8.7 cm x 7.4 cm) separate from that of columns II and III. Column IV is unusually narrow, only 5.9 cm in width. Its twelve partly preserved lines correspond to 1QS X,4-12. The margin between columns IV and V (0.9 cm) is also narrower than the other margins of this manuscript (1.2 cm). In column V only one or one and a half words at the beginning of eight lines have been preserved. They provide a parallel to 1QS X,12-18.

---

[55] This palaeographical date was suggested by H. Stegemann, whom I consulted personally. It has been confirmed by Cross 1994, 57. In the recent radio-carbon dating given by Jull et al. (1995, 11-19), using both 1σ and 2σ confidence intervals, the (second) sample of 4Q258 (4QS[d]) resulted in the dates 11 B.C. - A.D. 78 (1σ) and 95 B.C. - A.D. 122 (2σ) (p. 14).

[56] To be more precise, the last preserved letter of column III corresponds to 1QS X,3, but the unpreserved end of the last line of column III must have reached as far as 1QS X,4a.

Fragment 3 is very small (1.2 cm x 0.8 cm) and has preserved only four letters, but it can be identified. The fragment provides a parallel to 1QS XI,7.

## 2.4.2. Material Reconstruction of the Manuscript

There is a clear wave pattern discernible at the lower edges of the fragments, and the length of the wave grows as one moves from left to right, indicating that the scroll was rolled in the 'right' way, i.e. with the beginning of the text in the outer layers. None of the fragments have preserved any stitching, but there must have been some between fragment 2 IV and fragment 2 III: both fragments have preserved part of the margin, but since a direct join between the pieces is not possible, they must have preserved parts of a double margin.

The length of the first wave is 9.3 cm; the corresponding points of damage can easily be seen on the level of line 4 in the fragments (2.7 cm from the upper edge of the fragments; this is the level where the wave begins to curve in the fragments). The corner on the left-hand edge of fragment 2 IV corresponds well with the corner at the left-hand edge of the fragment 2 III.

Moving 9.5 cm to the right, there is once again a corner on the level of line 4. This corner stands 0.8 cm to the left from the right-hand margin of the column and corresponds with the corner of the left-hand edge of fragment 2 III. Beside the corner which is situated 0.8 cm towards the left from the right-hand margin of column III of fragment 2, there is a smaller corner on the left-hand side. This smaller corner (1.4 cm from the right-hand margin of column III of fragment 2) provides a point corresponding to the corner located on the level of line 4 in column II (frg.2). The distance between these corners which correspond to one another is 9.7 cm.

The leather in fragment 1 is thicker than in fragment 2, indicating that fragments 1 and 2 belong to different leather sheets and that there was stitching in between. Instead of 0.2 cm the circumference in fragment 1 increases by 0.25 cm.

In the leather of fragment 1 there are vertical breaks at the edges of the margins of columns I and II. In the middle of both columns I and II there are also areas which seem to have broken into small pieces. The vertical breaks as well as the broken areas were most likely placed one top of one another in the scroll. Presuming that the break at the left-hand edge of column II beside the margin and the break at the left-hand edge of column I beside the margin were placed on top of one another, the patterns at the lower edge of the fragment also match well. The distance between the corresponding points of damage (the breaks) is 10.85 cm.

The innermost preserved circumference in fragment 2 is 9.3 cm. The circumference increases by 0.2 cm, and in the outermost preserved part of fragment 2 it reaches 9.7 cm. In fragment 1, which has an increase of 0.25 cm per layer, the circumference is 10.85 cm in the outermost layer. With the sequence 9.3 cm - 9.5 cm - 9.7 cm - 9.9 cm - 10.1 cm - 10.35 cm - 10.6 cm - 10.85 cm, there were four columns in the first sheet of the scroll (frg. 1 I-III plus a column from which no material has been preserved) and four columns in the second sheet (a column from which no material has been preserved plus frg. 2 I-III). Columns IV-V of fragment 2 belong to the third sheet. The columns in the first and the second sheet regularly have a width of approximately 10.7 cm (with the margin of 0.9 - 1.2 cm). The column of frg. 2 IV in the third sheet is narrower, 6.9 cm (with a margin). Between the sheets there is always a double margin.

Presumably the innermost circumference in the original scroll was about 4 cm.[57] In addition to the preserved nine columns[58] (approx. 98 cm) the length of the inner layers of the manuscript was 172 cm (the total length of the scroll was about 270 cm). For the rest of the material of the Community Rule (1QS X,12-XI,22) about 28 cm is needed, which makes either four narrow columns (columns X-XIII, 6.9 cm each) or one narrow column plus two wider columns (column X, 6.9 cm; columns XI-XII, 10.7 per column).[59] There remains 144 cm, i.e. twelve wide columns plus a handle sheet or nineteen narrow columns plus a handle sheet (including double margins alongside stitching), for some other text(s).[60]

It is a matter for consideration whether the Rule of the Congregation (1QSa) and the Words of Blessings (1QSb) were also included in the scroll of 4QS[d]. The estimated total number of words in 1QSa and b is 2145

---

[57] Cf. Stegemann 1990, 196: "First, there are large scrolls with more than 50 columns and a length of 7 m or more... Such large scrolls were closely wrapped and, therefore, the distances between corresponding points of damage in the innermost layers are very short, regularly about 3 cm... Secondly, there are shorter scrolls which had a length of only 1.5 or 2 m divided into, for example, 12 or 13 broader columns or about 20 smaller columns. If they were rolled with the beginning of their text in the outer layer of the scroll, they were not as tightly wrapped as the larger scrolls. The result is that the distances between corresponding points of damage in the innermost layers of those scrolls are greater than in the larger scrolls. Usually, they are about 5 cm." The scroll of 4QS[d] belongs in the category in between the examples provided by Stegemann. Therefore, the estimated length of the innermost circumference in the scroll is 4 cm.

[58] Column X (4QS[d] 2 V) has actually preserved its left-hand edge. The column has not been included here, since the point of damage which has been used in counting the circumference is very close to column IX.

[59] On the basis of the reconstructed text it can be estimated that the width of column X (4QS[d] 2 V) was presumably also 6.9 cm (see transcription). Column X covered the text of 1QS X,12-22.

[60] Although the number of columns per leather sheet may vary greatly, it has been calculated here that one sheet contained either 3-4 wider columns or 4-5 narrower columns.

(1QSa I-II: 537; 1QSb I-V: 1608). At least one, possibly two more columns (2 x approx. 350 words) belonged to the original text of 1QSb,[61] which makes a total of 2,495-2,845 words. The scroll of 4QS[d] has thirteen lines per column. A wider column (10.7 cm), comprising about fourteen words per line, had about 182 words per column, whereas a narrower column (6.9 cm), with ten words per line, included about 130 words. For the material of 1QSa and 1QSb fourteen to sixteen wider columns or twenty to twenty-two narrower columns would be needed. According to this calculation, there would not be quite enough room for the texts of 1QSa and 1QSb in the scroll of 4QS[d], but one may speculate over the possibility that a shorter version of their text once existed (cf. the parallel of 1QS V in 4QS[d]). It must be emphasized, however, that the inclusion of the texts of 1QSa and 1QSb is not at all self-evident, for the text of 4QS[e], for example, was followed by Otot. In the scroll of 4QS[d] the text(s) following the Community Rule may have been completely different from 1QSa and 1QSb, although the required amount of space is not very far short of that taken by the text of 1QSa and 1QSb.

The text of 4QS[d] is shorter than that of 1QS not only in its parallel to 1QS V (4QS[d] I-II). The reconstruction of the scroll indicates that the text in 4QS[d] III-V was also shorter than the corresponding section in 1QS. The distance between fragments 1 III and 2 I is, on the basis of the material reconstruction, calculated as 36.3 cm, which includes almost four columns. In the scroll of 4QS[d] these were columns III-VI (i.e. the column to which frg. 1 III belongs, the column of frg. 2 I, and two columns of which no fragments have been preserved. Between the two 'empty' columns there must have been stitching). The last word preserved from col. III is אשר from line 3 corresponding to 1QS VI,12. The first word in col. VI comes from line 1. It is לר[שעים which corresponds to 1QS VIII,6. Presuming that there were fourteen words per line and thirteen lines per column, each column had 182 words. An attempt to fill the 'empty' space with the text of 1QS reveals that the text of 4QS[d] in columns III-V was about 1/5 shorter than that of 1QS: In columns III-V there is space for 546 words, but 1QS VI,12-VIII,6 includes 683 words, i.e. 137 words more.[62]

---

[61] The text of 1QSb was in the outer layers of the scroll and was only partly preserved. The presence of at least one more column in the scroll is likely on the grounds of the content of the text. Milik 1955, 119, Stegemann 1993, 163-164.

[62] The possibility of one more column between the preserved fragments is practically ruled out: the circumferences can be measured accurately, and it is unlikely that there would have been a column of normal width having only 137 words when the normal number of words per column was 182.

## 2.4.3. Transcription and Variants

### Frg. 1 I (1QS V,1-19)

מדרש למשכיל על אנשי התורה המתנדים להשיב מכל רע ולהחזיק בכל אשר צוה   1

ולבדל מעדת אנשי העול ולהיות יחד בתור[ה] ובהון ומשיבים על פי הרבים לכל דבר   2

לתורה ולהון ולעשות ענוה וצדקה ומשפט ואהבת] חסד וה[ה]צנע לכת בכל דרכיהם   3

[אשר ]לא ילך איש בשרירות לבו לתעות כי אם ליסד] מוסד ]אמת לישראל ליחד לכל   4

המת[נ]דב לקדש באהרן ובית אמת לישראל והנלוי[ם] עלי[ה]ם ליחד וכל הבא לעצת   5

הי[ח]ד יקים על נפשו באסר ל[שוב א]ל [ת]ורת מש[ה ]בכל לב ובכל נפש כל הנגלה מן   6

[       ] [ל]    [עצת אנש]י[ ] היחד] להבדל מכל אנש]י העול ואש[ר] לא ינעו לטהרת אנשי   7

[הקוד]ש ואל יוכל אתו ב[י]חד ואשר לא ישיב א[י]ש מאנשי היחד על פיהם לכל   8

[תורה] ומשפט ואש[ר] לוא יבו עמו    [ע]בודה ואל יואכל איש מאנשי הקדש   9

[              ] [ל]  [      ] [ ° ] ולא ישנעו על [כל מע]ש[י ההבל כי הבל ]כל אשר[ לא ידעו]   10

[את בריתו וכל מנאצ]י דברו להשמיד מחבל ומעשיהם לנד]ה לפניו [   11

[   ] [ ] נוים ושבעות וחרמים ונד]רים בפיהם [   12

[   ] [ ] [ל]  [ ]רשל[ ]   13

Remarks:

1. The text has the same title as 4QS[b]: Instead of זה הסרך לאנשי היחד (1QS) both 4QS[b] and 4QS[d] read מדרש למשכיל על אנשי התורה. The scribe has made a spelling error in המתנדים; Vermes (1991) has erroneously given the correct form המתנדבים in his transcription. García Martínez (1996) suggests that tthe scribe had intended that the final *mem* of this word should be omitted, but I cannot see any dot to substantiate this. 1QS reads Qal infinitive construct לשוב, 4QS[d] hiph'il infinitive. 1QS has the *plene* spelling מכול.

2. After אשר צוה 1QS reads לרצונו. 1QS has the niph'al infinitive construct להבדל without the conjunction ו. Before the substantive יחד 1QS has the preposition ל. Instead of הרבים 1QS has בני צדוק הכוהנים שומרי הברית ועל פי רוב. Then 1QS continues with the words אנשי היחד המחזקים בברית. אנשי היחד יצא תכון על פיהם. Then 1QS continues with the words הגורל.

3. 1QS adds ולמשפט after ולהון, and אמת יחד ו- after לעשות. The scribe first wrote לכל by mistake, but he himself corrected it to לכה.

4. The negative לא is in the *plene* form לוא in 1QS. After לתעות 1QS adds אחר לבבו ועיניהו ומחשבת יצרו (read כיא אם) ואאם, and after ליחד למול ביחד עורלת יצר ועורף קשה 1QS continues with the words ברית עולם לכפר.

5. 1QS uses the plural form התמנדבים, gives the *plene* forms לקודש and באהרון, and varies in preposition and article ולבית האמת בישראל. After ליחד 1QS continues with the words ולריב ולמשפט להרשיע כול עוברי חוק ואלה תכון על כול החוקים האלה בהאספם ליחד. The conjunction ו is missing before כל in 1QS and the word is in the *plene* form כול.

6. After הי[ח]ד 1QS reads יבוא בברית אל לעיני כול המתנדבים, and the verb יקים, which in 1QS is also to be understood as hiph'il (יָקֵם), has the conjunction ו in front. 1QS has בשבועת אסר. After the *plene* form מושה 1QS continues ככול אשר צוה. In all occurrences of כול in this line 1QS uses the *plene* form. 1QS adds a preposition in לכול הנגלה.

7. Qimron's reconstruction [התורה] ל[רוב] at the beginning of the line is very probable. Instead of [עצה אנש]י[ ] היחד 1QS has לבני צדוק הכוהנים שומרי הברית ודורשי

After .רצונו ולרוב אנשי בריתם המתנדבים יחד לאמתו והתלך ברצונו ואשר יקים בברית על נפשו

1QS continues with the words החשבו לוא כיא הרשעה בדרך ההולכים מכול אנשי העול

בבריתו כיא לוא בקשו ולוא דרשהו בחוקיה לדעת הנסתרות אשר תעו בם לאששמה והנגלות עשו

ביד רמה לעלות אף למשפט ולנקום נקם באלות ברית לעשות בם [מ]שפטים גדולים לכלת עולם

1QS reads אל יבוא, ואשׁ֗ לא ינעו לטהרת אנשי הקודש. Whereas 4QS[d] has לאין שרית

במים לנעת במטהרת אנשי הקודש.

8. 1QS has כיא ואל יוכל אתו בי֗ח֗ד כיא לוא יטהרו כי אם שבו מרעתם. Whereas 4QS[d] reads

טמא בכול עובדי דברו ואשר לוא יוחד עמו בעבודתו ובהונו פן ישיאנו עוון אשמה כיא ירחק ממנו

בכול דבר כיא כן כתוב מכול דבר שקר תרחק. At the end of the line, 1QS reads the

plene form לכול instead of לכל.

9-10. For עׄבׄודה] there is no correspondence in this place in 1QS, but see the text
earlier in 1QS V,14. Instead of [ ל֗] [ מאנשי הקדש 1QS ואל יואכל איש

ואשר לוא יוכל מהונם כול ולוא ישתה ולוא יקח מידם כול מאומה אשר לוא במחיר כאשר has

כתוב חדלו לכם מן האדם אשר נשמה באפו כיא במה נחשב הואה כיא כול אשר לוא נחשבו בבריתו
להבדיל אותם ואת כול אשר להם.

10. 1QS gives the plene forms כיא and כול. Instead of ולא ישנעו על 1QS reads ולא ישען
איש הקודש על. The verb ישנעו in 4QS[d] contains a scribal error and should be
corrected to ישענו (cf. 1QS).

11. 1QS reads ישמיד instead of ל + infinitive construct. Qimron provides a plausible
suggestion for the reconstruction of the end of the line: לׄ[פניו וטמא בכ֗]ל [הונם].

12. The wording has no correspondence in 1QS. The noun גוי, גוים does not occur in
1QS at all but it appears in other Qumran sectarian manuscripts, such as
1QpHab, 1QM and CD. The word שבעות appears only in the singular in 1QS
referring to the candidate's vow to commit himself to the law of Moses (1QS
V,8). In CD there is also mention of other kinds of vows, cf. IX,12; XV,1;
XVI,7; XVI,10-11. See also 1QH XIV,17. Neither חרם nor נדר occurs in 1QS,
but in CD VI,15 they appear together in the words ולהנזר מהון הרשעה הטמא בנדר
ובחרם ובהון המקדש. For חרם see also CD IX,1 (as a verb), and for נדר see CD
XVI,13 (as a verb) and 18 (as a participle). No direct parallel to ונדרים כפיהם
occurs in the Qumran texts or in the Old Testament (cf., however, Num 6:21).

## Frg. 1 II (1QS V,21-VI,7)

1 ואת מעשיהם בתורה על פי בני אהרון המתנדבים להקים את בריתו ולפקוד את כל חקיו אשר צוה
2 לעשות על פי רוב ישראל המתנדבים לשוב ביחד ולהכתב איש לפני רעה בסרך איש לפי שכלו
3 ומעשיו בתורה להשמע הכול איש לרעה[ו] הקטן לנדול ולהיות פוקדים את רוחם ומעשיהם
4 בתורה שנה בשנה לה֗עלות איש כפי שכ֗ל[ו] ולאחרו כנעותיו להוכיח איש את רעה ואהבת חסד
5 ואל ידבר איש אל רעהו באף או בתלונה א֗ו בקנאת רשע ונם אל יבא איש על רעהו דבר לרבים
6 אשר לא בהוכח לפני ע֗[ד]ים ]ב֗אלה יתהל֗כ֗ו֗ בכל מנורייהם כל הנמצא את רעהו וי֗[שמעו הקטן]
7 לנדל למלאכה ולׄ[ממון ויחד יא[כלו ]ו֗יח֗ז]ר֗ יברכו ויחד יועצ֗[ו ו]ב֗[כול מקום אשר יהיה שם עשרה]
8 אנשים מ֗[עצת היחד אל ימש מ[א]תם כ֗ה[ן ואי[ש] כתכונו יש֗[בו לפניו וכן ישאלו לעצתם לכול דבר]
9 והיה כי [יערוכו השולחן לאכול או התי֗[רוש] לשתות ה[כ]והן יש֗[לח ידו לרשונה להברך בראשית הלחם]
10 והתירוש[ יש[ק[ד ] [

Remarks:

1. 1QS has the 3rd masc. sg. suffix instead of the 3rd masc. pl. suffix in מעשיהם
(4QS[d]), and 1QS lacks the nota accusativi את. After המתנדבים 1QS adds ביחד.
Note the plene spelling כול in 1QS.

2. 1QS adds the conjunction ו before the preposition על. In 1QS הוב has been written *defective*. After ביחד 1QS adds לבריתו. Instead of ל + niph. inf.cstr. 1QS has a suffixed finite form וכהבם and בסרך before the words איש לפני רעה. The second איש is missing in 1QS.

3. The word בתורה is missing in 1QS. Presumably the copyist of 1QS meant the same form פוקדים as the copyist of 4QSᵈ when he wrote פוקדם (cf. the vocalization by Lohse פּוּקְדָם).

4. 1QS lacks בתורה and has a different preposition: לפי שכלו. Then 1QS adds והם דרכו. Instead of a plural noun 1QS has the singular: כנעיתו. After איש את רעהו 1QS adds בא|מה| וענוה, and after אהבת הסד 1QS adds לאיש.

5. The conjunction ו is missing in 1QS. Instead of איש אל רעהו 1QS has אלוהיהו (read אליהו). After the second א 1QS continues with the words קשה או בעורף| ואל ישנאהו |בעורלה| לבבו כי ביום יוכיחנו ולוא ישא עליו |בקנאת| רוח רשע. 4QSᵈ is lacking עוון (1QS). Instead of the Qal form 1QS has hiph'il יבי, or alternatively the form יבא in 4QSᵈ is to be understood as hiph'il spelt *defective*. The preposition is different in 1QS: לפני הרבים instead of לרבים.

6. Instead of בהוכח 1QS reads בתוכחה. There is an ink mark before באלה in 4QSᵈ; possibly there was the conjunction ו.1QS has כל in the *plene* form in both its occurrences. 1QS provides the idiomatic expression for the the complete form of the reciprocal relation: איש את רעהו, whereas 4QSᵈ expresses the same by means of ellipsis.

7. 1QS uses the *plene* form לנדול. The word following למלאכה is either ולממון (1QS) or ולהון (4QSⁱ).

8. 1QS: מאתם איש כוהן.

9. The word כי is spelt *plene* in 1QS.

10. If the word of which two letters are preserved is ישק|ד (cf. 1QS VI,7 ישקודו), the text in 4QSᵈ must have been shorter than that of 1QS, for there is no room for seventeen words here in 4QSᵈ after והתירוש.

## Frg. 1 III (1QS VI,9-12)

| | |
|---|---|
| ובמושב| | 1 איש את מד|עו |
| | 2 הרבים אל ידב|ר איש כול דבר אשר לוא להפץ הרבים וכיא האיש המבקר| |
| | 3 לרבים אשר |יש אתו דבר לדבר לרבים אשר לוא במעמד האיש השואל את עצה| |
| | 4 ה|י|ה|ה| |

Remarks:

1. The text of 1QS is here about twice as long as in 4QSᵈ. 1QS: לעצה היחד אל ידבר איש בתוך דברי רעהו טרם יכלה אחיהו לדבר *vacat* וגם אל ידבר לפני תכונו הכתוב לפניו האיש הנשאל ידבר בתרו. Presumably at least the words after the *vacat*, starting with וגם, were missing.

3. 1QS reads על הרבים instead of לרבים, and וכול איש אשר instead of אשר.

## Frg. 2 I (1QS VIII,6-21)

| | |
|---|---|
| ל|הׄשיב לרשעים | 1 | |
| 2 |נמולם היאה חומת הבחן פנת יקר בל יזדעזעו יסודותיהו ובל יחישו ממ|קומם מעון קודש קודשים | |
| 3 |לאהרון בדעת עולם לברית משפט ולקריב ריח ניהוח ובית תמים ואמת בישרא|ל להקים ברית לחקות עו | |

4  [והיו לרצון לכפר בעד הארץ ולחרוץ משפט רשעה ואין עולה בהכין אלה בי]סוד היחד שנתים ימים

5  [בתמים דרך יבדלו קודש בתוך עצת אנש]י היח[ד וכול דבר] נ[סתר מיש]ראל ונמצא

6  לאיש [הדורש אל יסתרהו מאלה מיראת רוח נסונה] *vacat* ובהיות אל[ה בישראל י]בדלו מ[תוך מושב]

7  אשנ[י העול ללכת למדבר לפנות שם את דרך האמת היא מדרש התור]ה אשר צוה בי[ד מושה לעש]ו[ת כל] הננלה]

8  ע[ת בעת וכאשר גלו הנביאים ברוח קודשו וכול אי[ש מאנשי ברית ה]יחד אשר יסור מכול המצוה דבר ביד]

9  [רמה אל יגע בטהרת אנשי הקודש ואל ידע בכול עצתם עד אשר יזכו מעשיו מכול עול]

10 [להלך בתמים דרך וקרבהו בעצה על פי הרבים ואחר יכתב בתכונו וכמשפט הזה לכול]

11 [הנוסף ]ליחד [ואלה המשפטים אשר ילכו בם אנשי תמים הקודש איש את]

12 [רעהו ]כל ה[ו]בא ]ל[ו]עצת הקודש ההולכים בתמים דרך כאשר צוה כול איש]

Remarks:

2. After ממקומם 1QS has a *vacat* which is lacking in 4QS[d]. Presumably the words added by the second scribe above the line in 1QS were included in 4QS[d].

3. It is uncertain whether the word רוח added above the line in 1QS was included in 4QS[d]. In 4QS[e] it was most likely absent. Cf. the orthography of 1QS: להקם (also hiph'il) and לחזוק. The verb נמצא is in the plural form נמצאו in 1QS.

4. The words והיו לרצון לכפר בעד הארץ ולחרוץ משפט רשעה ואין עולה are written above the line in 1QS.

5. In 1QS the definite article has been added above the line before נסתר.

6.-7. The words ליחד and בתכונים האלה written above the line in 1QS were not included in 4QS[d]. Manuscript 4QS[d] also lacks the words כאשר כתוב במדבר פנו דרך ···· ישרו בערבה מסלה לאלוהינו (Isa 40:3).

7. 1QS has the preposition כ before כל.

8. The phrase וכול איש מאנשי היחד ברית היחד in 1QS is syntactically difficult; the first occurrence of היחד is unnecessary and apparently a mistake, as indicated by 4QS[d].

12. 1QS uses the *plene* form כול and has a different preposition: בעצת הקודש.

## Frg. 2 II (1QS VIII,24-IX,10)

1  והבדילהו מן הטהרה ומן העצה ומן המשפט שנת[ים ימי]ם ושב במדרש ובעצה אם לא הלך עוד

2  בשננה עד מלאות לו שנתים כי על שגגה אחת יענש שנתים וליד הרמה לא ישוב עוד אך

3  שנתים [י]מים יבחן לתמים דרכו ולעצתו על פי הרבים ונכתב בתכונו ליחד קודש

4  [בהיו]ת אלה בישראל ליחד כתכונים האלה ליס[ד רוח קודש לאמת עולם לכפר על אשמת פשע

5  [ומעל חטא]ת ולרצון לאר[ו]ץ מבשר] עלות ולחלבי זבחים ותרומות ונדבת שפתים למ[שפט]ט כניחוח

6  [צדק ותמים ]ד[ר]ך כנדב[ת מנחת ר]צ[ו]ן בעת ההיא יבדלו בית אהרן לקודש לכל ך[    ]ל[    

7  [    ]ליש[ר]אל ההלכים בתמ[י]ם רק בני אה[ר]ן ימשל[ו]ו ב[משפט ובהון ועל פיהם *vacat* והון] אנשי הקודש]

8  [ההולכי]ם בתמים אל יתע[רב הונם עם] הון] אנשי הר[מ]ה[ אשר לא הזכ]ו דרכם להבדל מעול]

9  [    ]ר[    ] ל[התה]לך ב[    ]     [    ונשפטו במ[שפטים הרשונים אשר החלו אנשי היחד]

Remarks:

1. Instead of hiph'il והבדילהו 1QS reads hoph'al without a suffix: הובדל. Note 1QS: אשר לוא ישפוט איש. Before שנתים ימים 1QS has the addition ומן העצה ודרשו המשפט. and after שנתים ימים 1QS continues with the words: ולוא ישאל על כול עצה. Instead of הלך 1QS has שנג. Instead of אם תתם דרכו במושב במדרש ובעצת [על פי הרבי]ם.

2. 1QS lacks the preposition ב and the noun שׁגגה, but there is a verb from the same root before it (see the note on the previous line). The orthography differs in 1QS: מילאה. Instead of שׁנתים alone 1QS has שׁנתים ימים. 1QS reads the *plene* form כיא. After the second occurrence of שׁנתים 1QS adds ולעושׂה, and has the semi-preposition ביד without the conjunction ו instead of וליד. The article is lacking in front of רמה in 1QS. After עך 1QS adds the subject השׁוגג.

3. The word order in 4QS<sup>d</sup> (שׁנתים [י]מים יבחן) differs from that in 1QS: יבחן שׁנתים ימים. 1QS lacks the preposition ל before עצתו. Instead of niph'al נכתוב 1QS reads ואחר יכתוב. Orthographically, the Qal form appears unambiguous in 1QS, although a niph'al, as suggested by Lohse (1986, 32), is what one would have anticipated (cf. Kuhn 1960, 106 n. 1).

4. 1QS lacks the word ליחד and has ככול התכונים האלה instead of כתכונים האלה. In 1QS the word ליסד (4QS<sup>d</sup>) is written *plene* (ליסוד).

5. 1QS gives the *plene* form עולה and has the preposition מן in ומהלכי while 4QS<sup>d</sup> has ל. The following nouns זבחים and ותרומת (4QS<sup>d</sup>) are in the singular in 1QS, and ונדבת is completely absent in 1QS.

6. 1QS has the longer form of the personal pronoun ההיאה in the function of a demonstrative pronoun (בעת ההיאה), whereafter the text continues as follows: יבדילו אנשי היחד בית קודש לאהרון להוחד קודש קודשים. The text in 4QS<sup>d</sup> differs from that of 1QS so that it is difficult to fill up the last gap of line 6 and the first one of line 7.

7. Presumably the scribe first wrote בתוֹכ, but then changed the word to בתוֹכמ by adding a *mem* above the line (in many instances there is practically no difference between *waw* and *yod* in this manuscript). The sentence ועל פיהם יצא ויהנגורל (הנורל) לכול תכון אנשי היחד (corr.) included in 1QS is missing here.

9. The text at the beginning of the line differs from that of 1QS.

## Frg. 2 III (1QS IX,15-X,3)

1 ולפי שׂכלו להגישׂו וכן אהבתו עם שׂנאתו ואשׂר לא יוכיח אישׂ ולא יתרובב עם אנשׂי השׂ֯ח֯<ע>ת
2 ולסתר עצתו בתוך אנשׂי העול ולהוכיח דעת אמת ומשׂפט צדק לבחירי דרך אישׂ כרוחו וכתכון
3 העת ל[ה]נחות[ם] בדעה וכן להשׂכילם ברזי פלא ואמת בתוך אנשׂי היחד להלך תמים אישׂ את
4 [רעהו בכול ה]נגלה להם היא עת פנות הדרך ל[מ]דבר להשׂכילם בכל הנמצא לעשׂות *vacat* בעת
5 [הזואת והבדל] מכל אישׂ אשׂר לא הסיר דרכיו מכול עול *vacat* ואלה תכוני הדרך למשׂכיל בעת[ים]
6 [האלה לאהבתם עם ]שׂנאתו שׂנאת עולם עם אנשׂי השׂחת ברוח הסתר ולעזוב למו הון ובצע
7 [כעבד למושׂ]ל בו וענוה לפני הרודה בו ולהיות אישׂ מקנא לחוק ועתו ליום נ֯ק֯ם֯ ל[עשׂות]
8 [רצון בכול משׂלח כפים וב]כ֯ו֯ל ממשׂלו כאשׂ[ר] צוה וכו[ל] הנעשׂה בו ירצ֯ה בנדבה וזולת רצון [אל לא]
9 [יחפץ ובכול אמרי פיהו ירצה ולוא יתאוה ב]כו֯ל֯ אשׂר לא צוה ולמשׂ[פט אל יצפה ת֯[מיד]
10 [ ] ובכול אשׂר יהיה יס[פ]ר [הרומה שׂפתים י]ברכנו עם [קצים אשׂר]
11 [חקק אל ברשׂית ממשׂלת אור ע[ם] ת[קופתו ובהא]ספו אל מעון חקו ]בראשׂית֯ א[שׂמורי]
12 [חושׂך כיא יפתח אוצרו וישׂתהו עלה] ת[בתקופתו עם האספו מפ]נ֯י אור בהופע[ מאורות מזבול קודשׂ]
13 [עם האספם למעון כבוד במבוא מועדי]ם[ ל]ימי חודשׂ יחד תקופתם עם מסרותם זה לזה[]

Remarks:

1. 1QS has ואשׂר לא יוכיח אישׂ ולא instead of ואשׂר לוא להוכיח ולהתרובב אם אנשׂי השׂחת יתרובב עם אנשׂי השׂח<ע>ת.

2. Instead of the suffixed noun עצתו 1QS gives את עצה התורה. 1QS has the Qal participle (ל)בוחרי, and 4QS[d] the Aramaic passive participle (ל)בחירי. 1QS lacks the conjunction ו before כתכן.

4. 1QS gives a longer (Qumranic) form of the personal pronoun 3rd fem. sg. היאה. Qimron transcribes [ו]להשכילם, but I cannot detect any defect in the leather or text before this word. The preposition ב is missing in front of כול in 1QS.

5. 1QS has a different clause connector: only ו instead of איש אשר. The verb is in the form הסר in 1QS, and instead of דרכי 1QS reads דרכו (an interchange of י־ and ־ֵ; יו = o).

6. שדה is an indefinite form in 1QS, and לעזוב is without the conjunction ו. Instead of ובצע 1QS reads ועמל כפים.

9. The name of God אל has been written in palaeo-Hebrew letters.

11. Note the different orthographies in 1QS: על instead of אל and ברשת instead of בראשית (towards the end of the line).

12. 1QS has an error in the laryngeal (באופיע), but 4QS[d] has skipped yod (בהפע).

13. The fragment located in PAM 43.246 in this line most likely does not belong here.


Frg. 2 IV (1QS X,4-12)

1  בהתחדשם יום נדול לקודש קודשים ואות למפתח חסדו עולם
2  לראשי מועדים בכל קץ נהיה בראשית ירחים למועדיהם וימי
3  קודש בתכונם לזכרון במועדי־]הם תרומת [ש]פ̇ת̇]ים ]אברכנו כחק
4  [ח]ר]ות לעד בראשי שנים ובתקו]פת מועדיהם בהש]לם חוק
5  תכונם יום משפטו זה לזה מוע̇ד לקיץ ומועד ז]רע למועד
6  דשא מועדי שנ]י[ם לשבועיה]ם ובראש ש]ב]ועיהם למועדו דרור
7  ובכל היותי חוק] ח]רות בל]שוני לפרי ]תהלה ומ]נת] שפתי א̇ומרה̇
8  בדעת וכל ננינתי לכבוד א]ל ]כה נבל]י] לחכו]ן קודש וחליל]
9  [שפתי א]שא בק]ו מ]שפט]ו עם מבוא] יומ] ולילה ]אבואה בברית
10 [אל ועם מוצא ערב ובוקר אמר חוקיו ]ובהיותם אשיב
11 [נבולי לבלתי שוב ומשפטו אוכיח כנעויתי ופ]שעי לננד עיני
12 [כחוק חרות ולאל אומר צדקי ולעליון ]מכין טוב̇י̇ מק̇ו̇ר]
13 [דעת ומעון קודש רום כבוד ונבורת כול להפאארת עולם אבחרה]


Remarks:

1. Due to an orthographical error (יו has been confused with ה) 1QS has the personal pronoun הם instead of יום. 1QS reads the plural חסדיו instead of the singular חסדו. The form in 4QSd might also be an example of a specifically Qumranic spelling, where we find ־ו instead of ־יו.

2. Note the different orthography in 1QS: בכל and ברשת.

3. 1QS has a laryngeal error in הברכנו whereas 4QS[d] gives the correct form אברכנו.

6. 1QS has the plene form לשבועיהם and reads למועד without a suffix.

7. 1QS has the plene form ובכול.

8. Again, 1QS uses the plene form וכול. The name of God, which is only partly preserved, is written in palaeo-Hebrew letters in 4QS[d] (aleph is visible). 1QS reads נבלי וכנור. Qimron suggests א̇כה נבל]י] in 4QS[d].

10. The last word of the line is אשים in 1QS. A difference of one letter alters the
root.

Frg. 2 V (1QS X,12-18)

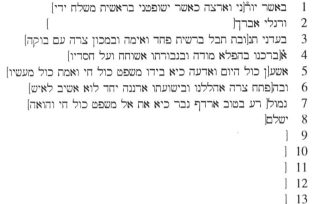

| | |
|---|---|
| באשר יור[]ני וארצה כאשר ישופטני בראשית משלח ידי[ | 1 |
| ורנלי אברך[ | 2 |
| בעדני תנ[ו]בה חבל ברשית פחד ואימה ובמכון צרה עם בוקה[ | 3 |
| א[ברכנו בהפלא מודה ובנבורתו אשוחח ועל חסדיו[ | 4 |
| אשע[ן כול היום ואדעה כיא בידו משפט כול חי ואמת כול מעשיו[ | 5 |
| ובה[פתח צרה אהללנו ובישועתו ארננה יחד לוא אשיב לאיש[ | 6 |
| נמול[ רע בטוב ארדף גבר כיא את אל משפט כול חי והואה[ | 7 |
| ישלמ[ | 8 |
| ] | 9 |
| ] | 10 |
| ] | 11 |
| ] | 12 |
| ] | 13 |

Remarks:
2. The gap has room for only 10-12 words, but 1QS reads here שמו בראשית צאת
ובוא לשבת וקום ועם משכב יצועי ארננה לו ואברכנו תרומת מוצא שפתי ממערכת אנשים ובטרם
אים ידי להדשן.

Frg. 3 (1QS XI,7)

 וינחיל[ם בנו]רל  1

Remarks:
The orthography of the fragment, insofar as it is preserved, is identical with that of
1QS.

Unidentified fragments of 4QS[d] (frgs. A,B,C are to be found in PAM
43.244, frgs. D,E,F,G in PAM 43.246):

A. [ליחה[       B. [ דו מ ֺ[       C. [בֺר כ[
   [כל ֺ ]ל[

D. [ בנ ]ם[     E. [בֺר       F. [חֺ[
                    ֹֹ[              ]ֹֹ[

## 2.5. 4QSᵉ (4Q259)

### 2.5.1. Description of the Fragments

Manuscript 4QSᵉ has been regarded as the oldest copy of the Serekh ha-yaḥad. J.T.Milik dated the manuscript to the second half of the second century B.C.,[63] whereas F.M.Cross states in his recent list of the dates of the 4QS manuscripts that the manuscript was written "about the same time as 4QpapMMTᵉ, 50-25 B.C.E."[64] The remarkable difference between the dates may be explained by the fact that the hand of 4QSᵉ is very extraordinary and contains elements of several known script types. Since the palaeographical date of a manuscript is not decisive for the analysis presented in this work, the question as to the dating of 4QSᵉ may be left open at this point.

Material from four columns has been preserved. Fragment 1 has pieces of three columns. Twelve lines from column I have been preserved in a piece (8.2 cm x 10.1 cm) which has a partly preserved margin (1.4 cm) and belongs at the right-hand edge of the column. It provides a parallel to 1QS VII,8-15. Column II is preserved in two parts. A piece from the lower right-hand corner (6.9 cm x 6.5 cm) with margins provides a parallel to 1QS VIII,3-9. A block of pieces from the left-hand side of the column parallels 1QS VII,20-VIII,10. This block of pieces (8.6 cm x 12.3 cm) has preserved the margin (1.7 cm) between columns II and III as well as a part of the text from column III. Almost half of the column is preserved in a block of pieces (7.6 cm 14.6 cm) from the left-hand side of column III. Together the preserved pieces from column III provide a parallel to 1QS VIII,11-15 + IX,12-20. The lower margin of columns II and III shows that column III contained one line more than column II.[65]

Fragment 2, consisting of three pieces (3.0 cm x 1.9 cm; 6.0 cm x 1.4 cm; 3.4 cm x 2.3 cm), belongs in the upper part of the next column (col. IV). The fragment corresponds to 1QS IX,20-24. The fragments of column

---

[63] Milik 1956, 60 ff. and 1976, 61. He designated the manuscript 4QSᵇ, but the present signum used for this manuscript in the inventory lists of the Rockefeller Museum is 4QSᵉ. There is no doubt that the manuscript which Milik refers to is 4QSᵉ, for in his article of 1976 he provides a transcription of one of the fragments of 4QOtot in the same connection. The text of Otot, written by the same hand as 4QSᵉ, was included in the same scroll with 4QSᵉ. F.M. Cross states in his Haskell lectures (1958, 89) that 4QSᵉ was written at the beginning of the first century B.C., but it remains unclear whether he is actually talking about the same manuscript, for he refers to 4QSᵉ as being a *papyrus*. Note a more tentative comment in the second edition (1961, repr. 1980), p. 119.

[64] Cross 1994, 57: "The scroll is written in an unusual Jewish Semicursive with mixed Semicursive and Semiformal script features, *e.g.*, Semiformal and Semicursive (looped) *Taw*."

[65] Fragments from columns I-III are to be found in PAM 43.264 and 43.263.

four are to be found in PAM 43.283 together with fragments of Otot, a calendric text which was written on the same scroll by the same copyist.[66] Uwe Glessmer, the editor of this document, showed me the fragments of the Rule in his photographs and discussed their significance. There are three relatively well-preserved columns from the beginning of 4QOtot. According to Glessmer, only a couple of introductory lines may be missing from the beginning of the text, and no more.

### 2.5.2. Material Reconstruction of the Manuscript[67]

The fragments of 4QS$^e$ and 4QOtot have preserved six column-dividers, none of which shows marks of stitching. Although the evidence of the number of columns per leather sheet in the scrolls ranges from one column to seven,[68] one would not usually expect more than three or four columns per leather sheet. Between the fragmentarily preserved columns of 4QS$^e$ and 4QOtot, there may have been at least one line of stitching. The preserved column-dividers rule out every possibility of stitching anywhere except in the space between columns III and IV of 4QS$^e$, and the measurements taken in the reconstruction to be described below support the view that there was stitching between these columns.

The fragments belonging to 4QS$^e$ and those belonging to 4QOtot show a remarkable resemblance. They cannot have been at a great distance from each other in the scroll. Surprisingly, there are no fragments parallel to 1QS X-XI. One may ask whether these columns were included in the scroll at all. F.García Martínez has left one empty column for the rest of the Serekh material in his translation of 4QS$^e$ - 4QOtot.[69] The question arises as to whether it is possible to envisage one missing column between six relatively well-preserved columns.

The parts which are left of the scroll show a pattern of vertical blocks separated from one other. Only one fragment, that of Otot published under the siglum 4QS$^b$ (4Q260B) I vi 6-13 by Milik,[70] has preserved a circumference of 9.5 cm in one piece. The vertical break in the leather beside the edge of the left-hand-side margin corresponds to the vertical break in the narrow block in the right-hand part of the column. This circumference provides a solid starting-point for the material reconstruction of the scroll. Although in some places the text of 4QS$^e$ follows 1QS rather

---

[66] Milik 1976, 62 f. See also Glessmer 1991, 124-164. I am grateful Uwe Glessmer, who kindly lent me his photograph PAM 43.283 for reproduction in this book.
[67] The substance of this chapter has been previously published in the *Journal of Jewish Studies* (Metso 1993, 303-308).
[68] Stegemann 1990, 197-198.
[69] García-Martínez 1992, 73.
[70] Milik 1976, 61.

accurately, this circumference makes it possible to determine the measurements of the original scroll without basing the starting-point for the reconstruction on the parallel text of 1QS alone.

The upper left-hand edge of another Otot fragment belonging in the column next to 4QS<sup>b</sup> (4Q260B) I vi 6-13 on the right-hand side - following Milik's classification this would be column 4QS<sup>b</sup> I v - forms a line corresponding to the break in the narrow block of 4QS<sup>b</sup> (4Q260B) I vi 6-13. The distance between these corresponding points is 10.0 cm. Moving 10.5 cm to the right, the left-hand edge of 4QS<sup>e</sup> 1 III provides a corresponding line for the next circumference. Again, the outermost right-hand edge of the said fragment 4QS<sup>b</sup> I v corresponds well to the right-hand edge of the block belonging to the left-hand part of column 4QS<sup>e</sup> 1 III. Between these edges there is a distance of 11.0 cm. This block belonging to the left-hand part of column 4QS<sup>e</sup> 1 III has a break going right through the block. This break has its correspondence in the break in the middle of the margin between 4QS<sup>e</sup> 1 III and II (circumference 11.5 cm). The break in the margin between 4QS<sup>e</sup> 1 III and II corresponds to the break in the fragment belonging at the right-hand side of column 4QS<sup>e</sup> 1 II. The distance between these breaks is 12.0 cm. The outermost edge of the fragment which belongs at the right-hand side of 4QS<sup>e</sup> 1 II corresponds to the right-hand edge beside the margin in fragment 4QS<sup>e</sup> 1 I. This circumference of 12.5 cm is the outmost one which is preserved in the remaining fragments of 4QS<sup>e</sup>. The innermost circumference is 9.0 cm: the line of the break downward in the middle of 4QS<sup>b</sup> I vii corresponds to the smaller break which stands 3.6 cm towards the right from the margin between 4QS<sup>b</sup> I vii and vi.

The scroll of 4QS<sup>e</sup> - 4QOtot was rolled in the 'right' way, i.e. with the beginning of the text in the outer layers, for the distances between corresponding points of damage increase as one moves from left to right. In the outermost preserved layers the circumference is 12.5 cm, and in the innermost preserved layers it is 9.0 cm. The leather is very thick (about 0.8 mm); the circumference decreases by 5 mm. Thus eight layers are preserved. If one attempts to add an empty column (or two) for the rest of the Serekh material between the preserved columns of Serekh and Otot, there is a break in the sequence of 9.0 - 9.5 - 10.0 - 10.5 etc. and also in the relatively regular width of approximately 13 cm per column (including a margin). Between columns III-IV there is only room for a double margin caused by stitching. Since the last lines of 4QS<sup>e</sup> III are preserved giving a parallel up to 1QS IX,20a, there is no doubt that the fragments parallel to 1QS IX,20b-23 are a part of column IV. It is clear that the fragments parallel to 1QS IX,20-23 and the beginning of the Otot belong in the same column (col. IV).

Presumably the inner circumference of the scroll was not less than 6 cm, considering the thickness of the leather. In addition to the preserved material, the scroll had six inner layers totalling approxiamately 43.5 cm. With the average width of about 13 cm per column this would make three columns and a handle sheet. We cannot be certain how decay affected the scroll, or - to put it differently - which part of the scroll was preserved. One may speculate, however, that it was the middle part, and that the same amount of six layers was also destroyed in the outer layers. Six circumferences in the outer layers gives a total of 85.5 cm, which is about six columns and a handle-sheet. This is insufficient for the whole material of 1QS I-VII,6. In fact, six columns of 4QS$^e$ only leave room for about 1,080 words, which is about the same as in 1QS V-VII,6 (960 words). It is possible - but not certain - that 4QS$^e$ is another example of a version of Serekh containing only the text of 1QS V onwards (compare 4QS$^d$). If it was the middle part of the scroll that was preserved, the total length of the scroll would have been about 2 metres, and the total number of columns would have been fifteen plus the handle-sheets (nine and a half columns for the Community Rule, five and a half columns for Otot).

## 2.5.3. Transcription and Variants

Frg. 1 I (1QS VII,8-15)

1  [ששה חוד]שים[ וכן לנוקם לנפשו כול דבר ואשר ידבר בפיהו]

2  [דבר נבל שלושה חודשים ולמדבר בתוך דברי רעהו עשרת]

3  [ימים ]ואשר ישכב [וישן במושב הרבים שלושים ימים וכן לאיש]

4  הנפטר ממוש הרבים אש[ר] לוא בעצה ותנם עד שלוש פעמים]

5  [ע]ל מושב אחד ונענש עש[רת ימים ואם יקפו ונפטר]

6  [ונ]ענש שלושים יום ואשר יה[לך לפני רעהו  ערום ולוא]

7  היה אנ[ו]ש[ ]ונע[נש [ש]שה חו[ד]שים ואיש אשר ירוק אל תוך מושב]

8  הרבים ו[נענש שלושי[ם יו[ם] ואשר יוציא]

9  את [ידו מתוחת] בגד[ו] והו[א]ה פוח ונראתה ערותו]

10 ונענש ששים יום ואשר ישחק] בסכלות להשמיע]

11 קולו ונענש שלשים יו[ם ]וה[ו]מוציא את יד שמאולו]

12 ל[ושה

Remarks:
Possibly the text differed to some extent from 1QS, since the length of lines appears to be very irregular when the gaps are filled with the text of 1QS.
1. In 1QS the duration of the punishment (ששה חודשים) has been corrected to שנה אחת above the line.
2. There is no *vacat* in the line, but the surface of the leather has broken off. Therefore, the text has not been preserved.
3. 1QS gives the *plene* form ישכוב. In classical Hebrew the imperfect form usually has the vowel 'a'.

4. The copyist has made a spelling error. The word ממוש lacks the last letter ב. In 1QS the preposition connected to this word is not מן, but ב.
7. The leather is so defective and the text so unclear that it is very difficult to say whether אנוס (Qimron) instead of אנוש should be read here (interchange of consonants ס and ש).
9. The *nota accusativi* את is missing after יוציא in 1QS.
10. The numeral is שלושים in 1QS. Qimron reads ונענש שֹלֹשֹים here, but I find the reading less probable.

## Frg. 1 II (1QS VII,20-VIII,10)

1  [ובשנית לוא ינע משקה הרבים ואחר כול אנשי היחד יש]ב ובמל]אֹת לו[
2  [שנתים ימים ישאלו הרבים על דבריו ואם יקרבהו ונכתב ב]תֹֹכֹינו ואחר ישֹאֹל
3  [על המשפט וכול איש אשר יהיה בעצת] היחד עד מלאות לו
4  [עשר שנים ושבה רוחו לבנוד ביחד יוצא מלפני] הרבים ללכת
5  [בשרירות לבו לוא ישוב אל עצת היחד עוד ואיש מ]אֹנשי היחד אשר
6  [יתערב עמו בטהרתו או בהונו אשר ערב עם הון הרבים] והיה משפטו
7  [כמוהו לשלח הואה בעצת היחד שנים עשר ]אֹנשים ]ו[כוהנים שלושה
8  [תמימים בכול הנגלה מכול התורה לעשות] אמת צדקה ומשפט
9  [ואהבת חסד והצנע לכת איש אם רעהו לשמור א]מֹונה בארץ ביצר סמוך ובענוה
10 [ורוח נש]ברה ולרצת עֹוֹן בעושי משפט וצרה] מֹצרף הֹתהלך עם כול
11 [במדרת] האמת ובתכון] העת בהיות אלה ב]יֹשראל נכונה עצת היחד
12 [באמת למ]שֹפֹט עול]ם בית קודש לישראל וסוד] קֹדֹש קדשים לאהרֹוֹ]ן
13 עֹדי אמת למשפט ובחירי רצֹון לכפר בעד] הארֹ]ץ ולהש]ב לרשעים
14 גֹמולם והיא הוֹמֹה הבחן פֹ]נת יקר ב]אֹל[ יזדעזעו וב]ל יחישו ממקומם
15 מֹעֹון קודש קֹוֹ]דֹ]שים לאהרֹו]ן בדעת עולם לב]ריֹ]ת משפט ולקריב ]ניחוח ובית
16 תמים ואמת בֹ]ישראֹ]ל[ להקם ברית לחוקות עול]ם בהכין אלה

Remarks:
3. 1QS has a different preposition: על instead of עד. In 1QS the word מלאֹה is in the orthographical form מלואה, and the word לו is lacking.
7. Instead of the plural אנשים 1QS has the singular איש.
8. 1QS adds the conjunction ו before צדקה.
9. After the words ביצר סמוך 1QS continues directly with the words ורוח נשברה, omitting ובענוה (4QSᵉ). Note the medial *ṣade* at the end of בארץ in 4QSᵉ.
10. Qimron transcribes וֹתֹהֹלֹך, but the conjunction ו is not visible to me. 1QS reads ולהתהלך.
12. Instead of למ]שֹפֹט עולֹם 1QS reads למֹעֹה עולם (corrected from בעת עולם by the second scribe).
14. 1QS gives the longer form of the personal pronoun היאה without the conjunction ו. Apparently, the word יסודותיהו added above the line in 1QS, to be read after יזדעזעו, was not included in the text of 4QSᵉ.
15. Towards the end of the line, there are two ink marks above the line, the significance of which is unclear. Qimron suggests לֹם, and indeed, the head of a *lamed* is to be seen in line 14 before the two ink marks above line 15. Whether the two ink marks can be interpreted as final *mem*, seems somewhat questionable to me, but I am unable to offer any alternative reading.

16. The sentence והיו לרצון לכפר בעד הארץ ולחרוץ משפט רשעה ואין עולה added above the
line in 1QS is lacking in 4QS ᵉ.

## Frg. 1 III (1QS VIII,11-15 + IX,12-20)

1   [ביסוד היחד שנתים ימים בתמים דרך יבדלו] קדש בתוך [ע]צת אנ[שי]
2   [היחד וכול דבר הנסתר מישראל ונמצ]א לאיש הדורש אל י[ס]תרהו
3   [מאלה מיראת ר]וֹח נֹס[ו]נה ובהיות ]אלה ליֹהֹדֹ בֹלֹי־יבדלו מושב
4   °°° [העול ל]לכת המלֹבֹבֹה] לפנות שמֹ[ה את דרך האמת כאש]ר[
5   כתוב] במד]בר פ[נו דרך יהוה יש]רו בערבה מסלה לאלוהינו
6   היאה [מדרש התורה אשר ]צֹוה ביד משה אלה הח]וקים[
7   למ[שכיל להתהלך בם] עם כול חי לתכון עת] ועת[
8   ולמש[קל איש ואיש לעשות ]אֹת רצון אל ככול הנגלה ]לעת בעת[
9   [ולמוד את כול השכל ]הנמצא לפי העתים ואֹת] חוק[
10  הֹעתֹ] להבדיל ולש[קול בני הצדק לפי ר[ו]חֹמה
11  ובבחירי העת להחזיק ]על פי רצונו כאשר צוה ואיֹש[
12  [כרוחו כן לעשות משפטו ו]איש כבור כפיו לקרבו ול[פי]
13  [שכלו להגישו וכן אה]בתו עם שנאתו אשר לוא ל[הוכיח]
14  ול[התרובב עם א[נשי השחת ולסתיר את ע]צֹת[
15  התורֹהֹ] בתוך אנשי העול] להֹוֹכֹיח דעת אמת ומשפט
16  צדק לבחֹ[ירי דרך איש ]כרוחו וכהכנו העת להנחותם
17  בדעֹה וכן להשכילם בר]זֹי פלא ואם תיתם דרך סוד
18  יֹהֹר לֹ[הלך תמים איש ]את רערו בכל הנגלה להם
19  היאה [עת פנות הדרך ]למדבר ולהמשילם בכול

Remarks:

1. 1QS has the *plene* spelling קודש. Qimron transcribes מֹקֹרֹשֹ here, but if there was
a *mem* before this word, the lower stroke of the letter would be visible. The
surface of the leather has broken off only in the upper part of this line.
2. 1QS reads ונמצאו, which does not match the singular subject.
3-4. Before מושב 1QS has מתוך. Reading the second (preserved) word of line 3 of col.
III is problematical. Recognizing the letters is difficult; at first sight they do not
seem to constitute any word at all. Probably a second copyist corrected the text
of the first copyist and re-shaped at least two, possibly three, letters. In "A
Preliminary Concordance to the Hebrew and Aramaic Texts from Qumran
Caves II-X" (printed from a card index) this word is read as בישראל written in
cryptic letters. I have earlier argued (JJS 44/1993, 307-308) that the presence of
a cryptic text here is unlikely, since the same word occurs elsewhere in the
manuscript written in normal Hebrew letters (frg. 1 II 10 and 16). I suggested
instead that the second copyist attempted to correct the unclear text of the first
copyist and wrote ליחד, which is to be found above the line in 1QS. Stephen
Pfann has now studied the text in this line more carefully. In a personal
communication he shared with me his conclusion that the reading בישראל in
cryptic letters is indeed correct. According to him, the end of the word בישראל is
written above the line, where I have read כול. While I would like to maintain my
earlier reading as an alternative, I am now inclined to think that the reading

בישראל is more probable, especially since S. Pfann pointed out to me that
cryptic letters also occur at the beginning of the next line, where the word אנשי
(1QS) is to be anticipated. The words בתכונים האלה added above the line in 1QS
are absent in 4QSᵉ. Instead of המדבר 1QS reads למדבר, and instead of שמֹה 1QS
has שם. While 4QSᵉ reads האמה, 1QS gives the personal pronoun הואה, which is
syntactically difficult in this context.

5. The *Tetragrammaton* is marked with four dots in 1QS. In 4QSᵉ it is not
preserved, as indicated by the square brackets.

6. After ביד משה the text continues directly from 1QS IX,12. The word משה is in
*plene* form in 1QS.

8. Qimron's transcription לעֹלֹוֹת רצוֹן cannot be ruled out either.

10. 1QS reads בני הצדוק, which is possibly a scribal error (see, however, p. 137 n.
92), and uses the shorter form of the 3.m.pl. suffix in רוחום (4QSᵉ: רוחמה).

13. 1QS has the conjunction ו before אשר.

14. The hiphʿil infinitive construct ולסתיר has dropped the letter *he*. The *he* is also
lacking in 1QS, where the infinitive has furthermore been written without *yod*
(the form should still be understood as hiphʿil; in the Old Testament, too, a
hiphʿil infinitive construct form of this root occurs spelt without *he* and *yod*, see
Isa 29:15).

16. 1QS has a Qal active participle לבוחרי, 4QSᵈ the Aramaic passive participle
לבחירי. The form in 4QSᵉ (only partially preserved) may have been a *defective*
spelt Qal active participle or the Aramaic passive participle, as I have suggested
in my reconstruction.

17. 1QS reads פלא ואם תיתם דרך סוד יהֹד ואמת בתוך אנשי היחד instead of פלא ואם תיתם דרך סוד יהֹד.

18. To be grammatically correct, the definite article should be read before יהֹד.
Qimron transcribes היחד here, but the article is not visible to me. The word רערו
is a scribal error and should be corrected to רעה. Qimron has רעיו, but I find the
reading unlikely here, since the hook in the letter *yod* is usually sharper.

19. The word ולהמשילם probably also contains a spelling error; instead of the first
*mem* the letter *kaph* should be read (cf. 1QS). On the other hand, the root משל
(4QSᵉ) is not impossible in the context. The preposition ב is lacking in 1QS
before כל.

Frg. 2 (1QS IX,20-24)

1   [הנמצא לעשות] בֿעת הֹ[זואת ו]הֹבֿ[דֿל מכול איש ולוא הסר]

2   [דרכו מכול עול] ואלה הכֿוֹני [הדר]ֿך למשֿכיל] בעתים האלה לאהבתו]

3   עם שנא[תו שנאת עו]ל[ם ע]ם [אנשי שחת ב[ר]ו[ח] הֹסתר לעז[וב]

4   למו הוֹ[ן] ועמל כפים כעבד למושל בו וענוה] לפני הרודה בו ו]להיות]

5   איש מֹקֿ[נא לחוק ועתו ליום נקם לעשות רצון בכֿ]ול משל[ה כפים]

6   וֹבֿ[כ]וֹל [ממשלו כאשר צוה וכול הנעשה בו ירצה בנדבה וזולת]

Remarks:
The orthography in the preserved parts is identical with that of 1QS.

## 2.6. 4QS^f (4Q260)

### 2.6.1. Description of the Fragments

The upper part of five columns survives from the early Herodian manuscript 4QS^f.[71] Milik identified the preserved parts of this manuscript with the sigla 4QS^f 1 I-V, but actually fragment 1 has broken up into six smaller fragments.

The first small fragment, the size of which is 5.5 cm x 4.0 cm, has preserved two lines from the upper right-hand corner of column I parallelling 1QS IX,23-24, the margin between columns I and II, and five lines from the left-hand part of column II which provide a parallel to 1QS X,1-5.

The upper left-hand corner of column II parallelling 1QS X,1-5, the margin between columns II and III, and the upper right-hand corner of column III, which provides a parallel to 1QS X,9-11, are preserved in a fragment measuring 4.6 x 3.6 cm. To this upper right-hand corner of column III also belongs a small fragment (1.1 cm x 0.8 cm) which is not visible in PAM 43.265 but which is to be found in the Rockefeller Museum plate 366.

The upper left-hand corner of column III is preserved in a fragment measuring 3.1 cm x 2.9 cm which parallels 1QS X,9-11.

Column IV, providing a parallel to 1QS X,15-20, is preserved almost entirely in two fragments (4.3 cm x 7.3 cm; 3.3 cm x 7.4 cm) both containing half of a passage of ten lines.

The upper part of column V in its full width (7.9 cm) and the right-hand margin are preserved in a fragment 9.4 cm x 5.6 cm in size. Six preserved lines provide a parallel to 1QS X,20-24.

### 2.6.2. Material Reconstruction of the Manuscript

The fragments have preserved several margins, with the aid of which the original scroll can be reconstructed with great precision. Each column comprised only ten lines. The width of the columns varies to some extent (II 9.9 cm, III 10.5 cm, IV 8.4 cm, V 7.9 cm), but the margin is regularly 1.0 - 1.2 cm at the sides of the columns and 0.9 - 1.3 cm above. Presumably there was stitching between columns III and IV; a double margin has to be counted there.

The left lower edge of fragment 4QS^f 1 V curving downwards to the right and the lower left edge of the left-hand fragment 4QS^f 1 IV correspond in shape. These pieces were placed on top of one another in the scroll.

---

[71] I studied the palaeography of this manuscript with A. Steudel in Jerusalem in 1993. The date is consistent with that proposed by Cross 1994, 57.

Because there is hardly anything missing between the pieces - 4QS$^f$ 1 V has preserved the margin between the pieces and only about one word is missing at the end of each line in the left-hand piece of 4QS$^f$ 1 IV - determining the circumference here is a simple task. The distance of 9.4 cm can easily be seen at the level of line 4 where the lower edge begins to curve. This is the innermost circumference of the preserved part of the scroll.

The width of the upper left-hand fragment 4QS$^f$ 1 IV corresponds to the width of the left-hand fragment 4QS$^f$ 1 III. Also the shape of the lower edge of this fragment 4QS$^f$ 1 III is similar to the line of the edge of the left-hand fragment of 4QS$^f$ 1 IV curving downwards to the left from line 2. The points of circumference of 9.6 cm are to be seen in the small corners of line 2 of both fragments (there is a vertical break in the left-hand fragment 4QS$^f$ 1 IV).

Determining the corresponding points in the next level of circumference (9.8 cm) is more difficult, but I find it probable that the corner at the end of line 1 in the left-hand fragment 4QS$^f$ 1 III and the corner at the beginning of the same line in the right-hand side of the same column were placed one on top of another in the scroll.

The left-hand fragment 4QS$^f$ 1 II has a similar kind of lower edge curving to the left as has fragment 4QS$^f$ 1 I. The circumference of 10.0 cm, which is the outermost one preserved in the fragments of 4QS$^f$, is the easiest to see in the points at the level of line 2 where the edge begins to curve in both fragments.

The beginning of the text was written in the outer layers, and the circumference in the outer preserved fragments is 10.0 cm; in the inner preserved layers it is 9.4 cm. The leather is much thinner than in 4QS$^e$; the circumference decreases by 0.2 cm. Considering the thickness of the leather the inner circumference of the scroll was presumably 3 cm. In addition to the five columns that are preserved, the scroll must have had approximately 195 extra centimetres in its inner layers, i.e eighteen columns plus a handle sheet in its inner layers. The last line of column V presumably corresponded to 1QS X,26. For the last column of 1QS about three and a half columns are needed. This would leave us with fourteen and a half columns. The material of 1QSa would take up about six columns. For the material of 1QSb about 18 columns would be needed. Obviously the scroll could not have contained both of these manuscripts, even the material of 1QSb would be too much. Most likely the document following the Community Rule was neither of these two.

## 2.6.3. Transcription and Variants

### Frg. 1 I (1QS IX,23-24)

1  [לחוק ועתו ליום נקם לעשות רצון בכ]ל משלוח
2  [כפים ובכול ממשלו כאשר צוה ]וכול הנעשה

Remarks:
1. 1QS provides the lexical by-form משלח. Both forms are also attested in the Old Testament (cf. Isa 11:14 - Deut 15:10).

### Frg. 1 II (1QS X,1-5)

1  ברשית א[ש]מ̇ורות [חושך כיא יפתח אוצרו וישתהו עלת] תקופתו
2  עם האספו מ[פני אור בהופיע מאורות מזבול קודש עם האס]פם למעון
3  כבוד ובבוא[ מועדים לימי חודש יחד תקופתם עם מסרוחם ז]ה לזה
4  בהתחד[שם יום נדול לקורש קודשים ואות למפתח חסדיו עו]לם
5  לר[א]ש̇י מועדים בכול קץ נהיה ברשית ירחים למועדיהם וי̇מ̇י̇

Remarks:
1. 1QS has the *plene* spelling בראשית and the masculine ending אשמורי instead of the feminine one. Since there is an empty space (a word space?) before תקופתו, the conjunction ו and the preposition ב may have been absent in 4QS$^f$ (cf. 1QS: ובתקופתו). On the other hand, in the same word between the letters ו and פ there appears also a space in the manuscript.
3. Instead of ב plus infinitive construct 1QS has the preposition ב plus the noun מבוא (entrance; sunset; entering).

### Frg. 1 III (1QS X,9-11)

1  וכ̇[נ]ור נב[ל]י ]ל[ה]תכון קודשו וחליל שפתי א[שא בקו משפטו̇
2  ע[ם מבוא יום ולילה אבואה בברית אל ועם] מוצא ערב
3  [וב]וקר [אמר חוקיו ובהיותם אשים נבולי ל]בלתי שוב

Remarks:
1. At the beginning of the line, Qimron's reading אכ̇ה [ונב]לי is also possible. García Martínez (1996) prefers the reading וכ̇נור suggested in the Preliminary Concordance and here.

### Frg. 1 IV (1QS X,15-20)

1  בר[א]שית פחד ואימה [ובמכון] צרה עם בוקא [אברכנו]
2  ב̇הפלא מאדה ובנבורו̇[תו א]שוחח ועל חסד[יו אשען]
3  כול היום משפט כול הין ואמת כול מ[ע]ש̇יי ]ובה[פתח]
4  צרה אהללנו ובישועת̇ו̇ ארננה י̇חד לוא אש[יב]

5  לאיש נמול רע לטוב [ארדף [נבר כ]יא] את א[ל משפט]

6  כול חי הוא ישלם לא[י]ש נמו[ל]ו לוא אק[נא ברוח]

7  רשעה ולהון חמ[ס לוא האוה נ[פ]שי ור[י]ב אנשי

8  שחת לו[א] אחפוש ע[ד יום נקם ו[א]פי לו[א אשיב]

9  מאנשי עולה ו[לוא ארצה עד הכי[ן משפט] לוא]

10  [א[טור לש[ב]י] פשע]		[אנשי ]			[

Remarks:

1. The orthography of 1QS is different in ברשית and בוקה. The latter (interchange of *he* and *aleph*) is actually an error in the laryngeal caused by their weakening.

2. At the beginning of the line the surface of the leather has broken off and only a part of the letter ב is visible. Qimron transcribes וה.פלא, but I find this reading less probable here. Note the difference in orthography: 1QS reads מדה instead of מאדה. The noun is in the singular in the word ובנבורתו in 1QS, but it is in the plural in 4QS^f. The suffix ־יך is expected in 4QS^f, but the Qumranic suffix ־ may also have been used.

3. After כול היום 1QS adds ואדעה כיא בידו.

5. 1QS gives a different preposition: בטוב instead of לטוב.

6. 1QS has the longer form of the personal pronoun הואה with the conjunction ו.

8. 1QS reads an extra *aleph* in ואפיא.

10. At the end of the line the text must have differed from that of 1QS, since there is no correspondence to אנשי in 1QS. After אטור 1QS adds באף, and after לשבי פשע 1QS continues ולוא ארחם על כול סוררי דרך.

## Frg. 1 V (1QS X,20-24)

1  אר]חם על כול סוררי` דרך לוא אנחם בנכיהים עד תום

2  ד]רכ[ם ובליעל לו[א] אשמור בלבבי ולוא ישמע בפי

3  נבלוה וכחש עוון [ומ]ר[מות וכזבם לוא ימצאו בשפתי

4  ופרי קודש בלשני`		*vacat*	ושק[ו]צ[ם לוא ימצא

5  בה בהוד]ות אפתח[ה		*vacat*	פי] ו[צ]דקות אלחס[ופר]

6  לשוני תמ]יד ומעל [אנשים] עד ת[ום פשעם [רקים]

7  [אשבית משפתי נדות נפתלות] מ[דעה לבי בעצת תושיה]

Remarks:

1. What remains of the letter *yod* in סוררי is barely visible, since the surface of the leather has broken off. The form בנכיהים is impossible. It should be corrected with 1QS to בנכאים.

3. 1QS has the *plene* form וכוזבים. Qimron transcribes וכוזבין (4QS^f); since the leather has become rumpled, it is difficult to decide whether the last letter of the word is final *mem* or *yod* plus final *nun*. The Aramaic plural ending ־ין does not occur elsewhere in this manuscript. Therefore, I read a defectively written Hebrew plural ending, which in my opinion also corresponds better to the ink marks on the leather.

4-5. The *vacat* is due to a defect in the leather.

5. Read אלחס[ופר] (4QS^f) with a word space אל תס[ופר] as in 1QS.

## 2.7. 4QSᵍ (4Q261)

### 2.7.1. Description of the Fragments

Seventeen small fragments, many of them less than 1 sq.cm in size, have remained of 4QSᵍ. According to Cross, the script of the manuscript is Jewish Semicursive and dates to c. 50-1 B.C.[72] Due to the poor condition of the material, it is very difficult to read and identify the fragments. Transcriptions of only five fragments are provided here; three (possibly four) of them have been identified. All transcribed fragments come from the middle parts of columns, only two small unidentified pieces seem to have preserved parts of the upper column(s). Reconstruction of this scroll is impossible.

Fragment 1 is in two pieces (1.6 cm x 4.8 cm; 3.9 cm x 3.0 cm), which in their six partly preserved lines provide a parallel to 1QS V,22-24.

Fragment 2 (3.9 cm x 2.5 cm) with its four partly preserved lines corresponds to 1QS VI,22-25.

Fragment 3 (4.3 cm x 5.2 cm), the largest of the fragments of this manuscript, is a parallel to 1QS VII,9-13.

Fragment 4 (3.3 cm x 2.2 cm) possibly forms a parallel to 1QS VII,16-18.

Fragment 5 (1.3 cm x 3.6 cm) is legible but cannot be identified.

### 2.7.2. Transcription and Variants

Frg. 1 (1QS V,22-24)

1 [את ב]ר̇י̇]ת̇ו̇ ול]פקוד את כול הו]ק̇ו̇' אשר צוה לע̇]שות]

2 [ועל פי ר]ב יש]ראל המתנדבים ]לשבת̇ יחד ולכת̇]וב בסרך]

3 [איש לפנ]י רע]הו לפי ]ש̇כלו ומעשי ה̇ת̇ו̇ר̇]ה להשמע הכול איש]

4 [לרעהו] הקטן̇ לנדול ולהיות פוקד]ם̇ א̇]ת רוחם]

5 [ומעשי]הם ש̇]נה בשנה להעלות איש לפי שכלו ותום דרכו]

6 [ולאחרו כ]נעו]י̇תו להוכיח איש את רעהו באמת וענוה]

Remarks:
The handwriting is very irregular. It is very difficult to estimate whether line 4 really was shorter than the corresponding text in 1QS.
1. 1QS has הוקיו, but this variant is merely an example of the Qumranic non-standard spelling (ו- instead of י -).
2. 1QS: לשוב ביחד לבריתו וכהבם בסרך. Charlesworth's translation "to return to the community" is incorrect and appears not to have taken account the variant in 4QSᵍ. The verbal root concerned is ישב 'to dwell,' not שב as in 1QS.
3. Instead of ומעשי הת̇ו̇ר̇]ה 1QS has ומעשיו.

[72] Cross 1994, 57.

## Frg. 2 (1QS VI,22-25)

1   [לתורה ולמש]פّّט ולؤّّ[ה]הרה ולערב את הונו ויהי עצתו ליחד ומשפטו ואלה]

2   [המשפטים א]שר ישפטו על פ]י הדברים אם ימצא בם איש אשר]

3   [ישקר במ]מון והוא יודע וה]בדילהו מתוך טהרת רבים שנה אחת]

4   [ונענש את רבי]עית לח]מ]ו ואשר ישיב את רעהו בקשי עורף ידבר]

**Remarks:**

Neither the right-hand nor the left-hand margin is preserved in the fragment. Therefore, it is possible that it belongs more to the left or to the right in the column, and the lines should accordingly be divided in a different way.

1. Qimron transcribes עלצתו לי‍ח]ד, but I find his reading less likely here.
2. The words בם במדרש יחד included in 1QS are missing after ישפטו.
3. 1QS reads בהן instead of במ]מון and uses the longer form ה)האה) of the personal pronoun 3rd masc. singular. Instead of ות]בדילהו 1QS has ויבדילהו. The letter before the gap is either a *he* or a *yod* with an unusually long hook.

## Frg. 3 (1QS VII,9-13)

1   [ידבר בפיהו דבר נבל שלושה חודשים ולמדב]ר [בתוך]

2   [דברי רעהו עשרת ימים ואשר ישכוב וّיّשן במ]ّוّש]בّ [הרבים]

3   [שלושים ימים] כן] לאיש הנפטר במושב הרבים] אשר לא ב°צה

4   [והנם עד שלו]ש] פעמים על מושב אחד ונענש עשר]ת ימים

5   [ואם יזקפו ונפטר ונענש ש]לושים ש]לושים יו]ם וא°שّّر

6   [יהלך לפני רעהו ערום ולו]א היה אנוש

7   [ונענש ששה חודשים ואיש אשר ירוק אל תוך מו]שב הّّّרّבّים

8   [ונענש שלושים יום ואשר יוציא ידו מתו]ّחّت בנדו

9   [°°°ר]

**Remarks:**

Apparently there were differences in comparison with the text of 1QS, since filling up the gaps gives very irregular line lengths.

1. One letter is preserved from this line, a *resh* at the end of a word which is located above the word וישן of the following line. Filling up line 1 with the aid of 1QS does not produce such a word in exactly this position, however. The words ולמדבר and דבר occurring nearby are the most probable alternatives for the word from which the letter *resh* has been preserved.
3. 1QS reads לוא instead of לא.

## Frg. 4 (1QS VII,16-18 ?)

1   [°°ר]

2   י]שלחוהומאّّّ‍ה‍ם וّלוא

3   [°היחד לש]לח ול]וא

4   [°°°מّ]

Remarks:

2. After ‏י[שלחוהו‎ read a word space (‏י[שלחוהו מא֗ת֗ם‎). 1QS has ‏לשלח הואה מאתם‎.

3. 1QS reads ‏ישלחהו‎.

Frg. 5[73]

‏א °[‎  1
‏[באן‎  2
‏[נה א]‎  3
‏[לרבים]‎  4

## 2.8. 4QS^h (4Q262)

### 2.8.1. Description of the Fragments

In the upper part of photograph PAM 43.267 three fragments of fairly similar shape have been placed together, but presumably only fragments 1 and 2 (4.7 cm x 3.3 cm and 4.8 cm x 3.3 cm) belong to the same manuscript.[74] The colour of fragment 3 (5.1 cm x 4.3 cm) is darker, the distances between the lines as well as the handwriting (cf. esp. ‏ם‎, ‏נ‎, ‏ל‎, ‏ק‎) are clearly different from those of fragments 1 and 2. According to Cross, the script of 4QS^h is Vulgar Semiformal and dates to about the first half of the first century C.E.[75]

Fragment 1 alone has a parallel in 1QS, whereas fragment 2 cannot be identified. There is a good likelihood that the manuscript is not a copy of the Community Rule at all, but some other manuscript (a collection of hymns?) quoting a phrase from the Community Rule. Interestingly, the text in fragment 1 is the same, 1QS III,4-5, as that cited in manuscript 5Q13. With only two fragments, it is impossible to reconstruct the original scroll.

### 2.8.2. Transcription and Variants

Frg. 1 (1QS III,4-5)

‏[בכפורי]ם ולא יטהר ב]מי נדה ולא]‎  1
‏[יתקד]ש֗ בימים ונהרות] ולוא יטהר]‎  2
‏[בכול מי ]רחיצה טמ]א טמא יהיה]‎  3
‏[כול יומי ]מ֗ו֗א]סו במשפטי אל]‎  4

---

[73] This fragment is not included in Qimron's transcription.

[74] Fragments 1 and 2 even have similar worm-holes.

[75] Cross 1994, 57.

Remarks:
1. 1QS has the *plene* form ולוא.
3. The noun רחצה has an extra *yod* or else this is a case of differing vocalization (cf. Biblical Hebrew רחצה, Cant 4:2; 6:6). 1QS has the synonym רחץ.
4. Qimron suggests יומי מואֹֹ בֹ]משפטי. There is so little remaining of the letters that it is difficult to say which of the readings is more probable.

Frg. 2

1   ]נכסו לכול ק[ֹ
2   ]רום נו ֹֹם[
3   במפצ אב ]

Remarks:
1. The scribe has rewritten the first word of the line.
2. It is very difficult to read the word commencing with a *nun*. The third letter might very well have been *qoph*. It may be asked, for example, whether the word was Qal masc. participle of the root נקם. This root occurs quite often in 1QS both as a noun and as a verb, especially in the columns surrounding the doctrine of the two spirits. After *qoph*, however, there seems to be another letter, possibly *yod*, and it would be rather unusual for this form to have been written with a *yod* (cf. BH נקם). Alternatively, the word may have been some form from the root נקה, although נקה does not occur elsewhere in the Community Rule (cf., however, CD V,15). The masc. pl. participle of נקה may have been spelt נקים. The adjective נקי may have had a cognate form נוקי, for *waw* instead of *qames* is attested in the Qumran texts (Qimron 1986, 39-40). In the latter case, the form in the text would have been masc.pl.st.abs. נוקים or נקים (cf. BH נְקִיִּם/נְקִיִּים).
3. Note a medial *ṣade* in the final position of במפצ.

Frg. 3 (This fragment most likely does not belong to the same manuscript as frgs. 1 and 2.)

1   ]הת דליתו ישתו עֹ[ֹ
2   ]שחקים ודליותו עֹ[ֹ
3   ]ֹֹ מרום ינובב פרי[
4   ]ֹ[ שבעה בזוהר ]
5   ]שֹמו טוהר ֹ[ ]
6   ]מלקי ֹ[ ]

## 2.9. 4QSⁱ (4Q263)

### 2.9.1. Description of the Fragment

Only one fragment 4.1 cm x 3.6 cm in size is preserved of this early Herodian manuscript (30-1 B.C.).[76] The fragment provides a parallel to 1QS VI,1-3.

### 2.9.2. Transcription and Variants

Frg. 1 (1QS VI,1-4)

| | |
|---|---:|
| [ ° ] [ונם ]אל יבא| | 1 |
| [ °] לפני עדים ובאלה יההל[כו בכול מנוריהם כול הנמצא| | 2 |
| [איש את רעהו וישמ]ע הקטן לנדול למלכאה ולה]ון ויחד יואכלו ויחד יברכו| | 3 |
| [ויחד יועצו ובכול מ]קום אשר יהיה שם [עשרה אנשים מעצת היחד אל ימש| | 4 |
| [מאתם איש כוהן ואי]ש כת]כנו ישבו לפניו וכן ישאלו לעצתם לכול דבר| | 5 |

Remarks:
1. Before אל יבא ונם 1QS has ולוא ישא עליו עוון. In 4QSⁱ, however, there seems to have been something else. Before the gap there is a blank space of about three letters, and this space is preceded by traces of one letter at the edge of the fragment. A final *nun* of עוון is to be expected, but the traces do not match with the final *nun* which can be seen two lines below. An *ayin* of עוון, as suggested by Qimron, is ruled out as the letter is clearly followed by blank leather. The version preserved by 4QSᵈ lacks the whole of ואל ישנאהו [בעורלת] לבבו כיא כיום [בעורלה] יוכיחנו ולוא ישא עליו עוון. It is likely that 4QSⁱ followed the text of 4QSᵈ here and that the *ayin* belongs to the word רשע. Instead of יבא 1QS reads יביא. The form in 4QSⁱ is either Qal or a *defective* written hiph'il. The hiph'il form, as attested in 1QS, is more suitable in the context.
2. Before לפני there is בתוכחה in 1QS, but the last partly preserved letter of the word before לפני in 4QSⁱ is certainly not ה. It seems rather to be כ. The word ובאלה lacks the conjunction ו in 1QS.
3. 1QS has a different orthography in למלאכה and reads ולממן instead of ולהון.

## 2.10. 4QSʲ (4Q264)

### 2.10.1. Description of the Fragment

Only one fragment (4.4 cm x 4.3 cm) is left of this manuscript, as well, dating from the second half of the first century B.C.[77] The fragment is from the very end of the Community Rule and provides a parallel to 1QS XI,14-22. The left edge of the fragment has marks of stitching. If manuscript

---

[76] So also Cross 1994, 57.

[77] I consulted A. Steudel when dating this manuscript. Our tentative conclusion has been confirmed by F.M. Cross (1994, 57): "This little fragment is written in a characteristic late Hasmonean or early Herodian Formal script of c.a. 50-25 B.C."

4QSj ended with the same line as 1QS,[78] the leather sheet on the left-hand side of the fragment was probably a handle sheet.

## 2.10.2. Transcription and Variants

Frg. 1 (1QS XI,14-22)

[ברחמיו הגישני ובחסדיו יבוא משפטי בצדקת ]אֿמתו שפטני̇ וברוב טֿ[ובו]     1

[יכפר בעד כול עוונותי ובצדקתו יטהרני מנדת אנ[וש וחטאת בני אדם להודות     2

[לאל צדקו ולעליון תפארתו ברוך אתה אלי הפותח לדעה ]לֿב עבדך הכן ב[צד]ק כל מע[שיו]     3

[והקם לבן אמתכה כאשר רציתה לבחירי אדם להתי]צֿב לפניך לעד כי מבלעדיך     4

[לוא תתם דרך ובלי רצונכה לוא יעשה כול אתה ה]וֿרית כל דעה וכל הנהיה     5

[ברצונכה היה ואין אחר זולתכה להשיב על עצ]תך ולהשכיל בכל מחשבת     6

[קודשכה ולהביט בעומק רזיכה ולהתבונן ב]כל נפלאותיך עם כוח [ג]בורתך     7

[ומי יכול להכיל את כבודכה ומה אף הואה בן ה]אֿדם במעשי פלאך וילוד אֿשֿהֿ     8

[מה ישב לפניכה והואה מעפר מגבלו ולחם רמ]ה מדורו והוא מצור דֿק̇ חֿמֿר     9

[קורץ ולעפר תשוקתו מה ישיב חמר ויוצר י]ֿדֿ לעצת מה יבין     10

Remarks:

3. 1QS has different orthography in עבדכה and כול. In the passage XI,14-22 1QS systematically uses the 2nd person masc. sg. suffix form כה-.

4. 1QS: כיא.

5.-7. 1QS has an orthographical by-form הוריתה which is also common in Biblical Hebrew. All three occurrences of כל in lines 5-7 are written *plene* in 1QS.

9. 1QS, too, has מדורו and not סדורו, which is the reading of Burrows (1951). (Qimron has corrected the reading error of Burrows in his transcription of 1QS.) 1QS gives the longer form of the personal pronoun 3rd person masc. sg. הואה (ו).

10. It is not quite clear whether there is a word-space before לעצת or not. If there is a space, the partly preserved letter after the gap is most likely the ד of יד (cf. 1QS XI,22). In the case that the letter should be read as belonging together with לעצת, it is most certainly the conjunction ו, which is also to be found in 1QS (ולעצה).

---

[78] Cf. 4QS[b] frg. 12.

### 3. Manuscripts 5Q11 and 5Q13

#### 3.1. 5QS (5Q11)

##### 3.1.1. Description of the Fragment

One fragment of a Herodian copy of the Community Rule has been found in Cave 5. The size of the fragment is 3.1 cm x 4.8 cm, and it has preserved six lines in two columns with stitching in the middle. Only the column on the right-hand side, which forms a parallel to 1QS II,4-7, can be identified with certainty. On the left-hand side, remains of only about six letters at the beginnings of the lines are recognizable. Milik suggests that they correspond to 1QS II,12-14.[79] If Milik's identification is correct, and if the text in the unpreserved part of column I followed 1QS, there were fourteen lines per column in this manuscript.[80]

Filling up the lines of the fragment with the aid of 1QS reveals that there were differences between the two manuscripts, omissions and additions.[81]

##### 3.1.2. Transcription[82] and Variants

Frg. 1 I (1QS II,4-7)

| | |
|---|---|
| °°°[ | ] 1 |
| מקל]לים | ] 2 |
| [את כול אנשי נורל בליעל וענו ואמרו ארור] אֹתה | ] 3 |
| בכול מעשי רשע אשמת]כֹּה יתנכה | ] 4 |
| אל זעוה ביד כול נוקמי נקם ויפקו]דֹ אֹחריכה | ] 5 |
| כלה ביד כול משלמי נמולים ארו]דֹ אתה | ] 6 |

Frg. 1 II (1QS II,12-14?)

1 וֹהֹי]ֹה בשומעו את דברי הברית הזות יתברך
2 בֹ]לבבו לאמור שלום יהי לי כיא בשרירות לבי אלך ונספתה רוחו הצמאה
3 עֹם ]הרויה

[79] Milik 1962, 181.

[80] This estimate based on about 39 letters per line is a very rough one, for the fragment does not form any identical parallel for the text of 1QS.

[81] Cf. Milik 1962, 180: "Bien que les mots, ou des parties de mots, du fragment se retrouvent, avec les mêmes séquences, en 1QS II,4-7 et 12-14, l'irrégularité du nombre des espaces par ligne suggérerait des variantes, des omissions ou des additions dans le texte de 5Q."

[82] The transcription follows that of Milik (1962, 181), only the lacunae have been reconstructed by the present writer. Charlesworth (1994, 106) considers the first letter after the lacuna in lines 5 and 6 uncertain, but Milik's transcription seems correct to me.

] 4

] 5

ſ 6

Remarks:
Presumably there were 36-39 letters per line in 5Q11. The text in line 4 in column I seems to have been longer in 5Q11 than in 1QS, for the text of 1QS gives only 22 letters to the line. Of course, there may have been a *vacat* in the line. On the other hand, in column II line 2 could not have contained all the text of 1QS (61 letters). The latter part of the quotation, i.e. the words כיא בשרירות לבי אלך, may have been missing in 5Q11, for the conjunction כיא is often used by redactors as a link. Without the latter part of the quotation the number of letters per line is 40.

## 3.2. 5Q13 Citing the Community Rule

### 3.2.1. Description of the Fragment

A citation of 1QS III,4-5 occurs in another sectarian text, which contains a review of the holy men of the past in a form of meditation addressed to the God of the universe (2nd person singular). In fragment 4, where the citation occurs,[83] the term מבקר is also mentioned. In the manuscripts of the Community Rule מבקר never occurs in connection with liturgical material. Milik has dated 5Q13 to the first century A.D.,[84] whereas most of the copies of the Community Rule come from the last century B.C.

### 3.2.2. Transcription[85] and Variants

5Q13 frg.4

1   יע[מֹוד לֹפֹנֹי המבקר ]

2   [ ] ולוא יזכה בכפורֹ]ים

3   [טֹמא טמא יֹהיֹהֹ] כול] יֹמי

4   הֹ]אֹלֹה יעשו שנה כֹ]ול ימי

5   [ֹא] [ ] לרוחֹ ]

Remarks:
If the citation in lines 2 and 3 followed the text of 1QS III,4-5 accurately, there were about 79 letters per line in 5Q13, which means that the lines were remarkably wide (cf. 1QS V which has about 80 letters per line).

---

[83] Schiffman (1994, 133) correctly points out that "the author may have drawn from an already existent *Rule of the Community* or, alternatively, may share sources with the *Rule of the Community*."

[84] Milik 1962, 181.

[85] The transcription follows that of Milik 1962, 183.

## 4. Conclusions

Of the ten copies of the Community Rule from Cave 4 four manuscripts - 4QS<sup>c</sup>, 4QS<sup>d</sup>, 4QS<sup>e</sup> and 4QS<sup>f</sup> - can be fully reconstructed, and one - 4QS<sup>b</sup> - partially reconstructed.

The preserved fragments of 4QS<sup>c</sup> are from the beginning of the Community Rule. Although the reconstruction of a papyrus is more difficult to carry out with precision than in the case of a leather manuscript, and a very large part of this particular manuscript has been destroyed, it is very likely that it contained text from all parts of the Community Rule except for the final psalm (par. 1QS IX,26b-XI,22).

Apparently, the manuscript 4QS<sup>d</sup> did not include the material of 1QS I-IV at all, but commenced with the parallel to 1QS V,1 onwards. The beginning of the manuscript has been preserved; the margin is unusually wide here and it bears no marks of stitching. The text corresponding to 1QS V-VII was considerably shorter in 4QS<sup>d</sup> than in 1QS. The parallel to 1QS V has been preserved in 4QS<sup>d</sup>, and the existence of a shorter version in the parallel to 1QS VI-VII can be demonstrated with the aid of material reconstruction. Besides the Community Rule, the scroll of 4QS<sup>d</sup> included a further text or texts. There was not quite enough space, however, for the material of both the Rule of the Congregation (1QSa) and the Blessings (1QSb). The text following the Community Rule may have been a completely different document.

The manuscript 4QS<sup>e</sup> might also have commenced with the parallel to 1QS V,1. In half of the manuscripts found at Qumran, the remains of badly damaged scrolls contain only their middle sections. The material reconstruction of 4QS<sup>e</sup> - 4QOtot indicates that it was probably the middle section of this scroll that was preserved, and the same amount of the text (six layers) which had deteriorated in the inner layers was also destroyed in the outer layers. With a much higher degree of certainty, the manuscript 4QS<sup>e</sup> did not include the final psalm (par. 1QS IX,26b-XI,22) at all, but contained the calendric text 4QOtot directly attached to the regulations addressed to the *maskil* (par. 1QS IX,12-26a).

The fragments of 4QS<sup>f</sup> have preserved parts from the parallel to 1QS IX-X. Some other text, which remains unidentified, must have followed the Community Rule in 4QS<sup>f</sup> (there would not have been enough space for 1QSa and 1QSb). It is also unclear whether the text of the Community Rule in 4QS<sup>f</sup> commenced with the parallel of 1QS I,1 or with 1QS V,1.

The manuscript 4QS<sup>b</sup> can be reconstructed only partially. The measurements of several columns can be calculated, and with the information provided by the parallel manuscript 4QS<sup>d</sup> it can be estimated that the text of the Community Rule in 4QS<sup>b</sup> consisted of twenty columns.

The manuscript 4QS[b] appears to be the only preserved copy of the Community Rule from Cave 4 containing all the major parts of the text of 1QS. The text corresponding to the end of the manuscript 1QS (XI,22) has been preserved in 4QS[b]. It is followed by the beginning of another text, or of a final formula.

Some copies of the Community Rule cannot be reconstructed: the fragments of the papyrus 4QS[a] are relatively large, but very different in shape. The places with corresponding damage cannot be determined. The manuscript 4QS[h] has been preserved in two fragments; without the existence of a third one it is impossible to determine the direction in which the scroll was rolled, thus enabling us to proceed in the reconstruction. Both 4QS[i] and 4QS[j], as well as 5Q11, have survived in one fragment only.

Almost all the fragments of the manuscripts of the Community Rule can be transcribed and identified; the present work includes more fragments than does the edition by Qimron, and provides a number of alternative readings to those suggested by him. The variants in comparison with 1QS have been pointed out in the remarks attached to the transcriptions. The fragments which cannot be transcribed come mainly from 4QS[g], which has been preserved in minute pieces. The manuscripts 4QS[a] and 4QS[h] include two fragments which have no direct parallel in 1QS. The vocabulary of the fragments indicates that at least the fragment of 4QS[a] belonged to the doctrine of the two spirits.

# CHAPTER TWO

THE LINES OF TEXTUAL TRADITION
IN THE COMMUNITY RULE

The remarks attached to the transcriptions of the fragments in the previous chapter have already indicated that the copies of the Community Rule contain a large number of differences. Our task now is to take a closer look at the variants included in the preserved manuscripts of the Community Rule, in terms of both their linguistic features and their contents, and to determine the signs of redaction in the text. What are the characteristics of the major versions of this document? Does 1QS represent the oldest preserved form of the Community Rule or has the material from Cave 4 transmitted a more original version (or more original versions) of the text? Are there any common features to be seen in the redactional activity? Can we detect only one line of textual tradition in the manuscripts or are there several to be found?

Our analysis is primarily focused on the manuscripts which provide enough material for comparison and ones where the number and the nature of variants are particularly significant, i.e. manuscripts 4QS$^{a,b,d,e,h}$. The manuscripts 4QS$^{c,f,g,i,j}$ as well as the material from Cave 5 have been preserved in too fragmentary a form to enable us to draw any far-reaching conclusions, but the variants included in them will be briefly dealt with. Since the analysis can cover only the preserved parts of the manuscripts,[1] and the amount of the preserved text varies greatly from one manuscript to another, it is clear that the possibility of using the statistics of the variants for comparison of the manuscripts is fairly limited. The purpose of the statistics is rather to point out the particular features of the individual manuscripts.

*1. The Early Version of the Community Rule in 4QS$^e$*

*1.1. Orthography and Language*

The manuscript 4QS$^e$ appears to use *defective* spelling more often than does 1QS. There are two cases in the preserved fragments where 4QS$^e$ reads

---

[1] This difficulty involves the linguistic analysis in particular. As to the differences in the contents of the manuscripts, the reconstruction can provide some indication of the character of the original text.

*defective* when 1QS has a *plene* form,[2] whereas the number of reverse cases is one.[3] There is a case with an orthographic variation of מלואת/מלואה/מלואת caused by a silent *aleph*,[4] and a medial letter is used once in final position in 4QSᵉ.[5] The number of spelling errors in 4QSᵉ is four, which can be considered relatively a high number taking into consideration the amount of the preserved material.[6] The possibility of the presence of cryptic script in 4QSᵉ has been discussed in the remarks on fragment 4QSᵉ 1 III.

As to the morphological differences, there is one variant with a shorter form of a personal pronoun in 4QSᵉ where 1QS uses the longer form,[7] and one variant with a longer form of the 3rd masculine plural suffix.[8] Two cases involve the use of singular/plural variation,[9] but the second case is presumably the result of an error in 1QS: in 1QS VIII,11 a plural verb form occurs together with a singular agent (ונמצאו לאיש הדורש), whereas the form in 4QSᵉ 1 III,2 (ונמצא[א לאיש הדורש) matches the agent. Differences in syntax, on the other hand, are numerous. Seven of these differences are related to prepositions or the use of *nota accusativi*,[10] and in three cases 4QSᵉ lacks the conjunction ו, while 1QS has it.[11]

## 1.2. Variants of Contents

1QS VII,8: The manuscript 4QSᵉ has preserved the presumably earlier practice of the community, according to which the punishment for holding a grudge against one's neighbour lasted six months. In 1QS VII,8 the words ששה חודשים are omitted by placing them between brackets and the changed punishment of one year (שנה אחת) is written above the line.

1QS VII,14: The punishment for displaying one's nakedness lasts sixty days (ששים יום) in 4QSᵉ 1 I,10, while 1QS VII,14 reads a more lenient punishment lasting thirty days (שלשים יום). In 4QSᵉ there is thus evidence for a more lenient punishment than in 1QS (VII,8), as well as for a more severe punishment than in 1QS (VII,14). The comparison between the

---

[2] 4QSᵉ 1 I,3; 1 III,1.

[3] 4QSᵉ 1 III,14 ולסחיר (1QS ולסחר). Note that both 4QSᵉ and 1QS have dropped the *he*.

[4] 4QSᵉ 1 II,3.

[5] 4QSᵉ 1 II,9.

[6] 4QSᵉ 1 I,4; ; 1 III,10 (see p. 137 n. 92); 1 III,18; 1 III,19.

[7] 4QSᵉ 1 II,14.

[8] 4QSᵉ 1 III,10.

[9] 4QSᵉ 1 II,7; 1 III,2.

[10] 4QSᵉ 1 I,4 (1QS has a different preposition); 1 I,9 (1QS adds the *nota accusativi*); 1 II,3 (1QS has a different preposition); 1 II,3 (1QS lacks the preposition with a suffix); 1 II,10 (1QS adds a preposition); 1 III,4 (1QS adds a preposition); 1 III,19 (1QS lacks the preposition which is necessary in the context).

[11] 4QSᵉ 1 II,8; 1 II,10; 1 III,13.

manuscripts 1QS and 4QS^e indicates that one should not draw over-hasty conclusions as to the direction of the development in the penal code.[12]

1QS VIII,3: In the list of tasks and qualities required of the members of the council of the community, 4QS^e includes the word ובענוה before ורוח נשברה, while 1QS lacks it. The meaning of the word ענוה is very close to that of רוח נשברה, so adding or omitting it does not actually change the import of the sentence. The text in 4QS^e reads: "...that they may preserve faithfulness in the land by a constant mind, humility and a broken spirit."

1QS VIII,5: Instead of למ[שפט עול[ם (as eternal justice) 1QS reads למ°עת עולם (as an eternal plant). The words in 1QS have been corrected from בעת עולם (in eternal time) by the second scribe.

1QS VIII,13: In 1QS the text is syntactically very difficult, for the personal pronoun הואהא referring to God occurs instead of the possessive suffix: "They... shall go into the wilderness to prepare there the way of Him" (את דרך הואהא...). The fragment 4QS^e 1,III,4 gives a more intelligible text by presenting a genitive construction: את דרך האמת.[13] The form of the text in 4QS^e is likely to be more original, whereas 1QS provides a corrupt reading. It is to be noted that the reading in 1QS occurs in column VIII, where the scribe's *Vorlage* was particularly poorly preserved. Presumably he was able to read the letters *he* and *aleph* from his *Vorlage*, and he conjectured the rest of the word.

1QS VIII,15-IX,11:[14] An important passage is lacking in 4QS^e: the words ביד מושה of 1QS VIII,15 are directly followed by אלה החוקים in IX,12. The third occurrence of the threefold formula "When these exist in Israel", on which the structure of the so-called textual nucleus (Manifesto) of the Rule has been supposed to be based,[15] is located in this missing passage. The mention of the prophet and the two messiahs also belongs in this section.

---

[12] Baumgarten (1991, 274) also takes a very cautious view with regard to the direction of the development of the penal code, but he finds it "possible that Milik is right with regard to communal discipline in positing a development away from the strict rigour of earlier phases." Milik 1959, 83-93.

[13] The use of the 3rd person sg. pronoun instead of the name of God as the latter part of a genitive construction is extremely unusual. As the subject of a sentence the 3rd person sg. pronoun can naturally refer to God, cf. CD IX,5.

[14] I have previously published the major part of this passage in *Journal of Jewish Studies* 44 (1993), pp. 303-308.

[15] Sutcliffe 1959, 134-138. The view of Sutcliffe has been accepted by subsequent scholars: Leaney 1966, 211, Murphy-O'Connor 1969, 529, Pouilly 1976, 15, Dohmen 1982, 81-86, Knibb 1987, 129.

Hunzinger states that the missing section was omitted secondarily because of the tensions in the penal code,[16] and Murphy-O'Connor, Pouilly and Dohmen follow him in their analyses.[17] Puech proposes a technical slip on the part of a copyist.[18] So far all the scholars who have dealt with the question have maintained the view that the oldest material contained all three occurrences of the formula with the wording "When these exist in Israel".

I would suggest, however, that the whole passage of 1QS VIII,15-IX,11 is a secondary insertion. The sections 1QS VIII,16b-19 and VIII,20-IX,2 are clearly interpolations, as has been noted by several scholars.[19] Whereas the beginning of column VIII forms an introduction to the fundamental principles of community life, the sections 1QS VIII,16b-19 and VIII,20-IX,2 provide a penal code for judging cases of transgressions. The code falls into two parts, the second of which has a new heading, and the two parts appear in the manuscript as two separate paragraphs. A difference of practice can be observed in them, and this difference indicates two different stages in the development of the legislation.

The remaining section IX,3-11 with the heading "When these exist in Israel" appears to be a duplicate of the beginning of column VIII, for at least five common themes can be detected: expiation for the land (VIII,6,10; IX,4), grounding of the community in truth (VIII,5; IX,3), the holy house for Aaron and Israel (VIII,5-6,8-9; IX,6), the offering of a soothing odour (VIII,9; IX,4-5), separation of those who walk in the way of perfection (as holy ones VIII,10-11; IX,5-6, from evil VIII,13; IX,9).[20] The beginning of column eight functioned as a model for the third section with the formula "When these exist in Israel". A point of actualization can be perceived: Whereas VIII,14-15 speaks about studying the Law as "preparing the way", IX,9-10 warns against departing from it and emphasizes the importance of keeping "the first rules".[21]

The passage consisting of these three interpolations (1QS VIII,16b-19; VIII,20-IX,2; IX,3-11) is linked to the preceding material by means of ל +

---

[16] Hunzinger 1963, 242-243.

[17] Murphy-O'Connor 1969, 532; Pouilly 1976, 18; Dohmen 1982, 81-96.

[18] Puech 1979, 106-107.

[19] Denis 1964, 43, Guilbert 1959, 333-334, Hunzinger 1963, 242-245, Murphy-O'Connor 1969, 532-533, Knibb 1987, 136-137.

[20] Similar themes also occur in 1QS V,1-7, but the passage is likely to belong to a later stage, for the text shows that the structure of authority in the community has changed in the direction of democratization: In IX,7 the priests alone possess authority, whereas in V,2-3 it is shared between priests and laity. See Hunzinger 1963, 243-244, Klinzing 1971, 51-75, Murphy-O'Connor 1969, 534, Pouilly 1976, 55, Sanders 1977, 324-325.

[21] Cf. CD XX,31b-32a. For a recent discussion of the parallel see Stegemann 1990, 422-426 and Davies 1991, 277.

infinitive construct. This serves to introduce the clause עת הנגלה ככול לעשות
בעת וכאשר גלו הנביאים ברוח קודשו which completes the statement about
scriptural authority: It includes not only the law of Moses but also the
words of the prophets (compare 1QS I,2: כאשר צוה ביד מושה וביד כול עבדיו
הנביאים). The form of the text which we have in 4QSᵉ is syntactically fully
possible; there is no need to presuppose an error on the part of the copyist.
The sentence היאה מדרש התורה אשר צוה ביד מושה in 4QSᵉ is used in connection
with the preceding citation of Isa 40:3; "preparing the way" means the
study of the Law.[22] The heading אלה החוקים למשכיל then introduces a new
passage with the regulations for the wise leader.

1QS IX,18-19: The fragment 4QSᵉ 1 III,17-18 has preserved an interesting
variant which may indicate a change in the organization of the community. In the list of the duties of the wise leader 1QS points out that his
teaching duties concerning "the mysteries of wonder and truth" are to be
fulfilled "in the midst of the men of the community": וכן להשכילם ברזי פלא
ואמת בתוך אנשי היחד להלך תמים איש את רעהו (... and likewise instruct them in
the mysteries of wonder and truth in the midst of the men of the
community that they may walk perfectly with one another...). The text of
4QSᵉ makes no mention as to the forum in which the teaching takes place,
but it provides a further comment on the subject of the teaching: וכן להשכילם
בר|זֿי פלא ואם תיתם דרך סוד יֿחֿר לֿ|הלך תמים איש |את רערו {corr. רעהו} (... and
likewise instruct them in the mysteries of wonder and the perfection of the
way of the assembly of the community that they may walk perfectly with
one another...). The difference in syntax between the two versions of the
text is presumably caused by an error in the word division: 1QS reads
ברזי פלא ואמת..., but 4QSᵉ has בר|זֿי פלא ואם תיתם.... Particularly interesting
is the fact that whereas 1QS mentions "the men of the community" (היחד
אנשי), the text of 4QSᵉ speaks of "the assembly of the community" (סוד יֿחֿר,
corr. סוד היחד),[23] which also occurs in 1QS VI,19. It is unclear whether היחד
סוד is to be identified with עצת היחד (see 1QS V,7, VI,3,10,14,16,
VII,2,22,24, VIII,1,5) or whether they represent two different groups in the
organization of the community.

Although full certainty in the question as to the palaeographic age of 4QSᵉ
cannot be obtained,[24] the variants occurring in this manuscript, especially
those parallel to 1QS VII,8,14, VIII,13 and VIII,15-IX,11, indicate clearly

---

[22] Because of the interpolation, the referent of the pronoun היאה becomes less clear in 1QS.
The ambiguity has been noted by translators, see e.g. Knibb 1987, 128 and Vermes 1987, 73.

[23] Cf. 1QS VIII,5-6 וסוד קודש קודשים.

[24] On the problem of the palaeographical date of 4QSᵉ, see p. 48.

that 4QS^e has preserved a more original version of the Community Rule than has 1QS. The nature of the changes made in the text of 1QS varies to some extent, but a tendency towards actualization can be perceived. It remains unclear whether the corrections and additions were made by a single redactor or whether they are the result of successive revisions.

## 2. The Tradition Represented by 4QS^b and 4QS^d

A brief glimpse at the manuscripts 4QS^b and 4QS^d reveals that both of them contain a form of the text shorter than that of 1QS. Furthermore, the text of 4QS^b is practically identical with that of 4QS^d. The manuscripts even look alike: both of them are carefully written on well-prepared skins which have columns of about the same, rather small size. There is only one clear difference between these two manuscripts from Cave 4: whereas 4QS^b includes part of the text from all sections of the Community Rule, 4QS^d does not - and did not in its original form - contain any parallel to columns I-IV (liturgical and theological sections). The text beginning with the parallel 1QS V,1 (regulations for community life) was most likely also the beginning of the whole manuscript of 4QS^d, since the right-hand-side margin of column I in fragment 4QS^d 1 is unusually wide and it bears no marks of stitching. In spite of the difference in the amount of the text included in the scrolls, there is no question of manuscripts 4QS^b and 4QS^d belonging to the same textual tradition. The variants included in these manuscripts will be dealt with together.[25]

### 2.1. Orthography and Language

Of the linguistic variants, those involving differences in orthography are the most numerous, which is what one would anticipate. The total number of orthographical variants is thirty-six. In thirty cases, 4QS^{b,d} gives a *defective* spelling when 1QS has a *plene* form.[26] Six cases have the reverse - 1QS has a *defective* form when 4QS^{b,d} gives a *plene* spelling.[27] A clear difference between 1QS- and 4QS^{b,d}-manuscripts can be perceived: the copyists of 4QS^b and 4QS^d prefer *defective* spelling more often than does

---

[25] In fact, in the fragments of 4QS^b from the columns 1QS I-IV only two variants have been preserved. In the first case 1QS reads a *plene* form, while 4QS^b 3,1 has a *defective* one, in the second one 1QS uses the shorter form of the 2nd person sg. suffix, when 4QS^b 4,2 has הכ-. Both cases have been included in the next passage.

[26] 4QS^b 3,1; 4,2; 5,7; 10 II,1; 4QS^d 1 I,1; 1 I,4; 1 I,5 (3x); 1 I,6 (4x); 1 I,8; 1 I,10 (2x); 1 II,1; 1 II,6 (2x); 1 II,7; 2 I,3; 2 I,12; 2 II,2 (2x); 2 II,4; 2 II,5; 2 IV,2; 2 IV,6; 2 IV,7; 2 IV,8.

[27] 4QS^b 4,2 (may alternatively be a morphological error); 4QS^d 1 II,2; 1 II,3 (possibly a spelling error); 2 I,3; 2 III,11; 2 IV,2.

the copyist of 1QS. One must not, however, rely too much on the orthography as an indicator of the redaction or of the textual tradition of the text. Studies of the orthography of the Qumran scrolls have shown that the copyists retained a certain individuality in their use of *plene/defective*.[28]

Five of the cases of differences in orthography concern different laryngals.[29] A class of its own is formed by two cases where the scribe of 4QS[d] chose to use palaeo-Hebrew characters in the *Tetragrammaton* instead of the normal square script.[30] Four variants occurring in 4QS[d] belong in the group of scribal errors.[31]

The most numerous morphological variants concern pronouns and pronominal suffixes; there are three classified as pronouns and nine classified as pronominal suffixes. Very often the pronoun or the suffix is basically the same, but given in a different form (pronouns: 2 cases; suffixes: 3 cases).[32] 1QS is consistent in its use of longer forms of personal pronouns (היאה/הואה) but in both cases preserved in 4QS[d] the shorter form (היא) is used. In three cases 1QS lacks a suffix when it is present in 4QS[b,d].[33] The number of reverse cases is two.[34] Once the two versions have two completely different suffixes.[35] There is one case when 1QS reads a pronoun but 4QS[b] has a substantive instead.[36]

The number of cases of difference in the use of verbal stem forms is surprisingly high: six (all to be found in 4QS[d]).[37] Three cases involve the use of the infinitive construct combined with the preposition ל.[38] These constitute further evidence that the verbal system of the Hebrew language was in a stage of change at the time when the manuscripts were written.[39] Cases of different use of the article or definite or indefinite forms are five.[40] The manuscripts differ four times in the use of the singular or plural.[41]

The differences in syntax mainly involve the use of prepositions, *nota accusativi* and the conjunction ו. Thirteen variants belong in the first group. There are eight instances, when 1QS and 4QS[d] have a different preposi-

---

[28] See e.g. Tov 1986, 36.

[29] 4QS[b] 5,7 (may alternatively be a spelling error); 4QS[d] 2 III,12; 2 IV,3.

[30] 4QS[d] 2 III,9; 2 IV,8. For the use of palaeo-Hebrew in other Qumran manuscripts, see Tov 1986, 42.

[31] 4QS[d] 1 I,1; 1 I,10; 1 II,3; 2 III,11.

[32] Pronouns: 4QS[d] 2 II,6; 2 III,4. Suffixes: 4QS[b] 4,2; 5,4; 10 II,2.

[33] 4QS[b] 10 II,1; 4QS[d] 2,III,2 (a substantive attribute instead of a suffix); 2 IV,6.

[34] 4QS[b] 10 II,5; 4QS[d] 1 II,2 (a suffixed finite form instead of an infinitive construct).

[35] 4QS[d] 1 II,1.

[36] 4QS[b] 10,2.

[37] 4QS[d] 1 I,1; 1 II,2; 1 II,5; 2 II,1; 2 II,3; 2 III,2.

[38] 4QS[d] 1 II,2; 2 III,1 (2x).

[39] See e.g. Qimron 1986, 48-49.

[40] 4QS[b] 5,6; 4QS[d] 1 I,5; 1 II,6; 2 II,2; 2 III,6.

[41] 4QS[b] 4,2; 4QS[d] 1,I,5; 1 II,4; 2 IV,1.

tion.[42] In four cases the preposition is missing in 1QS when 4QS[b,d] has one,[43] and two times the preposition is missing in 4QS[d].[44] Once 1QS lacks a *nota accusativi*, when it is attested in 4QS[d].[45] The number of variants in the use of the conjunction is nine. In six cases 1QS lacks ו when 4QS[b,d] has it,[46] and four times the reverse is the case.[47]

## 2.2. Variants of Contents

1QS V,1: The heading for the section commencing a set of regulations for the community differs in the manuscripts 1QS and 4QS[b,d]. According to 1QS, what follows is "a rule for the men of the community" (סרך לאנשי היחד), whereas 4QS[b,d] entitles the passage "A teaching for the wise leader over the men of the law" (מדרש למשכיל על אנשי התורה).[48] The term סרך also occurs in the titles of 1QS I,1 and VI,8, and it is common in the headings of the sets of regulations in the Damascus Document (CD X,4, XII,19,22, XIII,7, XIV,3,12). The word is derived from the root שרך 'twist', 'adhere' (Jer 2:23).[49] According to M. Weinfeld, the original meaning of סרך is 'bond' or 'cord', and the Syriac, Arabic and Hittite cognates of שרך/סרך imply that סרך should be understood as 'bond' in the sense of the binding rules (= the code) as well.[50] The term is analogous with the Greek word τάξις and is used in the Community Rule with the same shades of meaning: 1. (battle) array, order; 2. post or place in the array; 3. ordinance, prescription.[51]

The word מדרש (4QS[b,d]), on the other hand, is derived from the root דרש, which in the Old Testament principially means 'to search', 'to seek', 'to examine' and 'to investigate' (cf. Lev 19:16; Deut 13:15; Isa 55:6 et al.).[52] The noun מדרש only occurs twice in the Old Testament (2 Chr 13:22 and 24:27); it is translated in the Septuagint by βίβλος and γράφη. In Jewish literature of the Second Temple period the word מדרש was first

---

[42] 4QS[b] 5,6; 4QS[d] 1 I,5; 1 II,4; 1 II,5; 1 III,3; 2 I,12; 2 II,2; 2 II,5.

[43] 4QS[b] 10 I,3; 4QS[d] 1 II,5; 2 II,3; 2 III,4.

[44] 4QS[d] 1 I,6; 2 I,7.

[45] 4QS[d] 1 II,1.

[46] 4QS[b] 5,2; 4QS[d] 1 I,2; 1 I,5; 2 II,2; 2 III,2; 2 III,6.

[47] 4QS[b] 11,3; 4QS[d] 1 I,3; 1 I,6; 1 II,2.

[48] For the translation of the clause, see C. Hempel 1993, 127-128.

[49] Baumgartner (HALAT) 1990, 1265.

[50] The word סרך can also be compared with תבל 'rope/cord' which likewise designates a guild or association. (1 Sam 10:5 and 10). Weinfeld 1986, 10-11.

[51] Cf. these meanings with the other occurrences of סרך in 1QS: I,1,16; II,20,21; V,23; VI,8,22. See Liddell - Scott 1973, Wernberg-Moeller 1957, 44, Schiffman 1975, 60-68, and Weinfeld 1986, 13.

[52] Baumgartner 1967 (HALAT), 223-224.

employed in the sense of education and learning generally (Sir 51:23),[52] and Vermes is correct in noting that מדרש appears here "in the non-interpretative sense of teaching or enquiry rather than the more common usage connecting it with the exposition of the Law."[53] The latter connotation of the term is apparent in 1QS VIII,15 and 4QMidrEschat III,14.[54]

The term אנשי היחד occurs in the Community Rule in columns of regulations only (V-IX). It refers to the members of the community in general and is somewhat synonymous with the term הרבים,[55] except that the latter has a more administrative connotation. Full certainty cannot be attained as to whether the term אנשי היחד also covers the members who were still on their probational period or whether the term, like הרבים, designated full members exclusively. In two out of the twelve occurrences אנשי היחד alludes to the lay members alone (1QS V,2-3; IX,7). In the contexts of these occurrences a differentiation has been made between the lay members (אנשי היחד or רוב אנשי היחד) and the priests (בני צדוק or בני אהרון).

In 4QSᵇ·ᵈ the teaching (מדרש) of the men of the Law (i.e. the men of the community) is said to be the responsibility of the wise leader, which is in agreement with the other occurrences of משכיל in the Community Rule. As one of the leaders of the community, he was to select, instruct and guide the members and avoid contacts with outsiders (cf. 1QS IX,12-26, III,13). Presumably he was a priest, for in 1QSb his duty is to bless the community, the high priest, the other priests and the prince of the congregation. The question has been raised whether משכיל can be identified with either the מבקר or פקיד, who are also mentioned as leading officers. It seems to me that whereas משכיל functioned as the spiritual leader of the community, the other two discharged administrative duties. Both מבקר and פקיד appear at the head of the rabbim (1QS VI,12,14), and the comparison with CD XIII,8-13 leads us to the conclusion that these two terms are synonymous.[56]

---

[52] Herr 1972, 1580.

[53] Vermes 1991, 254.

[54] Steudel (1994, 46) considers the usage of the term מדרש in 4QMidrEschatᵃ III,14 to be twofold: "...(ו)מדרש, welches zwar einerseits Einleitung zu Ps 1,1 und dessen Auslegung, andererseits und vor allem Überschrift zum gesamten folgenden Abschnitt ist." In the function of a heading, she maintains, the usage of the term is analogous to the one in the 4QSᵇ·ᵈ parallels of 1QS V,1.

[55] Weinfeld 1986, 14. For a broader discussion of the term היחד, see Dombrowski 1966, 293-307 and Wernberg-Moeller 1969, 56-81. For the background to and meanings of the term יחד, see Weinfeld 1986, 13-14 and Talmon 1989, 53-60.

[56] For the use of the term הרבים in the Qumran texts, see Brownlee 1951, 25 n. 27, Wernberg-Moeller 1957, 107, Milik 1957, 99-100, Cross 1958, 176, Priest 1962, 55-61, Vermes 1962, 19-25, Delcor 1979, 855, Newsom 1985, 3-4 Knibb 1987, 118.

1QS V,1: The gloss לרצונו, "according to his will," after "in all that he has commanded", has been inserted into the text in 1QS, presumably due to their close connection elsewhere in the Rule; see especially 1QS IX,15 and 23-24. Note that in the expanded part of the text in 1QS V,9-10 both of these sayings have been added.

1QS V,2-3: In 4QS[b,d] authority in the community has been said to belong to the *rabbim* (על פי הרבים)[57], whereas in 1QS the term is replaced by a long verse: "according to the sons of Zadok, the priests who keep the covenant, and the multitude of the men of the community who hold fast to the covenant. On the basis of their word the decision shall be taken" (על פי בני צדוק הכוהנים שומרי הברית ועל פי רוב אנשי היחד המחזקים בברית על פיהם יצא חכון הגורל). In spite of the use of different terminology, no difference can be perceived between the manuscripts in their description of the structure of the community, for 1QS VI,8 clearly states that the rabbim consist of both priests (הכוהנים) and laymen (הזקנים ושאר כול העם[58]). The motive for replacing הרבים with a long wording was undoubtedly theological: The redactor(s) wished to stress the purpose of הרבים as the true keeper of the covenant and, as Vermes has pointed out, to emphasize the Zadokite link of the priestly leaders of the community.[59]

1QS V,3: When recounting the matters concerned in the decision-making of the community - the law and wealth - 1QS adds ולמשפט (and with justice). In addition, at the beginning of the following sentence the words אמת יחד ו- have been inserted: "*Together* they shall practise *truth and* humility, righteousness and justice, kindly love and circumspection in all their ways."

1QS V,4-5: The sentence "Let no man walk in the stubbornness of his heart as to go astray" is attested both in 1QS and in 4QS[b,d]. In 1QS it has been expanded with a long phrase echoing several Old Testament verses (e.g. Num 15:39, Ezek 6:9, Deut 10:16, Jer 4:4): "...after his heart and his eyes and the thought of his inclination. Rather they shall circumcise in the

---

[57] For the meaning and translation of the term, see Huppenbauer 1957, 136-137, Carmignac 1971, 575-586, Kruse 1981, 548-549.

[58] This is the only occurrence of הזקנים in 1QS. The word also signifies a special group in 1QM XIII,1, CD V,4 and IX,4, and it may be somewhat synonymous with ראשי אבות העדה of 1QSa I,23-24. According to Baumgartner (1967 HALAT, 264), in the Old Testament the term is used in the sense "Gesamtheit der (den Vollbart tragenden) im reifen alter stehenden Männer, der Rechtsfähigen einer Gemeinschaft" (for example Josh 20:4, Deut 19:12; 21:3, Exod 3:16, 2 Kgs 23:1, Ezek 8:11, Lev 4:15, Deut 31:28, 1 Kgs 20:7, Exod 24,14).

[59] Vermes 1991, 254-255.

community the foreskin of their inclination and of their stiff neck" (אחר לבבו
(ועיניהו ומחשבת יצרו ואאם למול ביחד עורלת יצר ועורף קשה.

1QS V,5-6: The words "the eternal covenant" (ברית עולם) and "to make expiation" (לכפר), which have been added in 1QS, are essential concepts for the self-understanding of the community.[60] Having rejected the temple in Jerusalem as defiled, the community regarded itself as the only true keeper of the covenant of Sinai with Israel; joining the community actually meant entering this everlasting covenant (cf. 1QS III,11-12; IV,22; V,22). They were to make expiation, not by offering sacrifices in the temple in Jerusalem, but by the practice of justice and by enduring affliction (cf. 1QS VIII,3-4, 9-10). Adding theologically significant words to the text is a natural thing to do, but finding any reason for omitting them is very difficult. The text in 4QS$^{b,d}$ is undoubtedly more original.

1QS V,6-7: The following interpolation may have been produced at the same time as the previous gloss "and to lawsuits and judgements to declare guilty all those who transgress the statutes. These are their rules of conduct, according to all these statutes when they are admitted to the community" (ולריב ולמשפט להרשיע כול עוברי חוק ואלה תכון דרכיהם על כול החוקים האלה בהאספם ליחד). The themes of expiation and punishment belong closely together in 1QS VIII,6-7, but whereas the text in 1QS V,6-7 seems to refer to the wrongdoings of members of the community, in 1QS VIII,6-7 the punishment involves outsiders (note the mention of Aaron and Israel as in 1QS V,6-7). The manuscripts 4QS$^{b,d}$ indicate that the section referring to the binding oath to be taken by those desiring to become members of the community did not originally have any heading but begun directly with the words "Everyone who joins the council of the community."

1QS V,8: The emphasis on the community as the true keeper of the covenant is apparent again in the phrase absent in 4QS$^{b,d}$ but added in 1QS: "He shall enter into the covenant of God in the presence of all those who willingly offer themselves" (יבוא בברית אל לעיני כול המתנדבים).[61] Whereas the version 4QS$^{b,d}$ speaks of a binding obligation (אסר), 1QS stresses the nature of the commitment and by inserting the word 'oath' (שבועה) at the beginning. The same pair of words (שבועה אסר) is attested in CD XVI,7.

---

[60] For the use of the term ברית in the Qumran texts, see Ilg 1978, 257-263.
[61] The end of line 4QS$^b$ 5,6 has not been preserved, but counting the number of letters per line reveals that the words were absent there, as in 4QS$^d$ 1 I,6.

The gloss "according to all he has commanded" (ככול אשר צוה), added in 1QS after the words "to the law of Moses," is a phrase which occurs very often in 1QS, see I,3,17, III,10, V,1,22, VIII,15,21, IX,15,24.

1QS V,9-10: The text both in 4QS[b] and 4QS[d] has been preserved only fragmentarily in the parallel of 1QS V,9-10, but the equivalent to the term "the council of the men of the community" (עצת אנשי היחד) occurring in 4QS[b,d] appears to be the long phrase "to the sons of Zadok, the priests who keep the covenant and seek his will, and to the multitude of the men of their covenant who together willingly offer themselves for his truth and to walk according to his will" (לבני צדוק הכוהנים שומרי הברית ודורשי רצונו ולרוב אנשי בריתם המתנדבים יחד לאמתו ולהתהלך ברצונו). The phrase is similar to the one in 1QS V,2-3, where it replaces the term הרבים, and a comparison between 1QS VI,8 and 10 implies that the terms הרבים and עצת היחד are synonymous (see also e.g. 1QS V,7; VI,3,14,16; VII,2,22,24). A further addition in 1QS brings up again the theme of covenant: "He shall undertake by the covenant" (ואשר יקום בברית על נפשו).

1QS V,10-11: An attribute determining "the men of injustice" has been added in the text of 1QS: "those who walk in the way of wickedness" (ההולכים בדרך הרשעה).

1QS V,11-13: The necessity of separating from outsiders (the men of injustice) has been supported in 1QS with freely quoted and combined biblical citations which are lacking in 4QS[b,d]: "For they are not counted in his covenant because they have not sought or consulted him about his statutes in order to know the hidden things in which they have guiltily gone astray, whereas with regard to the things revealed they have acted presumptuously, arousing anger for judgement and for taking vengeance by the curses of the covenant to bring upon themselves mighty acts of judgement leading to eternal destruction without a remnant" (כיא לוא החשבו בבריתו כיא לוא בקשו ולוא דרשהו בחוקיהו לדעת הנסתרות אשר תעו בם לאששמה והנגלות עשו ביד רמה לעלות אף למשפט ולנקום נקם באלות ברית לעשות בם [מ]שפטים נדולים לכלת עולם לאין שרית). In the background can be detected Zeph 1:6, Deut 29:28, Num 15:30, Ezek 24:8 and Deut 29:21. הנסתרות (the hidden things) and הנגלות (the revealed things) are key terms for understanding the concept of divine revelation within the Qumran community. Even if the Mosaic law was recognized as the ultimate authority, there was an articulated emphasis on revelation as a continuing process involving a constant search for new illumination. The term הנסתרות, contrasted with הנגלות (the Torah), designates the esoteric halakhah of the community (such as the solar calendar).[62]

1QS V,13b-16a: In 4QS[b,d] the words "They shall not touch the purity of the men of holiness" (ואשר לא יגעו לטהרת אנשי הקודש) provide a loose parallel to 1QS V,13b: "He shall not enter the waters in order to touch the purity of the men of holiness" (אל יבוא במים לנעת לטהרת אנשי הקודש). The sentences begin somewhat differently, but the words לטהרת אנשי הקודש are identical. In 1QS the premises of conversion and thus of touching "the waters of purity" are stated explicitly in the text of 1QS, but they are lacking in 4QS[b,d]. The threefold conjunction כי serves as a link in 1QS: "... for men are not purified unless they turn from their evil; for he remains unclean amongst all the transgressors of his word" (כיא לוא יטהרו כי אם שבו מרעתם כיא טמא בכול עוברי דברו).

In 4QS[b,d] the prohibition to touch the purity of the men of holiness is followed by the sentence "He shall not eat with him within the community" (ואל יוכל אתו ביחד), which has nothing corresponding to it in 1QS. To be quite accurate, a similar kind of sentence does occur a little later in 1QS V,16, but it appears in 4QS[b,d] too. Thus the prohibition to eat with a man of injustice occurs twice in 4QS[b,d], which makes one wonder whether the first occurrence is the result of an error (יוכל - יוחד; the verb יוכל appears in both 4QS[b] and 4QS[d], however). Instead of the sentence ואל יוכל אתו ביחד 1QS has a long passage which includes a biblical citation: "No one shall join with him (i.e. with a man of injustice) with regard to his work or his wealth lest he burden him with iniquity and guilt. But he shall keep away from him in everything, for thus it is written, 'You shall keep away from everything false'" (ואשר לוא יוחד עמו בעבודתו ובהון פן ישיאנו עוון אשמה כיא ירחק ממנו בכול דבר כיא כן כתוב מכול דבר שקר תרחק). The sentence following the citation in 1QS "No one of the men of the community shall answer..." (ואשר לוא ישיב איש מאנשי היחד) is also attested in 4QS[b,d].

In this passage the basic statement of the oath to separate oneself from outsiders is clarified and confirmed with biblical proof-texts - Lev 22:16 and Exod 23:7.[63] The former is cited implicitly (cf. Lev 22:(15-)16 ...ולא והשיאו אותם עון אשמה), but the latter is a direct quotation. The citation is preceded by an introductory formula, כיא כן כתוב, which is followed by the citation מכול דבר שקר תרחק. Interestingly enough, the citation is in a form

---

[62] Baumgarten 1977, 29-32.

[63] Quite naturally, the citations which appear in 1QS were a subject of study long before the material from Cave 4 was available to the vast majority of scholars, see e.g. Wernberg-Moeller 1956, 40-46, Fitzmyer 1961, 296-333, Vermes 1989, 493-508, and Fraade 1993, 46-49.

which corresponds with the Septuagint rather than with the Masoretic text. The indefinite pronoun כול is missing in the Masoretic text (מדבר־שקר תרחק), but has an equivalent in the Septuagint (ἀπὸ παντὸς ῥήματος ἀδίκου). It is likely that the biblical manuscript used by the author contained this short word as a variant reading. Actually Exod 23:7 has to do with justice in lawsuits, but here - typically of Qumranic exegesis - it has been disconnected from its original context and applied to an entirely different matter. The catchwords here are רחק and דבר. The latter occurs not only immediately before the citation formula but also earlier in line 14, in the third of the sentences commencing with the conjunction כיא (note that there are five such sentences beginning with the conjunction כיא following one another).

1QS V,16b-18: The text parallel to 1QS V,16b-18 is fragmentary both in 4QS<sup>b</sup> and 4QS<sup>d</sup>, but quite clearly the words ואל יואכל in 4QS<sup>b</sup> 5,10b and 4QS<sup>d</sup> 1 I,9b correspond to the words ואשר לוא יוכל in 1QS V,16. In 4QS<sup>d</sup> they are followed by the phrase איש מאנשי הקדש, which is lacking in 1QS. Then there is a gap of about three words both in 4QS<sup>b</sup> and 4QS<sup>d</sup>, followed by the words ולא ישענו על ("They shall not rely on..."; note the scribal error in the verb in 4QS<sup>d</sup>, corr. ישענו). These words correspond to the words ולוא ישען איש הקודש על (No man of holiness shall rely on...) in line 18 of 1QS. No matter what the missing words in the gap were, it is clear that the whole of the passage 1QS V,16b-18b, with the citation from Isa. 2:22, was not included in the text of 4QS<sup>b,d</sup>. The missing passage beginning with ואשר לוא יוכל reads in full: "No one shall eat or drink anything of their property, or take anything at all from their hand except for payment, as it is written, 'Have no more to do with man in whose nostrils is breath, for what is he worth?' For all those who are not counted in his covenant, they and everything that belongs to them are to be kept separate" (ואשר לוא יוכל מהונם כול ולוא ישתה ולוא יקח מידם כול מאומה אשר לוא במחיר כאשר כתוב חדלו לכם מן האדם אשר נשמה באפו כיא במה נחשב הואה כיא כול אשר לוא נחשבו בבריתו להבדיל אותם ואת כול אשר להם).

The passage continues the prohibition of contact with the men of injustice, apparently with a concern to preserve the ritual purity of the community. The formula preceding the citation is here different from the one in the previous passage. Instead of כיא כן כתוב the text reads כאשר כתוב. The citation is in a form identical with the Masoretic text except for the Qumranic form of the personal pronoun הואה. 1QIs<sup>a</sup> uses the Masoretic הוא, but chooses the Qumranic form לכמה, which, however, in 1QS occurs in the Masoretic form. The quotation is followed by an interpretative comment. Note that in the context of the previous citation such an expository element is completely lacking. Obviously, the writer made a word-play on the verb

נחשב, 'to be accounted, be esteemed' and twisted its sense so as to make it bear the meaning 'being reckoned in the community' (cf. the occurrence of the same verb in 1QS V,11). In the text of Isaiah this verse counsels the people to cease trusting in the proud man, for on the day of God's judgement human pride will be humbled. Isaiah's prophecy has been given a totally different point of reference.

1QS V,21-22: In 1QS the glosses "in the community" (ביחד) before the words "to establish the covenant," and "to his covenant" (לבריתו) after the words "in the community," demonstrate again the need to emphasize the purpose of the community and reinforce its self-understanding.[64]

1QS V,23-24: Very rarely does the version from Cave 4 provide a longer text than does 1QS. Two of these instances occur in the context of a regulation concerning the registering and annual examination of the members. Whereas 1QS V,23 has "according to his insight and his deeds" (לפי שכלו ומעשיו) the text in 4QS[d] 1 II,3 reads "according to his insight and his deeds in Torah" (לפי שכלו ומעשיו בתורה). Similarly, while 1QS V,24 reads "They shall review their spirits and their deeds," 4QS[d] has "their deeds in Torah" (ומעשיהם בתורה).[65] The wording לפי שכלו ומעשיו בתורה appears a little earlier both in 1QS and 4QS[d] (1QS V,21; in 4QS[d] 1 II,1 the rest of the wording has been preserved in the form ואת מעשיהם בתורה), which explains both of the occurrences of the word בתורה in 4QS[d] 1 II,3 and 4. Interestingly, the second of the criteria for promotion in rank, ותום דרכו, (the perfection of his way) attested in 1QS, is lacking in 4QS[d], which reads merely: "that they may promote each man according to his insight."

1QS V,25-VI,1: The inserted words in 1QS V,25 "in truth and humility" (בא[מת] וענוה) and "towards men" (לאיש) echo the passage 1QS II,24-25, where the theme of conduct towards others is also dealt with. The expression "with a stiff neck" (בעורף [קשה]) is typical of passages describing the qualities of men who "walk in the way of darkness" (cf. IV,11, V,5, VI,26), but the wording "in a jealous spirit of wickedness" (בקנאת [רוח רשע] in ןQS, cf. בקנאת רשע in 4QS[d]) occurs nowhere else in 1QS. The verb יכח, 'to reprove' (1QS V,24), is likely to have functioned as a catchword for inserting the free quotation of Lev 19,17 (ואל ישנאהו [בעורלה] לבבו כי ביום יוכיחנו ולוא ישע עליו עוון) in the text of 1QS V,26-VI,1. The parallel to 1QS

---

[64] The parallel to 1QS V,21-22 is preserved in 4QS[d] only, but since 4QS[b] and 4QS[d] belong to the same textual tradition, it is highly probable that these variants were included in the text of 4QS[b] as well.

[65] The parallel of 1QS V,23-24 is not preserved in 4QS[b].

V,25-VI,1 is very short in 4QS[d]:[66] "They shall reprove one another (in)[67] kindly love. Let no man speak to his neighbour in anger or in complaint or in jealous wickedness." The text in 1QS: "They shall reprove one another in tr[uth], humility, and kindly love towards man. Let no man speak to his neighbour in anger or in complaint or with a [stiff] neck [or in a jealou]s spirit of wickedness, and let him not hate him in his [uncircumcised] heart. But let him reprove him on the same day lest he incur guilt because of him."

1QS VI,10-11: Very little has been preserved in fragment 4QS[d] 1 III, but line 1 seems to have contained a text approximately half the length of that in 1QS: the words איש את מד[עו corresponding to VI,9 are to be seen in line 1, and the words הרבים אל ידב[ר corresponding to VI,11 have been preserved from line 2; in between there is space for about eleven words, whereas 1QS has twenty-four.[68] At least the part reading "And no man shall speak before one registered in rank before him. A man who is asked shall speak in his turn" (ונם אל ידבר לפני תכונו הכתוב לפניו האיש הנשאל ידבר בתרו) must have been lacking in 4QS[d]. How much of the sentence אל ידבר איש בתוך דברי רעהו טרם יכלה אחיהו לדבר was lacking in the text of 4QS[d], or whether it was included in full, is difficult to judge. In 1QS this rule regulating the order of the right to speak in the community reads as follows: "No man shall interrupt his neighbour's words before his brother has finished speaking, or speak before one registered in rank before him. A man who is asked shall speak in his turn."

1QS VI,16-18: A very small fragment of 4QS[b] has been preserved from the section describing the second examination of the person applying for membership of the community. Only the very end of the sentence - "And afterwards, when he comes to stand before the *rabbim*, they shall all be asked about his affairs" - is left in 4QS[b], so we cannot be sure how accurately the text of 4QS[b] followed that of 1QS. The next sentence in 1QS, however, which is very emphatic about the authority of the *rabbim*, is lacking in 4QS[b]: "And as the decision is taken on the advice of the *rabbim*, he shall either draw near or keep away" (וכאשר יצא הגורל על עצת הרבים יקרב או ירחק). The prohibition against touching the purity of the *rabbim* during the first year of probation is attested in both 4QS[b] and 1QS, but the regulation concerning having no share in the wealth of the *rabbim* (ונם הואה אל יתערב בהון הרבים) appears to have been absent in 4QS[b]. Because

---

[66] The parallel of 1QS V,25-VI,1 is not preserved in 4QS[b].
[67] Actually, 4QS[d] 1 II,4 reads "*and* kindly love" (ואהבת חסד).
[68] The parallel to 1QS VI,10-11 is not preserved in 4QS[b].

of the insertion, the redactor has repeated the length of probation; the words
"When he has completed a year in the midst of the community" (ובמילאת
לו שנה בתוך היחד) are lacking in 4QS<sup>b</sup>.

1QS VIII,12-14: There is no preserved parallel to 1QS VIII,12b-16 in
4QS<sup>b</sup>, and a fragment in 4QS<sup>d</sup> has preserved only a part from the left-
hand-side edge of a column, which nevertheless allows a comparison with
the text in 1QS. Leaving out the orthographical differences, the text seems
in lines 1-5 of 4QS<sup>d</sup> 2 I to follow 1QS rather closely (the text above the
lines in 1QS VIII,9-11 was apparently included in 4QS<sup>d</sup>). In the middle of
line 6, however, from the sentence beginning with the words ובהיות אלה
בישראל (When these exist in Israel) onwards, the text begins to differ. The
words ליחד (as a community) and האלה בתכונים (in accordance with these
rules) written above the line in 1QS VIII,12 and 13 are lacking in line 6,
and the gap at the beginning of line 7 has room for only about ten words,
while in 1QS there are twenty. Obviously, some of the text of 1QS VIII,13-
15 was not included in 4QS<sup>d</sup>, and filling up the gap with the rest of the
sentence, which begins with the words ובהיות אלה בישראל, reveals that the
missing part was the citation from Isa 40:3.

The text of 4QS<sup>d</sup> thus reads as follows: "When these exist [in Israel],
they shall separate themselves fr[om the settlement] of the men of [injustice
and shall go into the wilderness to prepare there the way of him/the truth.
This is the study of the la]w which he commanded through[ Moses, that
they should d]o all [that has been revealed] from ti[me to time and in
accordance with what the prophets revealed by his holy spirit]" ( אלה ובהיות
בישראל ]יבדלו מ[תוך מושב אנשי העול ללכת למדבר לפנות שם את דרך האמת(?) היא מדרש
התור]ה אשר צוה בי]ד מושה לע[שות כו]ל הנגלה עת בעת וכאשר גלו הנביאים ברוח קודשו).
An alternative reading for "the way of him" is attested in 4QS<sup>e</sup>, which has
"the way of truth" (דרך האמת) instead of the syntactically difficult personal
pronoun הואה. It is interesting that both writers avoided the use of the name
'Yahweh' in this way. It may be noted that at the time of writing of the
Qumran texts the *Tetragrammaton* was no longer used outside explicit
biblical quotations. The more extensive version of 1QS has the phrases "as
a community" and "in accordance with these rules" added above lines 12
and 13 to be read after the words "When these exist in Israel", and the
citation of Isa 40:3 follows the words "to prepare there the way of him."
The text of 1QS reads: "When these exist as a community in Israel in
accordance with these rules, they shall separate themselves from the
settlement of the men of injustice and shall go into the wilderness to
prepare there the way of him, as it is written: 'In the wilderness prepare the
way of ••••, make level in the desert a highway for our God.' This (way) is
the study of the law w[hich] he commanded through Moses, that they

should act in accordance with all that has been revealed from time to time
and in accordance with what the prophets revealed by his holy spirit"
אלה ליחד בישראל בתכונים האלה יבדלו מתוך מושב אנשי הנשי (אנשי) corr. (העול ללכת למדבר)
הואהא כאשר כתוב במדבר פנו דרך •••• ישרו בערבה מסלה לאלוהינו היאה מדרש ובהיות
ביד מושה לעשות ככול הנגלה עת בעת וכאשר גלו הנביאים ברוח קודשו לפנוח שם את דרך
(התורה [אשר] צוה).

The introductory formula appears in the form of כאשר כתוב as earlier in
1QS V,17. The citation במדבר פנו דרך •••• ישרו בערבה מסלה לאלוהינו omits
the words קול קורא which appear at the beginning of the verse in the
Masoretic text, and instead of the *Tetragrammaton* the scribe of 1QS has
marked four dots. The use of four dots instead of the tetragrammaton is
also attested elsewhere in the scrolls (e.g. in 4QTest and 4QTanh). In some
cases the name of God is out of reverence written in paleo-Hebrew script
instead of in the square characters. The manuscript 4QS[d], in fact, provides
two examples of the latter in the parallels to 1QS IX,25 and X,9 (4QS[d] 2
III,9 and IV,8). The manuscript 1QIs[a] has a small variant from the
Masoretic text: instead of ישרו 1QIs[a] reads וישרו. In the book of Isaiah this
verse belongs to the Deuteroisaianic Book of Consolation of Israel.
Yahweh intends to place himself at the head of his people and lead them to
freedom from exile across the desert, as he did at the Exodus from Egypt
into the Promised Land. But the Qumran writer disregards the historical
context, and uses the verse to provide a motive for the community's
withdrawal into the desert to live a life of perfection in accordance with the
Law. The same verse from Isaiah is also used in the New Testament with
reference to John the Baptist by all four evangelists (Matt 3:3, Mark 1:3,
Luke 3:4-6, John 1:23). There the purpose of the verse is to explain John's
presence in the desert. The way in which the evangelists have detached the
verse from its original context and accommodated it into a new
environment is very similar to the one we find in the Community Rule.

1QS VIII,24-25: The need to provide a legitimation for the practices of the
community is again manifest in a passage included in 1QS but lacking in
4QS[d].[69] Whereas 4QS[d] reads "He shall be excluded from the purity and
from the council and from the judgement for two years" (והבדילהו מן הטהרה
ומן העצה ומן המשפט שנת[ים ימי]ם), 1QS adds a sort of citation, which, however,
has not been identified so far in any other rule text found at Qumran. The
version of 1QS: "He shall be excluded from the purity and from the council
and they shall consult the rule: 'He shall not judge anyone, or be asked for

[69] The parallel to 1QS VIII,24 is not preserved in 4QS[b].

any counsel for two years'" (והבדל מן הטהרה ומן העצה ודרשו המשפט אשר לוא
ישפוט איש ולוא ישאל על כול עצת שנתים ימים).

1QS VIII,25-IX,1: The redactor in 1QS has cleverly used the word ושב
(4QS<sup>d</sup>) when adding the words (אם תתם דרכו במ(ושב) to the text. He wished to
emphasize that after two years' punishment the offender can once again be
accepted as a full member only if his conduct was faultless in the minor
meetings of the community, which he was still allowed to attend while
undergoing his punishment. 4QS<sup>d</sup> reads simply "and he shall return to
study and to counsel" (ושב במדרש ובעצה).[70] The words על פי הרבי[ם] were
presumably also added to the text of 1QS - unfortunately there is a lacuna
in the manuscript - in order to point out that the final decision of
acceptance was to be made by the *rabbim*. A difference in syntax between
1QS and 4QS<sup>d</sup> may also be detected, cf. אם לוא שנב עוד (1QS) and
אם לא הלך עוד בשננה (4QS<sup>d</sup>). The absence of ימים after שנתים in 4QS<sup>d</sup> is
possibly just an error by the copyist. In 1QS we read ולעושה ביד רמה
whereas 4QS<sup>d</sup> has וליד הרמה.

1QS IX,1-2: In the regulation concerning the punishment for transgressing
the word of Moses inadvertently 4QS<sup>d</sup> reads: "Surely, he shall be tested for
two years with regard to the perfection of his way" (אך שנתים [י]מים יבחן לתמים
דרכו).[71] Although the aspect of inadvertence was set out a little earlier in the
text, the redactor of 1QS wished to repeat it emphatically: "Only if he has
sinned inadvertently he shall be tested for two years with regard to the
perfection of his way" (אך השונג יבחן שנתים ימים לתמים דרכו).

1QS IX,3: The formula "When these exist in Israel according to all these
rules" (בהיות אלה בישראל ככול התכונים האלה) appears in a slightly different
and longer form in 4QS<sup>d</sup>: "[When] these [exist] as a community in Israel
according to these rules" ([בהיות] אלה ליחד בישראל התכונים האלה).[72] Interestingly, the word ליחד is added above the line in the second occurrence of this
threefold formula in 1QS VIII,12 (cf. also 4QS<sup>e</sup> 1 III,3).

1QS IX,4: In the section where prayer and right conduct are described as an
atoning sacrifice, the version of 4QS<sup>d</sup> uses the plural forms of the words
זבח and תרומה, and reads the word (ו)נדבה ((and) freewill offering) after
ותרומת.[73] In this case there is no ambiguity as to which of the versions

---

[70] The parallel to 1QS VIII,25-IX,1 is not preserved in 4QS<sup>b</sup>.

[71] The parallel to 1QS IX,1-2 is not preserved in 4QS<sup>b</sup>.

[72] The parallel to 1QS IX,3 is not preserved in 4QS<sup>b</sup>.

[73] The parallel to 1QS IX,4 is not preserved in 4QS<sup>b</sup>.

represents the more original text. The term נדבה also occurs a little later in
both 4QS<sup>d</sup> and 1QS, and one might think that the similar context gave the
redactor the impetus for inserting the word in the previous line in 4QS<sup>d</sup>,
too. Alternatively, the first occurrence of נדבת was omitted secondarily in
order to avoid unnecessary repetition in the version of 1QS. Omitting the
first נדבת does not particularly affect the meaning of the sentence, since the
parallel word תרומת also signifies an offering. In the following translation
of the text of 4QS<sup>d</sup> the parts missing in 1QS are in italics: "...and that the
land may be accepted without the flesh of burnt-offerings and without the
fat of sacrifice*s* - and the gift*s and freewill offering* of the lips are like a
soothing (odour) of righteousness, and perfection of the way like an
acceptable freewill offering."

1QS IX,5-6: A variant which explicitly mentions "the men of the
community" is again to be detected through a comparison of 1QS and
4QS<sup>d</sup>. Whereas 4QS<sup>d</sup> has "At that time they shall be separated as a house
for Aaron" (בעת ההיא יבדלו בית אהרן),[74] 1QS reads "At that time the men of
the community shall separate themselves as a holy house for Aaron." The
subject of the sentence is included in the verb in 4QS<sup>d</sup> (niph. 3rd p. pl.
יבדלו) or בית אהרן must be understood as the subject of the clause, in spite of
the incongruence between the subject and the predicate (*constructio ad
sensum*). In 1QS it is stated explicitly (יבדילו אנשי היחד) and thereby the
incongruence is corrected. The purpose of this change was probably to
strengthen the self-understanding of the members of the community.

1QS IX,7: The regulation "Only the sons of Aaron shall rule in matters of
justice and wealth" is attested both in 1QS and 4QS<sup>d</sup>, but the sentence
"and on their word the decision shall be taken with regard to every rule of
the men of the community" (ועל פיהם יצא והגורל (הגורל .corr) לכול הכון אנשי
היחד), included in 1QS, is absent in 4QS<sup>d</sup>.[75] The motive for inserting this
sentence may have been to emphasize the authority of the priestly members
of the community. On the other hand, it is striking that "the men of the
community" once again appear in this addition.

1QS IX,17: Among the regulations addressed to the wise leader 1QS reads:
"He shall hide the counsel of the Law in the midst of the men of injustice"
(ולסתר את עצת התורה בתוך אנשי העול). The parallel text in 4QS<sup>d</sup> has עצתו
instead of את עצת התורה.[76] The referent of the 3rd masc. sg. suffix of the

---

[74] The parallel to 1QS IX,5-6 is not preserved in 4QS<sup>b</sup>.
[75] The parallel to 1QS IX,7 is not preserved in 4QS<sup>b</sup>.
[76] The parallel to 1QS IX,17 is not preserved in 4QS<sup>b</sup>.

word עצתו is not quite clear in the context of 4QS<sup>d</sup>; it might be the wise leader or God.

1QS IX,22: The term בצע (profit)⁷⁷ occurring in 4QS<sup>d</sup> is replaced by עמל כפים (the labour of the palms) in 1QS.⁷⁸

1QS X,10: A confusion between *bet* and final *mem* (4QS<sup>d</sup>: אשיב - 1QS: אשים) has presumably produced the difference between 4QS<sup>d</sup> 2 IV,10-11 and 1QS X,10. The change of the root does not greatly alter the import of the sentence, however: "While they (i.e. his statutes) exist I will restore⁷⁹ (4QS<sup>d</sup>) / I will set (1QS) my bounds without returning."

The comparison between the manuscripts 1QS and 4QS<sup>b,d</sup> indicates that 4QS<sup>b</sup> and 4QS<sup>d</sup> have preserved a more original text than has 1QS.⁸⁰ The Community Rule has gone through a process of redaction, which, on the one hand, strengthens the self-understanding of the community by stressing the rôle of the community as the true temple and guardian of the covenant as well as the true keeper of the Law, and which, on the other hand, provides a scriptural legitimization for the regulations of the community. Inserting theologically significant words into the text is a natural thing to do, whereas omitting them would be very difficult to explain. Omission of part of the text comes into question only when the text is obsolete, for example, or when it contains elements which are considered questionable in some way. Compared to 4QS<sup>b,d</sup>, the text of 1QS gains more authority when the community's own regulations obtain biblical legitimization. A further argument supporting the view that the shorter version, i.e. that of 4QS<sup>b,d</sup>, is the more original can be adduced by the observation that in the version of 4QS<sup>b,d</sup> the text runs smoothly without any breaks in the line of thought, whereas in 1QS the natural flow is interrupted in many places. The adding of biblical proof-texts may indicate that at the time when 1QS was copied (or a little earlier) enthusiasm within the community had begun to show signs of waning, and the strict rules needed to be justified by

⁷⁷ Cf. 1QpHab IX,5.

⁷⁸ The parallel to 1QS IX,22 is not preserved in 4QS<sup>b</sup>.

⁷⁹ The verb שב hiph. has a number of meanings in the Old Testament, but in my opinion the translation "restore" suggested earlier by Charlesworth (1994, 83) appears the most suitable in this context. The parallel to 1QS X,10 is not preserved in 4QS<sup>b</sup>.

⁸⁰ My analysis confirms the prefatory views expressed by Milik (1977, 78) and Vermes (1991, 255). I have also dealt with the question as to the more original version in my article "The Use of Old Testament Quotations in the Community Rule." *Qumran Between the Old and the New Testament*, eds. N.P. Lemche and T.L. Thompson. Copenhagen International Seminar Series. Sheffield Academic Press [forthcoming].

allusions to the Scriptures. The large number and the nature of grammatical variants indicate that the work of editing did not just mean joining passages together and adding glosses but modifying the text in a more profound manner.

Both 4QS[b] and 4QS[d] are palaeographically several decades later than 1QS, which was written about 100 B.C. The script of 4QS[b] belongs to the transitional period between Hasmonean and Herodian scripts and has been dated to 50-25 B.C. The latter 4QS manuscript is Herodian and was written in the last third of the last century B.C. If the 4QS manuscripts nevertheless represent a more original text, it is clear that the manuscripts 4QS[b,d] and 1QS cannot be directly dependent on each other or even belong to the same textual family. There must have been a split in the textual tradition at a very early stage, perhaps as early as the second half of the second century B.C. But the manuscripts 4QS[b,d] do not belong to the tradition represented by 4QS[e], either: the biblical proof-texts absent in 4QS[b,d] but present in 1QS are also attested in 4QS[e]. It seems that behind the versions of 4QS[e] and 4QS[b,d], both of which are more original than that of 1QS, there existed yet another version of the Community Rule, which is to be detected through a comparison of 4QS[e] and 4QS[b,d].[81]

### 3. 4QS[a] and the Doctrine of the Two Spirits

#### 3.1. Orthography and Language

The four preserved fragments of 4QS[a] provide relatively little material for our analysis. Only fragments 1 and 2 have direct parallels in 1QS. Fragment 3 is presumably part of the doctrine of the two spirits, whereas fragment 4 cannot be identified. Some indication as to the character of this manuscript might be observable, however.

*Defective* spelling seems to have been used in 4QS[a] more often than in 1QS. In three cases 4QS[a] uses *defective* spelling when 1QS reads *plene*,[82] whereas the number of reverse cases is zero. Medial letters appear to have been sometimes used in final positions in 4QS[a].[83]

Concerning the morphology it may be noted that in 4QS[a] 2,1 a genitive attribute is used instead of an adjectival attribute (1QS). In 4QS[a] 2,4 there is also a syntactical difference: 4QS[a] lacks the preposition ב before the word מי.

---

[81] See chapter III.4. *Redaction of the Community Rule*, esp. p. 146.
[82] 4QS[a] 2,2 (2x); 3,3.
[83] 4QS[a] 1,1; 3,5.

*3.2. Variants of Contents*

Fragment 3 provides a text which does not coincide with any of the known passages of 1QS but the vocabulary of which refers to the doctrine of the two spirits (1QS III,13-IV,26). The closest parallel is to be found in 1QS III,20-25 and the fragment may represent a shorter and divergent version of these lines. In the various literary critical studies of the doctrine of the two spirits it has been noted that the text was put together from passages which were originally independent. This fragment shows that the redaction involved more profound editorial work than merely joining passages together.

Translation:
1 ] [ ] [
2 the w]ays of man
3 ]... to instruct...
4 ]... the sons of man...
5 ] light and [   ] darkness

Except for fragment 3, the text of 4QSᵃ is very close to that of 1QS. Only one significant variant occurs: In line 8 of fragment 2 the words לפני אל (1QS III,11) are missing. Probably they were added as a gloss to 1QS, but there is not enough evidence to decide which of the manuscripts represents the more original text overall.

## 4. A Fragment of 4QSʰ which has no Direct Parallel in 1QS

*4.1. Orthography and Language*

Except for fragment 2 containing a text which has no direct parallel in 1QS, only two variants can be detected in the preserved parts of this manuscript: Fragment 1 contains the case of a *defective* spelling while 1QS uses a *plene* form, and offers the feminine by-form רחיצה for the noun רחץ occurring in 1QS III,5. It may also be noted that a medial *ṣade* is used in final position in 4QSʰ 2,3.

*4.2. Variants of Contents*

Fragment 2 has no direct parallel in 1QS. The text may be part of the doctrine of the two spirits (1QS III,13-IV,26); the themes of vengeance and destruction, even though expressed in different terms, are to be found in 1QS IV,12-14. The theme of concealment does not occur in the doctrine of the two spirits as such, but the doctrine speaks about the secrets of God in

1QS IV,6 and 18. It is impossible to say with any certainty, however, which part of the doctrine fragment 2 could correspond to.[84] As indicated earlier in chapter I, it may be asked whether 4QS[h] is a copy of the Community Rule at all, or whether it is a different manuscript quoting a phrase from the Rule.

Translation of frg. 2:

  1  ]they are concealed to all[
  2  ]the haughtiness of the one who takes vengeance[
  3  ]in the shattering. The father of ...[

### 5. The Other Manuscripts of the Community Rule from Cave 4

Half of the manuscripts of the Community Rule found at Qumran (4QS[c,f,g,i,j]) have preserved so little material that it is very difficult to draw any conclusions as to the textual tradition they represent. What follows is an attempt to create a picture of the variants included in these manuscripts.

### 4QS[c]

Although it is very difficult to draw any conclusions concerning the scribal character of 4QS[c] on the basis of the small number of variants included in the preserved material of the manuscript, it may be noted that fragment 1 III of 4QS[c] includes a variant, which uses *defective* spelling when 1QS reads *plene*.[85] A spelling error occurring in 1QS IV,5 (מתעב) should be corrected with the aid of 4QS[c] 2,2. In 4QS[c] 1 II,5 the word עו|נכה contains two variants in comparison with 1QS II,8 עווניך, that of different orthography and that of variation between singular/plural.

The identified fragments of 4QS[c] (frgs. 1-3) do not contain any variants of contents in comparison with 1QS.

---

[84] The third fragment placed in the same plate with fragments 1 and 2 most likely does not belong to the same manuscript with fragments 1 and 2 (see p. 72). Fragment 3 is presumably taken from a hymn or a liturgy. Translation:
  1  ]... (of) his (wine)foliage (?) they will drink until[
  2  ]clouds, and his foliage until[
  3  ]... the height, and it makes the fruits fall (?)
  4  ]the abundance in the brightness[
  5  ]his name is pure[
  6  ]...
[85] 4QS[c] 1 III,4.

## 4QS^f

Most of the variants included in 4QS^f involve orthography. In two cases 4QS^f uses *defective* spelling when 1QS has *plene*.[86] One variant of 4QS^f reads *plene*, when 1QS has a *defective* form.[87] Three cases concern differences in the use of laryngeals.[88]

Morphological variants are three in number: the variant in 1 IV,2 has a noun in the plural while 1QS uses the singular, and that in 1 IV,6 provides a shorter form of a personal pronoun when 1QS has a longer, Qumranic form. Most of the variants in syntax involve the use of prepositions and conjunctions: in 4QS^f 1 II,1 the conjunction plus the preposition may have been absent (the text is poorly preserved), 1 II,3 has the preposition ב plus an infinitive construct whereas 1QS reads the preposition כ plus a noun, 1 IV,5 is a case of a different preposition, and in 1 IV,6 the conjunction ו which is present in 1QS is missing. A variant containing lexical cognates occurs in 4QS^f 1 I,1.

The contents of 4QS^f in the preserved parts seem to follow 1QS fairly closely except for the words ואדעה כיא בידו, which are missing in 4QS^f 1 IV,3 and added as a gloss in 1QS X,16. The text seems to have varied also in 1 IV,10 (par. 1QS X,20), but due to the poor condition of the fragment the original variant can no longer be traced with greater accuracy.

## 4QS^g

The orthography of the manuscript 4QS^g is very close to that of 1QS. There is only one orthographical variant: 4QS^g 3,3 has preserved a *defective* form of a word which is written *plene* in 1QS. A minor spelling error occurs in 4QS^g 4,2, where a word-space is missing. An example of a non-standard spelling may be seen in 4QS^g 1,1 (יו = o).

Linguistic variants are also very rare in 4QS^g. In one case an infinitive construct is used instead of a perfect form with an object suffix (4QS^g 1,2), and there is a case where a perfect form occurs instead of an imperfect (4QS^g 2,3). In one case a construct infinitive is used instead of an imperfect form with an object suffix (4QS^g 4,3). In 1QS VII,16 a personal pronoun (הואה) is used to designate an object (לשלח הואה מאתם), while 4QS^g 4,2 uses an imperfect form with a normal pronominal suffix (יְֹשלחוהו מֹאֹתם).

As to the variants of contents, in a passage dealing with the admission of new members there is a statement concerning the "multitude of Israel"

---

[86] 4QS^f 1 II,1; 1 V,3.

[87] 4QS^f 1 IV,1.

[88] Interchange of *he* and *aleph* occurs in 4QS^f 1 IV,1. The word מאדה in 1 IV,2 is written מדה in 1QS X,16. The *aleph* at the end of ואפיא (1QS X,19) is missing in 4QS^f 1 IV,8.

(1QS V,22-23). According to 1QS, they have offered themselves "to return in the community to his covenant" (לשוב ביחד לבריתו). In 4QSᵍ 1,2 the words "to his covenant" are lacking, and instead of the wording concerning the return to the community 4QSᵍ reads: "to dwell together" (לשבת יחד). In the same passage 1QS reads simply ומעשיו referring to the works of the candidate, whereas 4QSᵍ 1,3 points out that the works in question are those related to the Law (ומעשי התור[ה]).[89]

In the heading of the large penal code the words בם במדרש יחד included in 1QS VI,24 are missing in 4QSᵍ 2,2. The text in 1QS reads "These are the rules by which they shall judge at a community inquiry according to the cases" (ואלה המשפטים אשר ישפטו בם במדרש יחד על פי הדברים),[90] whereas the version of 4QSᵍ is to be translated "These are the rules by which they shall judge according to the cases."

In 1QS VI,25 the manuscript 4QSᵍ (2,3) uses the synonym ממון (mammon) for הון (wealth) of 1QS.[91] The word ממון occurs, however, elsewhere in 1QS (VI,2).

## 4QSⁱ

The small fragment of 4QSⁱ provides a variant with regard to the use of *aleph* as a *mater lectionis*: whereas 1QS VI,2 reads למלאכה, 4QSⁱ 1,3 has למלכאה. A possible morphological variant is to be found in 4QSⁱ 1,1 where the form יבא, which is to be interpreted as Qal or *defective* hiphʻil, is used instead of the unambiguous hiphʻil (יביא) occurring in 1QS VI,1. A syntactical variant involving the use of the conjunction ו occurs in 4QSⁱ 1,2. As to the vocabulary, it may be noted that the word הון has been used in 4QSⁱ 1,3 instead of ממון (1QS VI,2).[92] The contents of the text in lines 1-2 of the fragment seem to be slightly different from the text in 1QS, but due to the small size of the fragment the proportions of the differences cannot be determined (see my remarks on this fragment in ch. I).

---

[89] Cf. Paul in the New Testament: τά ἔργα τοῦ νόμου (Rom 3:20 etc.).

[90] The term מדרש has been used here in a sense different from that in 4QSᵇ 5,1/4QSᵈ 1 I,1 (see pp. 76-77) and those in 1QS VIII,15 and 26. In the heading of the penal code (1QS VI,24) it signifies an enquiry or investigation, see Delcor 1955, 74.

[91] The word ממון may have had a negative, unethical connotation in the mind of the scribe, who chose the more neutral word הון instead. In Rabbinic literature, as well as in the New Testament, ממון often denotes unjust or unrighteous profit. The word ממון is not attested in Biblical Hebrew, but the Hebrew word בצע 'unjust gain, profit' is translated in the Targums by ממון (e.g. Gen 37:26; Judg 5:19; 1 Sam 8:3; Isa 33:15; Ezek 22:13,27). 'Mamon' is presumably a Phoenician loan-word in Hebrew, Targumic Aramaic and NT Greek. See Hauck 1942, 390-392 and Cox 1988, 86.

[92] Note that a variant on the same words occurs in 4QSᵍ 2,3 (par. 1QS VI,25).

*4QSj*

On the basis of a single fragment alone, not very much can be said about the character of an entire manuscript, but it seems that the scribe of 4QSj clearly preferred *defective* spelling to *plene*. The small fragment has preserved six cases where a *defective* form has been used instead of a *plene* one, while the number of reverse cases is zero.[93] The scribe also systematically used the shorter form of the 2nd person singular suffix (ך-) instead of the form כה- prevalent in the parallel passage in 1QS XI,14-22, as well as the shorter form הוא of the 3rd masculine sg. personal pronoun. The contents of the fragment follows the corresponding passage in 1QS.

## 6. The Manuscripts from Cave 5

The material from Cave 5 is so scarce and poorly preserved that any discussion of the possible differences remains a highly speculative undertaking. The reader is well advised to read the remarks on these fragments in chapter I.

## 7. The Work of Scribes 'A' and 'B' in 1QS VII-VIII

The scribe of 1QS left several *vacats* in columns 1QS VII-VIII. Presumably the *Vorlage* he was copying was so poorly preserved that in some places he was unable to read it. A later copyist supplemented some of the empty spaces left by the first scribe, and made other additions and corrections in the text. The existence of two different scribes in 1QS VII-VIII was early noticed by the translators,[94] but Guilbert (1958) and Martin (1958) were the first to present more thorough analyses of the work of the two scribes (A and B).[95] Working independently, Martin and Guilbert distinguished the typical features of the two hands and separated the work of scribe B from that of scribe A. In general, Martin attributes more of the text to B than Guilbert does. As to the nature of the scribal intervention by B, Martin supposes that B used a revisor-exemplar, from which he corrected and supplemented the work of A.[96] Guilbert suggests that most of the additions and corrections were made without the aid of another, perhaps better

---

[93] 4QSj 1,3; 1,4; 1,5 (2x); 1,6; 1,7.

[94] See e.g. Brownlee 1951, 29 n. 15 and Wernberg-Moeller 1957, 113 n. 3.

[95] Guilbert 1958, 199-21, Martin 1958, 439-442.

[96] Martin 1958, 464, 466. Martin claims that after the revision by B scribe A returned to the text and made further corrections. This hypothesis remains unproven.

preserved manuscript than 1QS. In his opinion, scribe B edited the text in a rather personal way.[97]

Subsequently Puech made a further analysis of the work of scribes A and B.[98] Unlike Martin and Guilbert, Puech was able to make use of the list of 4QS variants which had meanwhile been published by Milik.[99] Puech came to a similar conclusion to Martin's. According to Puech, at least some of the corrections in column VII were based on another manuscript which, in his view, was perhaps 4QSᵉ. Although Puech admits that some of the additions made by B are not included in 4QSᵉ, he argues that they may have been present in another manuscript more contemporary with 1QS.[100]

The complete evidence provided by the 4QS manuscripts, which was not yet included in the list by Milik, is now available. Unfortunately, the fragments parallel to 1QS VII-VIII appear to be relatively small in number.[101] For the study of the redaction history of the Community Rule it is nevertheless a matter of great importance and worth further consideration as to whether the work of scribe B represents a genuine, new phase in redaction or whether it should be seen merely as a revision based on a manuscript more or less identical to 1QS.

It can safely be argued that at least the following text originated with scribe B:[102]

VII:
1. ‏או לכול דבר אשר לו‎.
5. At the end of the line ‏ואם‎.
6. Above the line ‏יתרמה‎.
7. ‏ברושו‎.
8. Above the line ‏ששים יום‎ and ‏שנה אחת‎, perhaps also ‏ר‎ above ‏יט‎ and ‏ב‎ above ‏משפט‎.
10. ‏ט‎ above ‏ר‎ ‏הנפש‏<>‎ (?)
11. ‏ק‎ above ‏פו‏<>‏י‎ (?)
19. At the end of the line ‏ינע בטהרת הרבים‎.
20. Above the line ‏משקה‎ and at the end of the line ‏ובמלואה‎.

---

[97] Guilbert 1958, 212.
[98] Puech 1979, 35-43.
[99] Milik 1960, 410-416.
[100] 1QS VII,10 and 12-13, Puech 1979, 43.
[101] 4QSᵇ 9 (1QS VII,7), 4QSᵈ 2 I (1QS VIII, 6-21), 4QSᵉ 1 I (1QS VII,8-15) 4QSᵉ 1 II (1QS VII,20-VIII,10), 4QSᵉ 1 III (1QS VIII,11-15 + IX,12-20), 4QSᵍ 3 (1QS VII,9-13) and 4 (1QS VII,16-18).
[102] With the exception of VII,19, the list follows that of Guilbert 1958, 199-200; cf. Martin 1958, 439-442.

21. At the beginning of the line לו and after the *vacat* על דבריו ואם יקרבהו
ונכתב בתכונו ואחר ישאל אל המשפט.

22. The complete line וכול איש אשר יהיה בעצת היחד על מלואת עשר שנים.

23. The last word of the line לפני.

VIII:

5. למט in front of עת in the middle of the line after the *vacat*.

6. י above ובֿ<>חֿרֿי.

7. פנת יקר בל.

8. Above the line יסודותיהו.

9. Above the line רֿיֿח.

10. קֿ above the line in the word לֿחֿוֿקֿוֿת. Above the line והיו לרצון לכפר בעד
בתמים דרך. At the end of the line הארץ ולחריץ משפט רשעה ואין עולה.

11. Above the line יֿבֿדֿלֿו. The letter ה above the word נֿסֿתֿר.

12. Above the line לֿיֿחֿד.

13. Above the line בתכונים האלה.

VII,1 (no parallel preserved in 4QS): Scribe A envisaged that he or another scribe would later complete the text, for he left a blank space of about sixteen letters in the middle of line 1. Scribe B later added או לכול דבר אשר לו in the *vacat*. He also erased about ten letters following the space left by A.[103] No parallel fragment for this line is preserved in 4QS to help us to judge whether B was here using a revisor-exemplar or whether he independently edited the text here. The fact that B had to erase some of the text of A in order to make his addition better fit the context may speak against the availability of another manuscript similar to 1QS. The possibility that B personally edited the text, as proposed by Guilbert, is worth considering. Having noted the conjunction או without any part of the sentence corresponding to it scribe B added another או and continued או לכול דבר אשר לו. Possibly scribe A originally intended to write ואם קלל או, i.e. the adverb או instead of the conjunction או.[104] Indeed, the hook of the *waw* appears almost non-existent. On the basis of this supposition, the sentence as intended by scribe A was: "If he then has blasphemed through being terrified while he is reading the book or praying, they shall exclude him, and he shall never return to the council of the community." After the addition made by scribe B the text reads: "If he has blasphemed, either through being terrified by distress or for whatever reason he may have,

---

[103] Martin 1958, 439.
[104] Guilbert 1958, 201.

while he is reading the book or praying, they shall exclude him, and he
shall never return to the council of the community."

VII,5-6 (no parallel preserved in 4QS): It is difficult to say whether A
accidentally left line 5 shorter than most of the others in column VII or
whether he intentionally left a *vacat* at the end of the line where B later
added ואם. At the beginning of line 6, there is an obvious *vacat*, but it was
not supplemented by scribe B, who added יתרמה above the line instead.
Scribe B may have used a revisor-exemplar here. On the other hand,
Guilbert has pointed out that this kind of correction can also be made
without the aid of another manuscript:[105] In the text written by scribe A the
word ברעהו remains in the air. It cannot alone constitute the transgression
for which the punishment is a three months' fine. Presumably B noticed
that in the sentence which comes a little later the object of transgression is
also denoted by the preposition ב, and the transgression by the verb יתרמה.
Scribe B added the same verb above line 6 after the word ברעהו, and
separated the sentence from the preceding one by adding ואם at the end of
line 5. Thus he created a parallel with the following sentence. Without the
correction made by B the text of A is incomprehensible: "Whoever speaks
deceitfully to his neighbour or knowingly acts deceitfully shall be fined for
six months... to his neighbour, he shall be fined for three months." In the
corrected form the text reads: "Whoever speaks deceitfully to his neighbour
or knowingly acts deceitfully shall be fined for six months. If he is
negligent towards his neighbour, he shall be fined for three months."

VII,7: Scribe B added the word ברוש in order to clarify the meaning of the
preceding verb ושלמו. A small fragment of 4QS^b (frg. 9) containing only
one word provides a parallel to this addition in 1QS VII,7. Scribe B was
also probably the one who erased two words at the end of line 6, in order
to make the word he had added better match the verb.[106] The word ברוש is
followed by a large *vacat*. At first sight it appears inexplicable; the text
seems to continue logically without any break in the content. A look at the
original manuscript, however, reveals something that cannot be seen in the
photograph. The reason why scribe A left the *vacat* lies in the poor quality
of the leather: from the end of line 6 onwards there runs a long break in the
leather towards the middle of line 8 (after the *vacat*). The break was most

---

[105] Guilbert 1958, 202.

[106] Martin 1958, 439. From the remaining marks of the erased letter Stegemann considers
it possible that the word which follows ישלמו was ברושו, i.e. the same word which is added by
B at the beginning of line 7. Because of the poor quality of the leather in this place, B erased
the word and wrote it anew at the beginning of the next line.

likely caused by a bone, and the hole which it caused can be seen in the left-hand-side margin of lines 11-12 in the original manuscript.[107]

VII,8: It is difficult to say which of the two scribes erased two letters and corrected two spellings (ר above יטי and ב above משפט),[108] but certainly it was scribe B who made two additions concerning the duration of punishments. In the first case where A, perhaps by mistake,[109] had not written the duration of the punishment at all, B added above the line יום ששים, "sixty days." In the second case, where A had written ששה חורשים, "six months," B put these two words in brackets and wrote above the line a more severe punishment, שנה אחת, "one year". Scribe B either knew that the practice had changed in the community, or the different punishment was written in the revisor-exemplar he may have been using. The first line of fragment 4QSᵉ 1 I, though very fragmentarily preserved, appears to coincide with the text copied by scribe A (ששה חורשים).

VII,10-11 (no parallel preserved in 4QS): Two letters above lines 10 and 11 (ט above הנפ<>ר and ק above יז<>פו) probably come from B,[110] but it was presumably A who rewrote the first letter of the fourth word in line 11. It is not obvious whether וחנם was corrected to והנם or vice versa, but the first alternative seems more probable (וחנם was corrected to והנם; וחנם is erroneous), for according to Milik's report, a similar wording is evident in 4QSD 1 II,2.[111]

VII,19-21: In line 19 A himself corrected אל to לוא.[112] Scribe B then continued with the words ינע בטהרת הרבים.[113] He also erased one word in line 20, above which he wrote משקה. Looking at the traces of the erased word it

---

[107] The bone-hole cannot be seen in the photographs of any edition of 1QS.

[108] Martin 1958, 439 suggests that A originally wrote יטיר and המשפט. Puech 1979, 38 agrees in the case of המשפט, but he argues that יטיר also originally stood in the text. Since the last letter seemed unclear, it was omitted and rewritten above the line, either by A himself or by B.

[109] Puech 1979, 38.

[110] Guilbert 1958,204, Martin 1958,440.

[111] Milik 1960, 413: "Cette phrase n'est conservée dans aucun ms. de 4QS, mais elle se retrouve dans un contexte similaire dans un autre ms. de 4Q, que je recours brièvement dans *Dix ans...*, p. 111, et *Ten years...*, p. 96. On y lit (référence provisoire: SD 1,II,2): [...] *ḥspr* [y]*nwm ʾd šlwš p ʾmym*; dans la lacune initiale on mettra quelque comme: *w'm bmqr'*."

[112] Considering what remains of the letter before לוא, the original word cannot have been על as suggested by Puech 1979, 39. The word was אל, as proposed by Martin 1958, 440.

[113] Martin (1958, 440) claims that only the last word of line 19 comes from B. Guilbert (1958, 204), on the other hand, attributes בטהרת הרבים to B. In my opinion, Puech (1979, 39) is right in arguing that the same hand which wrote בטהרת הרבים also wrote ינע.

seems that Milik is right in claiming that the erased word was בטהרה.[114] At the end of line 20 scribe B added ובמלואה and at the beginning of line 21 לו.[115] After the *vacat* he completed the sentence with a long addition, על דבריו ואם יקרבהו ונכתב בתכונו ואחר ישאל על המשפט, which appears to have been included in full in the text of 4QS^e. Only בת]כונו ואחר ישאל/ is preserved in 4QS^e 1 II,2, but counting the number of letters per line of column II of 4QS^e indicates that the whole phrase stood there. The text of A in its original form reads: "In the first year (he shall) not, and in the second he shall not touch the *rabbim*, and he shall sit behind all the men of the community for two years. (Then) the *rabbim* shall be asked." After the additions made by B the text runs as follows: "In the first year he shall not touch the purity of the *rabbim*, and in the second he shall not touch the drink of the *rabbim*, and he shall sit behind all the men of the community. When he has completed two years, the *rabbim* shall be asked about his affairs. If they allow him to draw near, he shall be registered in his rank, and afterwards he may be asked about judgement."

VII,22-23: The hand of line 22 is that of B: וכול איש אשר יהיה בעצת היחד על מלואת עשר שנים. In 4QS^e, a text almost identical to this is to be found. The end of line 4QS^e 1 II,3 (= 1QS VII,22) reads ....[היחד עד מלאות לו. Obviously, B was using a revision-exemplar here, but because of two significant variants, עד and לו, it cannot have been 4QS^e. There are marks of erased words in the same line, and it was probably B who erased them.[116] At the end of line 23 scribe B added the word לפני, and presumably he was also the one who remoulded one letter before the same word.[117] The translators have read the letter as *mem*[118] - מלפני is perfectly suitable in the context - but looking at the photograph the letter seems to be a final mem (ם) rather than a medial one (מ). The lack of a normal word-space, however, is explained by the fact that B used a previous mark in the text. The text of A begins in the middle of line 23, after the *vacat*: "... and whose spirit turns back so that he betrays the community and who leaves... the *rabbim* to walk in the stubbornness of his heart, shall ever

---

[114] Milik 1951, 148, n. 2.

[115] Puech 1979, 39 ascribes the words ובמלואה לו to scribe A.

[116] Guilbert (1958, 206) claims that scribe B erased the words, but he admits that full certainty cannot be attained. Martin (1958, 441) thinks that the erased words were written by A, but that they were erased only after B had made his additions in the vacats left by A. Puech 1979, 39 claims that the erased words were עד מלואה לו עשר שנים. If Puech is right, which is possible, then it is likely that it was B who erased the words - having realised that they were exactly the same as the ones he had just added at the end of line 22.

[117] Guilbert 1958, 206.

[118] See e.g. the translations by Wernberg-Moeller 1957, 33, 42, Leaney 1966, 199, Lohse 1986, 28-29, and Knibb 1987, 124.

return to the council of the community." The text of B starts at the beginning of line 22: "But no man who has been in the council of the community for ten full years and whose spirit turns back so that he betrays the community, and who leaves in front of the *rabbim* to walk in the stubbornness of his heart, shall ever return to the council of the community."

VIII,4: Either B or A himself erased the *yod* in בימדת.[119]

VIII,5: The definite article was omitted before עצה by either one of the scribes. Scribe B corrected the fifth word by adding one letter in front of it, reshaping one, and by writing one letter above the line, thus producing the word למטעת. Scribe A had originally written בעת עולם, which in terms both of spelling and content is a faultless expression.[120] Unfortunately, the text in 4QSᵉ breaks down in the middle, but there seem to have stood the words למ[שפט עולם...[121] If B made this correction independently from any other manuscript, he may here have wanted to actualize the text. Scribe A refers to the future by his expression, whereas B connects the text to the contemporary life of the community.[122] The text of A was: "When these exist in Israel, the council of the community shall be established in truth. In the eternal time the holy house in Israel and the most holy assembly for Aaron shall be witnesses of truth for the judgement..." After the correction by B the text reads: "When these exist in Israel, the council of the community shall be established in truth. As an eternal plant, a holy house in Israel and a most holy assembly for Aaron, witnesses of truth for the judgement..."

VIII,7-8: Scribe B supplemented the quotation of Isa 28:16 touched on by A by adding the words פנה יקר בל.[123] Scribe B also wrote יסורותיהו above line 8.[124] The text is somewhat fragmentary both in 4QSᵈ and 4QSᵉ, but the

---

[119] So also Puech 1979, 40. Martin 1958, 441 suggests that the scribe started to write the word עצה after the preposition.

[120] Milik 1951, 149 n. 2.

[121] Reconstruction by Qimron 1994, 87.

[122] Guilbert 1958, 207.

[123] Guilbert 1958, 207-208; see also Wernberg-Moeller 1957, 126. According to Martin (1958, 441), these words are not written in the handwriting of B. It is noteworthy, that in 1QS there are vacats at both ends of the citation. In 4QSᵈ the citation is absent.

[124] Indeed, after וחם singular verbal forms are to be expected (cf. יזעזע and יחישו), see Guilbert 1958, 208. Puech 1979, 40 thinks the subject of יזעזע was יסורותיהו in the Vorlage of 1QS: Scribe A was not able to read the word, but he left an empty space for this word at the end of line 7. I do not find this suggestion very probable, for in this case the sentence would have had an inverted word order.

material reconstruction of these manuscripts indicates that there cannot have been space for the whole amount of text contained by A and B together. In 4QS^e בל יקר פנת is attested, while יסודותיהו seems to have been absent.[125] The case of 4QS^d is less certain, for neither פנת יקר בל nor י סודותיהו is preserved there. Counting both additions of B in 4QS^d 2 I,2, the number of letters per line remains within a possible range, so I have included both of them. Qimron, however, follows 4QS^e and leaves out י סדותיהו in his textual reconstruction of this line, whereas he includes פנת יקר בל.[126] The text of A was: "It shall be the tested wall which shall neither shake nor stir from its place." The text of B reads: "It shall be the tested wall, the precious cornerstone, whose foundations shall neither shake nor stir from their place."

VIII,9: Scribe B supplemented the text of A by writing the word ריח above the line. Together with ניחוח it forms a pair of words often used in the Old Testament (e.g. Ex 29:18,25,41, Ezek 20:41). The text is again very fragmentary in 4QS^e, but it is likely that ריח was not included in 4QS^e 1 II,15. This suggestion is based on the distance in two fragments in the material reconstruction of 4QS^e. Between the fragments, there is space for only about thirteen letters (...]לברי[ת משפט ולקריב ]ניחוח ובית). In 4QS^d 2 I,3 less than one third of the line is preserved, so it is practically impossible to judge whether this little word was included there or not.

VIII,10-11: In the third word of line 10 scribe B erased one or more letters and wrote קו above the line, thus producing the word לחוקות. Several proposals concerning the original word have been made: 1) Scribe A wrote לחומת as in line 7.[127] 2) Scribe A wrote לחוקת, but since two of his letters partly slipped below the line, he rewrote the word which seemed unclear to him.[128] 3) The word was corrected two times. The original לחוקת (sg. or pl. *defective*) was changed into a *plene* form by adding *waw*, which slipped slightly below the line. Then both קו were erased and written anew above the line.[129] What remains of the erased letters (interlinear *qoph*, *waw* partly

[125] The hand of 4QS^e is very irregular, so the exact number of letters varies from one line to another. Line 14 of 4QS^e II has been preserved relatively well, however. It has two gaps, both of which had approximately ten letters. If the word יסודותיהו is included in line 14, the total number of letters may have just about remained within the possible range, but in this case the second gap would have included twenty letters instead of ten. To me it seems improbable that the word יסודותיה was included in line 14.

[126] Qimron 1994, 76.

[127] Brownlee 1951, 33 n.22.

[128] Guilbert 1958, 208.

[129] Puech 1979, 41.

below the line) suggests that the third proposition is the correct one. It is noteworthy that in 4QS<sup>d</sup> 2 I,3 the word is attested in the orthographical form לחקות. Above line 10 scribe B wrote a long addition והיו לרצון לכפר בעד הארץ ולחרוץ משפט רשעה ואין עולה to be read after the word עולם. Interestingly, this phrase is attested in 4QS<sup>d</sup> but it is not included in 4QS<sup>e</sup>. At the end of line 10 scribe B added the words בתמים דרך partly below the normal writing line. There are traces of an erased word above בתמים. Guilbert thinks the omitted word was ברוח, for together with the word קודש it forms a natural combination. Provided that the erasure was made by B - which I consider likely - and he wanted to change the phrase, he presumably did so because he was disturbed by the fact that only a little later the same expression is used in connection with the holy spirit of God (1QS VIII,16). The words that scribe B chose are the same as in 1QS VIII,18.[130] Above the beginning of line 11 scribe B added a predicate which the sentence he had created now needed (יבדלו), and changed a perfect form נסתר into a participle.[131] Neither בתמים דרך יבדלו nor (ה)נסתר is preserved in 4QS<sup>e</sup>. Since the hand of the scribe of 4QS<sup>e</sup> is rather irregular, counting the number of letters per line does not give an unambiguous solution to the question whether the additions were included in the text of 4QS<sup>e</sup>.[132] From the point of view of the syntax, however, it is likely that at least יבדלו was there. The text of A was presumably the following: "It shall be a house of perfection and truth in Israel that they may establish the covenant according to the eternal statutes/wall when these have been established in the fundamental principles of the community for two years in the holy spirit within the council of the men of the community." The text of B reads: "It shall be a house of perfection and truth in Israel that they may establish the covenant according to the eternal statutes. And they shall be accepted to make expiation for the land and to determine the judgement of wicked; and there shall be no more injustice. When these have been established in the fundamental principles of the community for two years in perfection of way, they shall be set apart as holy within the council of the men of the community."

VIII,12-13: Scribe B made the text more accurate by adding ליחד and בתכונים האלה above the lines. It may be asked whether the reshaped word in

---

[130] Martin 1958, 442, Guilbert 1958, 208-209.

[131] Guilbert 1958, 209. Martin 1958, 442 believes that A first erroneously wrote תסדר, but that he himself corrected the word by adding *he* between the lines and by erasing a part of *taw*, which thus became *nun*.

[132] I have included these words in the reconstruction of the lacunae in 4QS<sup>e</sup> 1 III,1-2 producing lines which are longer than usual in column 4QS<sup>e</sup> 1 III. Qimron has not attempted to reconstruct lines 1 and 2.

4QS<sup>e</sup> 1 III,3 is ליחד. Alternatively, the word in 4QS<sup>e</sup> is בישראל written in
cryptic letters.[133] In 4QS <sup>d</sup> ליחד is absent. The second addition by B in 1QS,
בתכונים האלה, does not appear in 4QS<sup>d</sup> nor in 4QS<sup>e</sup>. In the interlinear
correction of line 13, it was probably scribe A himself who wished to
correct his own text by writing מתוך over another word. Guilbert thinks that
A originally wrote מבד, whereas Martin considers that the word was ככול.[134]
Puech, whose proposed solution I find the most probable, suggests בכול.
Guilbert's suggestion is ruled out, for *mem* is clearly a result of rewriting.
Martin's alternative seems unlikely to me, for the letter *kaph* of scribe A is
usually higher than the one originally written here. In 4QS<sup>e</sup> there is no
preposition at all between יבדלו and מושב (מושב יבדלו כול אלה ליחד בהיות). The
text of A was the following: "When these exist in Israel, they shall separate
themselves in all the settlement(s) of the men of injustice..." Moulded by B
the text reads: "When these exist as a community in Israel in accordance
with these rules, they shall separate themselves in the middle of the
settlement of the men of injustice..."

The picture evolving from the comparison of the work of scribe B in the
light of 4QS<sup>b,d</sup> and 4QS<sup>e</sup> is somewhat confusing. It can be shown that in
some places B did follow a revisor-exemplar, but this exemplar does not
seem clearly to belong to either of the two lines of tradition represented by
4QS<sup>b,d</sup> and 4QS<sup>e</sup>.[135] Sometimes B follows 4QS<sup>b,d</sup>, sometimes 4QS<sup>e</sup>, and
there are cases where the text of B is attested in neither of these two
manuscripts. The fact that B had to erase some of the text of A in order to
make his additions fit the context of A poses a further problem. Scribe B
did not merely supplement but also moulded and corrected the text of scribe
A.

Should we reckon with the possibility that B's work reveals a textual
tradition of the Community Rule so far unknown? Or was the work of
scribe B selective, so that he knew several forms of the text from which he
borrowed? Does the absence of some of B's additions and corrections in
4QS<sup>b,d</sup> and 4QS<sup>e</sup> indicate that scribe B independently edited the text? There
does not seem to be an easy way to definitively rule out any of these
options. It seems probable to me, however, that scribe B both used a
revisor-exemplar(s?) and took the liberty of independently editing the text.

<hr>

[133] See the discussion on pp. 53-54.

[134] Guilbert 1958, 210, Martin 1958, 442. Martin thinks the addition בתכונים האלה above
line 13 was also made by A.

[135] It has been shown in the previous chapters that 4QS<sup>d</sup> and 4QS<sup>e</sup> belong to two different
lines of textual tradition, both of which are earlier than that of 1QS.

It is especially difficult to interpret the work of B in the large part of column 1QS VII for which there is no parallel preserved in 4QS.[136]

In terms of time, the work of scribe B cannot be very far from that of scribe A. The analysis of the work of the two scribes provides further support for the hypothesis that there were several legitimate versions of the Community Rule in co-existence. Changes in the practice of the community had their effect on the text (cf. the change in one of the punishments of the penal code), but it may be asked whether there ever was any attempt to produce only one, legitimate and up-to-date version of the Community Rule.[137]

## 8. Conclusions

Among the copies of the Community Rule which have preserved sufficient material for a proper analysis the manuscripts 4QS$^b$ and 4QS$^d$, on the one hand, and the manuscript 4QS$^e$, on the other hand, have preserved a form of the text different from that of 1QS. Several variants included in these manuscripts indicate that there are two versions of the Community Rule, both of which are different from and older than that of 1QS. A comparison between the manuscripts 1QS and 4QS$^{b,d}$ reveals a process of redaction in 1QS, the purpose of which was to provide a Scriptural legitimation for the regulations of the community and to reinforce the community's self-understanding. The editorial changes, which are to be traced through a comparison between 1QS and 4QS$^e$, were motivated by a need to bring the text of 1QS up to date.

Since the amount of the text preserved varies greatly in the different copies of the Community Rule, it is very difficult to compare them linguistically. Of all the copies of the Community Rule the manuscript 1QS appears to have transmitted the features of Qumranic orthography most consistently. In the manuscripts from Cave 4 the *plene* spelling is less prevalent. This is particularly apparent in both the version of 4QS$^{b,d}$ but also in 4QS$^e$. Other manuscripts from Cave 4, all of which have preserved less material than 4QS$^{b,d}$ and 4QS$^e$ and therefore contain a smaller number of variants, also seem to prefer the use of *defective* spelling more often than

---

[136] The manuscript 4QS$^g$ has preserved parallels to 1QS VII,9-13 and 16-18(?). None of the corrections and additions made by B in 1QS VII have anything corresponding to them. The material is insufficient to reconstruct the size of the column and the length of its lines.

[137] I have dealt with this issue at greater length in a separate article entitled "In Search of the *Sitz im Leben* of the Community Rule" to be published in the proceedings of the 1996 International Dead Sea Scrolls Conference, 15-17 July, 1996, Provo, Utah (eds. D. Parry and E. Ulrich).

does 1QS. Only the manuscript 4QS<sup>g</sup>, very little of which has remained, is perhaps close to 1QS in its orthography. The manuscripts 4QS<sup>b,d</sup> also deserve attention because of the remarkable number of different linguistic variants they contain. In 4QS<sup>e</sup> the syntactical variants are more frequent than in other manuscripts.

The manuscript 4QS<sup>a</sup>, which on paleographical grounds is to be dated perhaps even earlier than 1QS, has preserved a fragment which has no direct parallel in 1QS but which presumably is part of the doctrine of the two spirits. There is a real probability that the fragment is related to the doctrine of the two spirits, the form of which in 4QS<sup>a</sup> may have been more original than that in 1QS. The manuscript 4QS<sup>h</sup> has also preserved a fragment which has no direct parallel in 1QS. Identifying this fragment is even more difficult than in the case of 4QSa, but t is possible that this fragment too is connected with the doctrine of the two spirits. Although the process of redaction in the doctrine of the two spirits can no longer be exactly determined, it is important to acknowledge that this section too underwent editorial work.

Being paleographically later than 1QS, the manuscripts 4QS<sup>b</sup> and 4QS<sup>d</sup>, which have preserved an earlier form of the text than has 1QS, cannot be directly dependent on 1QS. According to Milik the manuscript 4QS<sup>e</sup> is paleographically older than 1QS, but according to the recent dating by Cross, it is in fact paleographically later than 1QS. It nevertheless represents a form of the text which is earlier than that of 1QS. The form of the text in 4QS<sup>e</sup> is not, however, the same as the one in 4QS<sup>b,d</sup>: the final psalm, which is present in manuscripts 1QS and 4QS<sup>b,d</sup>, is replaced by the calendric text Otot in 4QS<sup>e</sup>, whereas the biblical quotations attested in 1QS and 4QS<sup>e</sup> are absent in 4QS<sup>b,d</sup>. Our comparison between 4QS<sup>e</sup> and 4QS<sup>b,d</sup> reveals that behind these manuscripts there existed yet another version of the Community Rule, older than that of 1QS.

The signs of the presence of a second scribe in columns 1QS VII-VIII most likely represent the latest phase of the redaction. In some places the second scribe seems to have corrected the text of the first scribe from another manuscript which, however, is not to be identified with any of the known copies of the Community Rule. Some of the changes and additions point in the direction that the second scribe also independently edited the text.

# CHAPTER THREE

# THE LITERARY DEVELOPMENT
# OF THE COMMUNITY RULE

All studies of the redaction history of the Community Rule have so far been based almost entirely on the manuscript 1QS. The material from Cave 4 provides concrete evidence of the different stages of this document and makes it possible to test the theories which have been presented earlier. In the previous chapters I have determined the variants between 1QS and the manuscripts of the Community Rule from Caves 4 and 5. The purpose of this chapter is to bring together these results, to combine them with the internal evidence of 1QS, and to create, if possible, an overall picture of the literary development of the Community Rule.

## 1. The Main Structure of the Community Rule

It is unlikely that every individual stage of the redactional process of the Community Rule can be detected on the basis of the twelve preserved manuscripts. Some of them are to be discovered through internal indicators in the text. The stages which have left their physical marks in the manuscripts must be able to be accomodated in the overall theory of the redaction of the Community Rule. The physical evidence of the manuscripts provides a framework for constructing the theory.

The material of the Community Rule from Cave 4 indicates clearly that columns 1QS I-IV did not originally appear at the beginning of the document. Manuscripts 4QS$^d$ and 4QS$^e$, both of which contain a form of the text more original than 1QS, are examples of manuscripts containing only the text with the parallel of 1QS V,1 onwards.[1] Only one of the

---

[1] In 4QS$^d$ the beginning of the manuscript is preserved and it begins with the text of 1QS V,1. The case of 4QS$^e$ is less certain, since it is based on the material reconstruction of this manuscript and on the assumption that the same amount of material as was destroyed in the inner layers of the scroll was also destroyed in the outer layers of the scroll. See pp. 49-51. The difference in character between the first four columns of 1QS and the following material was early on noticed by commentators, but it was not until the investigation by Murphy-O'Connor (1969, 541-543) that the liturgical and theological material was proposed to have been brought into the composition later than the legislative material. In Murphy-O'Connor's view, columns 1QS I-IV, together with 1QS X,9-XI,22, were joined with the rest of the material in the final stage of the redaction (stage IV). Accepting the views of H.-W. Kuhn (1966, 29-33) and Weise (1961, 79 n. 2), Murphy-O'Connor regarded the *Sitz im Leben* of 1QS X,9-XI,22 as being the same as that of section 1QS I,16-II,25a: the annual renewal of

manuscripts found in Cave 4, namely 4QS^b, has preserved material from both parts of the composition. On the basis of the reconstruction of 4QS^c it seems probable that this manuscript also contained material from both parts of the composition.

The final psalm corresponding to 1QS X-XI did not belong to the composition in the first stages of redaction, either.[2] In 4QS^e it was replaced by the calendric text 4QOtot, and on the basis of the material reconstruction of 4QS^c, the presence of the final psalm in the scroll of 4QS^c seems improbable, too.[3]

None of the manuscripts from Cave 4 displays physical evidence that columns 1QS V-VII and VIII-IX ever existed separately. The scribal sign at the end of column 1QS VII suggests a major break in the text there, but on the basis of the preserved manuscripts it cannot be determined, whether either one of the sections was introduced into the document earlier than the

---

the covenant (pp. 544-545). He considered that columns I-IV were intended to serve as an exhortative preface for the legislative corpus of the Community Rule, and that they were added in a situation where the community had lost its initial enthusiasm and was in danger of falling into legalism. Stegemann (1988, 98) saw the distinction between columns 1QS I-IV and V-XI even more profoundly. He considered columns 1QS I-IV to have formed a work which is completely independent of the material of columns V-XI ("Doch ganz unabhängig davon, was sich den 4QS-Befunden nach deren Edition einmal wird entnehmen lassen, so ist jedenfalls bereits jetzt literarkritisch eindeutig festzustellen und für unseren Zusammenhang wichtig, dass 1QS I-IV ein gegenüber 1QS V-XI völlig eigenständiges Werk ist..."). Whereas Murphy-O'Connor is correct in his estimation that the sections of columns I-IV were brought into the composition later than the material of columns V-IX, no connection between columns 1QS I-IV and X-XI can be demonstrated in the material from Cave 4. The view of Stegemann, that the material parallel to columns V-XI was originally independent of the preceding material, is supported by the analysis of the Cave 4 manuscripts, but none of the manuscripts of the Community Rule found at Qumran contains only the material of columns I-IV.

[2] Scholarly opinions about the position of the final psalm in the composition have varied greatly. According to Weise (1961, 5-7), the position of the calendaric section 1QS IX,26b-X,8 (Weise: Kultordnung) in the context depends on whether col. X is seen as an immediate continuation of col. IX. He recognizes similar wordings between the section IX,24b-X,1 and later parts of col. X (e.g. 1QS X,6,15 f. and 23; X,8b,14,17 and 19), and concludes that the columns do belong together. This view, which had been earlier put forward by van der Ploeg (1951, 114-115), Milik (1951, 153), Reicke (1952, 88) and Bardtke (1952, 103-104), has also been adopted by Murphy-O'Connor (1969, 529-530) and Pouilly (1976, 30), who argue that although the calendar may have had an independent existence, it has been brought into the nucleus of the Rule (stage I) in connection with column IX. Rabinowitz (1953, 175 n.2), Habermann (1952, 82) and Leaney (1966, 115-116) reject the view that columns IX and X belong together. Leaney argues that both VIII,1-IX,26 and X,1-XI,22 were originally separate. He thinks that columns X-XI are "manifestly composite," and that the author, "if composing from a number of already existing elements, nevertheless fused them into a whole." Leaney speculates about the possibility that the author of the final psalm may have been the Teacher of Righteousness himself, who - he thinks - was also the author of the Hodayot.

[3] The manuscript 4QS^c has been dated as contemporary with 1QS (100-75 B.C.). Although the text of 4QS^c in its preserved parts is very close to that of 1QS, the absence of the final psalm in 4QS^c favors the conclusion that the composition in 4QS^c is prior to that of 1QS.

other.[4] At the time when the scriptural proof-texts and the additions strengthening the self-understanding of the community were added to the text (about 100 B.C. or even earlier),[5] the sections parallel to 1QS V-VII

[4] The different nature of columns VIII-IX in relation to the preceding and following material has been acknowledged by most scholars. Even Guilbert (1959, 333), who suggests that 1QS forms a literary unity, writes about VII,25: "La Règle de la Communauté aurait pu, semble-t-il, s'arrêter là." Stegemann (1990, 422; 1993, 156) is of the opinion that the regulations starting with 1QS V,1 continue as far as IX,10 (the following sections 1QS IX,12-21 and IX,21 ff., in his view, form two secondary appendices). The majority of studies on 1QS VIII-IX have been influenced by the idea of Sutcliffe (1959, 134-138) that the threefold formula "When these exist in Israel" (VIII,4,12 and IX,3) refers to the future, to a community which was soon to be established and that the columns represent the oldest material in the Rule. Leaney (1966, 116) was the first to adopt this view, and he dated the material to about 130 B.C. Murphy-O'Connor (1969, 529-533) developed the idea further. He separated two interpolations, VIII,16b-19 and VIII,20-IX,2 (stage II), and argued that sections VIII,1-16a + IX,3-X,8a (Manifesto) form the nucleus on which the other sections in the Rule had been composed in four stages. Pouilly (1976, 19-34) defined the limits of the Manifesto slightly differently (VIII,1-10a + VIII,12b-16a + IX,3-X,8a), but substantially agreed with Murphy-O'Connor. Dohmen (1982, 81-96) separated three layers in the composition of columns VIII-IX alone: 1) VIII,1-7a + 12b-15a + IX,16b-21a (das Manifest), 2) VIII,7b-12a/IX,12-16a + IX,21b-26 (die Erweiterung des Manifestes), 3) IX,3-11 + VIII,15b-19/VIII,20-IX,2 (die "erste Regel" und ihre Erweiterung). Klinzing (1971, 50-55) also stressed the heterogeneity of the material in his analysis of 1QS VIII,1-IX,11. He regarded VIII,4-10, VIII,12-16, VIII,16-19, VIII,20-IX,2, IX,3-6, IX,7, IX,8, and IX,9-11 as individual passages. His interpretation of the nature of the columns differed significantly, however. He pointed out that the formula "When these exist in Israel" reminds one of similar sayings in apocalyptic literature. Three of the passages describe the self-understanding of the community with the aid of the image of a temple. In his view the community's separation and its self-understanding as a temple should most likely be understood eschatologically. Davies (1992, 158-159) has also argued quite recently that the section describes not an actual community but an ideal one. He parallelled 1QS VIII-IX with 1QSa, which is generally designated as an 'eschatological' or 'messianic' rule. Davies speculated about the possibility of some Qumran texts representing the genre of utopian literature.

[5] This stage of redaction is to be discerned by a comparison of manuscripts 1QS and 4QS[b,d], and it is particularly apparent in the parallel to 1QS V-VII. The heterogeneous character of these columns was acknowledged by many scholars even before the Cave 4 material was available. Leaney (1966, 114-115), for example, made an attempt to subdivide the halachic section V,1-VII,25, although he doubted whether the origin and chronological order of the sections can ever be fully determined. He saw V,7b ff. as repeating V,1-7a, and V,13b-20a as repeating some of the teachings in II,25-III,12, a passage which he ascribed to the compiler. According to Leaney, "it is possible that either he (the compiler) is the author of the regulations here or that V,13b-20a illustrates the fact that already existent halakah guided him in the earlier comment which he made on the ceremony of initiation." A.-M.Denis (1964, 39) described sections V,13-20 (la loi de l'impie) and V,23 - VI,13 (le règlement interne) as interpolations. Becker (1964, 42) regarded V,20-25 and VI,13-23 as parallel passages representing two different stages in the development of the community. He also noted two formal breaks in the content in V,13 and V,25. Murphy-O'Connor (1969, 546-547) used Becker's observation in discerning an interpolation in V,13b-15a: the third person plural changes to the third person singular, and it is difficult to interpret lines 13b-15a as referring to outsiders. The passage concerns rather a person whose conversion is insincere. Pouilly (1976, 45-50) argued that the interpolation reaches as far as VI,8a.

and VIII-IX had already been combined.[6]


## 2. Smaller Sections of the Document

Since 1QS is the best preserved of all the copies of the Community Rule, it is most convenient to use this manuscript when considering the contents and the detailed structure of the document. Methodologically this is by no means unproblematical. Since there existed no standardized text, and since the redaction not only meant combining larger units but also involved editing the smaller sections of the document, the structure of the text varies greatly from one manuscript to another. In what follows I have tried to take into consideration the differences included in the Cave 4 material. Determining the different sections included in the Community Rule is essential for the later comparison of the thematically parallel passages.

1QS I,1-15: The passage clearly serves as an introduction, and it is to be compared with 1QS V,1-7a and VIII,1-15a.[7] Several themes essential for the life of the community have been introduced with a series of infinitive constructs.[8] It has been argued that the latter part of the text (I,11b-15) is

---

[6] As early as 1956 Milik reported the existence of a shorter and more original version of 1QS V in manuscripts 4QS^(b,d) (pp. 60-61; 1960, 410-416; 1977, 78), and several scholars have mentioned this in their commentaries. Leaney (1966, 162), however, has so far been the only scholar to attempt to relate the 4QS version to other parts of the document. He writes: "If the Cave 4 mss. do indeed represent an older text, this text seems to be that of an originally independent work and may belong to the same period to which in our view (following Sutcliffe) 8.1 - 9.16 belongs, that is the time when the community was being founded." Leaney writes that "the whole of V,1-VI,23 (though composite) may date from the time before the desert withdrawal (cf. VIII,1-IX,26)." He considers that "VI,1-7 clearly legislates for the life of the sect during this early period" and that VI,13b-23 is "part of regulations drawn up early, it is likely to have been incorporated rather than created by the compiler." The passage VI,24-VII,25, which Leaney regards as itself composite, is "appropriate to the foundation of the community." In the view of Murphy-O'Connor (1969, 533-535), most of the material in columns V-VII (V,1-13a + V,15b-VII,25) belongs to stage III in the development of the text. The community has become more institutionalized and more democratic. The legislation is more detailed and manifests a stable, developed community which has existed for several decades. As to the existence of the different versions from Cave 4, Murphy-O'Connor states only that the partial recensions may have reflected the development of practice in the community.

[7] For determining the introduction in column 1QS VIII, see pp. 117-118.

[8] Compared to Biblical Hebrew, the use of the infinitive has expanded considerably, for the infinitive is often used instead of a normal finite verb. Qimron (1986, 71) describes the use of the infinitive in I,1 ff., V,1 ff., VIII,2 ff., and IX,12 ff. as modal. Leahy 1960, 137-144 has separated eleven different ways of using the infinitive in 1QS. According to him, the function of the infinitives in 1QS I,1-15 "would be that of explaining the opening words. As such, they might be classified as explicative, as substantival in apposition to a word in the title, or as purpose - perhaps more correctly, as pertaining to all three of these categories." Parisius

directed to the candidates for admission to the community, while the beginning (I,1-11a) has been addressed at those who stand at its head.[9] No redactional links between the two parts can be detected, however, but the section forms a literary unity. Very little of this introducton has remained in the fragments from Cave 4. Two manuscripts have preserved some words from the first lines of the document (4QSª 1 par. 1QS I,1-5; 4QSᶜ 1 I par. 1QS I,2). They provide no readings differing from 1QS.

Unfortunately, none of the twelve manuscripts of the Community Rule has preserved the whole of the title of the document. The lacunae at the beginning of 1QS can be filled only partly with the aid of 4QSª and 4QSᶜ: לן .שים לחיון] [בכול לב ובכול נפש ל[עשות ספר סר]ך היחד לדרוש אל. The additions which have been suggested for the reconstruction differ greatly from one another. Brownlee's proposed reconstruction ל[וכול הקהל מטף עד נ]שים לחיו]ת בסרך היחד "for [the whole assembly, including children and wo]men: to live in the order of the Community"[10] is to be rejected for several reasons: First, 4QSª confirms that לחיו constitutes a complete word; no letter is missing. Secondly, the same manuscript has preserved the word ספר before סרך; it cannot be left out. The third reason for rejecting the proposition is that women and children are nowhere mentioned in the document. The suggestion of Carmignac [למשכיל...לאנ]שים לחיו [ספר סר]ך היחד "de l'instructeur..., aux hommes ses frères, le livre de la règle de la communauté"[11] is unconvincing, for the word חיים (life) occurs several times in 1QS, also with a singular suffix (1QS III,1), whereas לחיו as a orthographical variant of לאחיו appears, to my knowledge, nowhere in the Scrolls.[12] Dupont-Sommer has proposed in his translation: "Pour [l'homme intelligent, afin qu'il instruise les sa]ints, pour qu'ils viv[ent selon la règ]le de la Communauté."[13]

---

(1955, 103-105) argues that in the structure of the section two lines beginning with ל + infinitive construct always form a pair of either contradiction (6x) or of parallel ideas (3x). In his view, the first four lines of 1QS give the impression of an oral tradition.

[9] E.g. Knibb 1987, 79. According to Weise (1961, 64), section I,1-15 can only be understood in comparison with 1QS IX,12-24b, for both passages describe things to be hated or loved by the *maskil* (I,3 ff., 9 ff.; IX,16,21). In my view, the principles of community life introduced in 1QS I,1-15 involve all members of the community. See below my suggestion for the reconstruction of the first lacuna.

[10] Brownlee (1951, 6-7 n. 2) presumes that the first partly preserved line of 1QS was not the beginning of the whole text. Therefore, he adds two more words at the beginning: [החקים ואלה] "These are the ordinances..."

[11] Carmignac 1959,85-87. Leaney (1966, 117-118) and Pouilly (1976, 8) follow Carmignac's suggestion.

[12] Carmignac 1959, 87 has not attempted to fill the gap in its entirety, but writes in n. 13: "Reste à combler un espace d'environ 14 millimètres, contenant 4 ou 5 lettres."

[13] Dupont-Sommer 1956, 12.

The first gap of 1QS has space for about seventeen letters (3.5 cm). The restoration ל[משכיל is supported by the titles in 1QS III,13, 4QS^b 5,1 (cf. 1QS V,1), 4QS^d 1 I,1 (cf. 1QS V,1), 1QS IX,12 and 21, and thus accepted by me. In the passages addressed to the wise leader teaching has been mentioned as his primary duty: The title in 1QS III,13 states that he shall "instruct and teach all the sons of light" (להבין וללמד את כול בני אור), and according to 1QS IX,13 he shall "teach all the wisdom which has been found throughout time" (ולמוד את כול השכל הנמצא לפי העתים). It is likely that the title in 1QS I,1 also referred to this responsibility of his, as Dupont-Sommer has proposed. Therefore I add ללמד as the second word. The possibility that מדר[שים is part of the title of 1QS I,1, which has to be considered in the light of 4QS^b 5,1 and 4QS^d 1 I,1 (מדרש למשכיל in both manuscripts), is less probable here, for the terms סרך and מדרש always seem to appear alternatively, and never simultaneously in the titles of 1QS, and מדרש is a word used only in the singular in the Community Rule. A natural parallel to את בני אור (1QS III,13), in my opinion, is את אנ[שים, which completes the number of letters needed for the gap (17).[14] There is no need to find a problem with the word לחיו in this context, for it forms a parallel to לאהבתו עם שנאתו in 1QS IX,21. The first line of 1QS is thus restored ל[משכיל ללמד את אנ[שים לחיו ספר סרך היחד "For the wise leader, to instruct the men for (during?) his life, the book of the order of the community." Although the contents of 1QS indicate clearly that the Community Rule was binding upon all members of the community, the manuscript was entitled as a sort of manual for the wise leader.

1QS I,16-III,12: The liturgical section starts without an apparent heading, but Weise is certainly correct in suggesting that the first sentence functions as a transitional passage (Übergangspassus).[15] It was presumably added by the compiler. The text can be divided into three parts: 1QS I,16-II,18 describes the ceremony of entry into the covenant, II,19-25a provides a rite for the annual renewal of the covenant, II,25b-III,12 condemns those who refuse to enter the covenant. After each unit ending with the exclamation "Amen, amen" by the congregation the scribe of 1QS has left a *vacat* in the

---

[14] The word קודשים suggested by Dupont-Sommer in his translation is less likely here, for it never occurs alone as a designation of the members of the community, but always in the form אנשי הקודש, see e.g. 1QS VIII,17,23, IX,8. Moreover, the reading קודשים (it would certainly have been written *plene*) exceeds the number of letters which the lacuna admits.

[15] Weise (1961, 68) compares I,16-18a with IX,24bβ-X,1aα, which in his opinion also forms a transitional passage. He concludes that the passages are "in formaler und weitgehender inhaltlicher Übereinstimmung."

text (I,20-21; II,11; II,18-19)[16]. There is also a *vacat* between the priestly blessing and Levitical curse in II,4.

The liturgical material probably had an independent existence before its insertion in the Rule.[17] Whether it was brought as a unity to the composition of the Community Rule or whether there are redactional joins within it, are questions that have so far received very little attention. It has been widely acknowledged that the section has numerous affinities with the Old Testament and has assimilated a number of ancient liturgical patterns.[18] The fragments of this section from Cave 4 include no major variants in comparison with 1QS, but the manuscript 5Q11, which has preserved parallels to 1QS II,4-5 and 12-14(?), displays differences in the contents of the text of the liturgy.

1QS III,13-IV,26: The section consisting of the doctrine of the two spirits has the heading למשכיל, and the passage clearly stands out distinctly from the preceding and following material. Nowhere else in the document are the community's theological concepts presented in such a systematic form. In 1QS the section starts on a new line with a *vacat* at the beginning, and the end of the previous line has also been left blank. The scribe left *vacats* in IV,1-2, 8-9, and 14-15, as well, in order to designate the beginning of subsections.

Some scholars have argued that the doctrine of the two spirits forms a literary unity,[19] but the manuscripts 4QS[a] and 4QS[h], which have preserved two fragments relating to the doctrine but which do not have direct parallels in 1QS, demonstrate that this section too underwent redaction.

---

[16] The *vacats* coincide with the marks of hooks (cryptic *ayin*, see p. 15) in the margin.

[17] This view has also been expressed by e.g. Murphy-O'Connor (1969, 538-539), Pouilly (1976, 65-75) and Delcor (1979, 854).

[18] Cf. Deut 27-30, Ps 106:6, 1 Kgs 8:47, Jer 3:25, Dan 9:5, Num 6:24-26, Neh 8:6. See e.g. Baumgärtel 1953, 263-265, Leaney 1966, 105-107. A similar kind of ritual is described in 1QM XIII,1-6.

[19] Licht (1958, 88-89) argued that the writer of the doctrine used a chiastic structure in composing the passage, but his presupposition of the literary unity of the doctrine has been questioned by some scholars. Von der Osten-Sacken (1969, 17-18) compared the two halves of the section, 1QS III,13-IV,14 and IV,15-26, and observed several differences between them in vocabulary and syntax. He concluded that they were originally separate, and took the view that the passage IV,23b-26 was added later as an explanation for IV,15-18. Duhaime (1977, 572-594) developed the theory of von der Osten-Sacken further, and argued that the text was composed in three stages: 1) 1QS III,13*-18a.25b-IV,14 with the additions III,18b-23a.23b-25a.13**, 2) 1QS IV,15-23a.23b-26, 3) 1QS IV,23b-26. The results of von der Osten-Sacken and Duhaime have recently been criticized by Puech (1993, 430-432), who argues that, taken as a literary unity, the text and its division with *vacats* and marks in the margin correspond best to the number of themes presented in the introductory sentence.

There is a possibility that at least the fragment of 4QS[a] represents a more original version than that of 1QS.

1QS V,1-7a: All manuscripts which have preserved the parallel to 1QS V,1 commence with a new column signifying the beginning of a major section.[20] In 4QS[d] the text starting with the parallel of 1QS V,1 was also the beginning of the whole manuscript. The heading in 1QS reads וזה הסרך לאנשי היחד, whereas 4QS[b] and 4QS[d] have entitled the text מדרש למשכיל על אנשי התורה. The versions of 1QS and 4QS[b,d] differ greatly one from another, the latter being shorter and more original.[21] Both versions set out the general ideas and principles of the life of the community in the form of an introduction, but in the version of 1QS the section has been separated more clearly from the following legislative material; the last sentence of the passage (1QS V,6b-7a) and also the heading of the following section are lacking in 4QS[b,d].

1QS V,7b-20a: The section speaks about the oath of those desiring to become members of the community. They were to bind themselves to the law of Moses (1QS V,7b-10a) and to separate from the men of injustice (1QS V,10b-20a). In 1QS the passage has a clear a title: ואלה תכון דרכיהם על כול החוקים האלה בהאספם ליחד, while 4QS[b,d] lacks it and commences with כול הבא לעצת היחד. The text of this passage has undergone a particularly thoroughgoing redaction; the version of 1QS is more than twice as long as that of 4QS[b,d].[22]

The scribe of 1QS left a *vacat* in the middle of line 13, and there is a mark in the margin. The 3rd person plural referring to the men of injustice changes into the singular, although the theme of separation remains the same. After the citation of Ex 23:7 in line 15b plural forms are again used with reference of the wicked. It is difficult to see 1QS V,13b-15a as referring to a person joining the community. The passage seems rather to speak about one of the men of injustice, or about a person whose conversion is insincere. Some commentators suspected that this passage was an interpolation even before the material from Cave 4 was available.[23]

---

[20] In 1QS there is also a large mark at the upper right-hand corner of column V.

[21] See the previous chapter, pp. 74-90.

[22] For the nature of the redaction in 1QS V,7-20, see the previous chapter, pp. 79-83.

[23] The break in the natural flow of the passage was first detected by van der Ploeg 1951, 114, and later by Becker 1964, 42. Murphy-O'Connor (1969, 546-547) was the first to draw the conclusion that 1QS V,13b-15a forms an interpolation, and this was accepted by Knibb 1987, 110. Pouilly (1976, 45,50) argues that interpolation reaches to VI,8a. Although some parts of the passage, as far as 1QS VI,8a, are actually missing in 4QS[b,d], it cannot be said that the whole of 1QS V,13b-VI,8a forms an interpolation.

The thought which is interrupted at the end of line 13 continues at the end of line 15. The syntax of the passage 1QS V,13b-15a is also very peculiar, for the particle כיא appears there five times. The problem of the person (sg. - pl.) does not come up at all in 4QS^b,d, for the long passage 1QS V,13b-15a is missing as well as the preceding passage in the plural form in V,11b-13a. Besides 1QS V,13b-15a, other insertions present in 1QS are not so apparent that they would have been recognized without the aid of the manuscripts 4QS^b,d.[24]

1QS V,20b-VI,1bα: The wording וכיא יבוא בברית לעשות ככול החוקים האלה introduces a passage dealing with the admission of new members and their annual examination. Except for a few glosses, the beginning of the section (1QS V,20b-25a) has very much the same contents in 1QS and 4QS^b,d, but the passage following the *vacat* in the middle of line 1QS V,25 (i.e. 1QS V,25b-VI,1b) is largely missing in the version of 4QS^b,d.[25] A different and more detailed account of the procedure of the admission of new members is to be found in 1QS VI,13b-23.

1QS VI,1bβ-8aα: The former passage is concluded with a reference to הרבים (1QS V,24b-VI,1a; also in 4QS^b,d). A new heading באלה יתהלכו בכול מגוריהם כול הנמצא איש את רעהו (VI,1b-2a) commences a section which is different from the surrounding material. At the end of the section, and at the beginning of the following passage (VI,7b-8aα) the term הרבים re-occurs. It seems that the redactor used the technique of inclusion when inserting the passage VI,1bβ-8aα into the composition.[26] The section must have been added to the text at a very early stage, for it is included in the manuscript 4QS^d.

The interpolation mentioned above is the only section in the Community Rule where the *Sitz im Leben* is very unlikely to be the settlement at Qumran. Leaney suggests that the passage regulates the life of the Essene movement in the period before the desert withdrawal "as it was lived in small scattered groups, kept together by acknowledging some

---

[24] Knibb (1987, 111) points out, though, that "the words of line 18, 'For all those who are not counted in his covenant, they and everything that belongs to them are to be kept separate', link back clearly to those of lines 10b-11a." In 4QS^b,d, the words in line 10bβ "He shall separate himself from all the men of injustice" are included in 4QS^b,d, whereas the rest of the passage 10b-11a is missing.

[25] Pouilly (1976, 48, 57) and Knibb (1987, 114) have earlier on suggested that the whole of the passage 1QS V,25b-VI,1a forms an interpolation. The passage has been edited heavily, but some parts of it are present in the version of 4QS^b,d, as well. For details, see the previous chapter pp. 83-84.

[26] Knibb (1987, 115) also refers to the particular character of the passage and assumes that it originates from a source different from the one of the surrounding material.

central authority as well as by their own community lives." Knibb is of the
opinion that the material describes the circumstances contemporary to those
at Qumran, but that the section alludes to the members of the Essene
movement living in towns and villages amongst their fellow Jews.[27] These
members are mentioned by Josephus and Philo,[28] and a basic group of ten
is also referred to in the text of Josephus.[29] Leaney and Knibb have a point
here. The term מגורים usually designates a place of sojourn and, indeed, the
idea of meeting a neighbour would be best suited to somewhere other than
Qumran. The question as to the function of this section and its relationship
to the surrounding material may be left open for the present, however, for it
involves a more fundamental question regarding the position of the entire
document in the Essene movement. As far as I am able to see, an answer
would require a comparison with the larger corpus of rule texts found at
Qumran, some of which are as yet unpublished.

1QS VI,8b-13a: A *vacat* and the heading הזה הסרך למושב הרבים mark the
beginning of a rule for the session of the *rabbim*. The manuscripts 4QS[b,d]
have preserved two small fragments belonging to this section. The form of
the text seems to have been shorter there, although it cannot be reconstructed in its entirety.[30]

    Interestingly enough, the groups of the members of the community
mentioned in this section are "priests, elders and the rest of all the people",
whereas in 1QS II,19-25b the groups are "priests, Levites and all the
people".[31] The terms elders (הזקנים) and Levites (הלויים) can hardly have been
used synonymously, so it seems that two different traditions are represented
here.

1QS VI,13b-23: One of the most important tasks of the *rabbim* was to
select new members to admit to the community. The section describing this
procedure commences without a formal heading or break in the text, but the

---

[27] Leaney 1966, 180 and Knibb 1987, 115.
[28] Josephus, Bell. Iud. II,124; Philo, Omn. Prob. Lib. 75-76.
[29] Josephus, Bell. Iud. II,146.
[30] 4QS[b] 7 par. 1QS VI,11-13 and 4QS[d] 1 III par. 1QS VI,9-12. For the variants in the
contents, see the previous chapter, pp. 83-84. Unfortunately, neither of the fragments has
preserved the sentence in 1QS VI,11-12 אל ידבר איש...וכיא האיש המבקר על הרבים, which is
difficult to translate. From the point of syntax it seems likely that וכיא does not start a new
sentence, but belongs to the former sentence as a particle connecting two parts, cf. Burrows
1955, 379. I consider the translation of Lambert (1951) followed by Lohse (1986, 23) "wenn...
auch" to be more likely than that proposed by Knibb (1987, 117): "and, indeed". For further
discussion on the alternatives, see Marcus 1956, 299-301.
[31] Yet another way of dividing the members of the Essene community into classes is to be
found in CD XIV, 5-6: priests, Levites, Israelites, and proselytes.

words וכול המתנדב מישראל להוסיף על עצת היחד designate the beginning of a
new thematic entity.[32] The passage is to be compared with 1QS V,20b-
VI,1a, where the procedure is recounted in more general terms and the terms
מבקר and פקיד referring to officials are not mentioned at all. A small
fragment of 4QS<sup>b</sup> (par. 1QS VI,16-18) indicates the existence of a shorter
and more original version of the section, while the fragment of 4QS<sup>g</sup> with
only one partly preserved line parallel to this passage (par. 1QS VI,22-25)
provides no significant variants here.

1QS VI,24-VII,25: A *vacat*, a paragraph sign in the margin and the new
heading ואלה המשפטים אשר ישפטו בם במדרש יחד על פי הדברים separate the
section consisting of the penal code from the preceding material, and a sign
at the end of column VII sets the section apart from the material of column
VIII. The section has a distinct character, most of the judicial cases being
introduced with the formula האיש אשר/איש אשר/ואיש/ואשר.[33] The offences and
punishments listed in the penal code appear to have been brought together
in no particular order. One would rather think that the list was supplemented in proportion as new cases came forward.

Two manuscripts, 4QS<sup>e</sup> and 4QS<sup>g</sup>, have preserved material parallel to
this section. The words בם במדרש יחד are lacking in the title in manuscript
4QS<sup>g</sup>, but except for some changes in the length of punishments no other
major differences are to be found in 4QS<sup>e,g</sup> in comparison with 1QS. The
order of the offences is the same, for example, which is quite surprising
considering the heterogeneous character of the offences. The marks of the
second scribe at the end of column 1QS VII largely follow the text of 4QS<sup>e</sup>
(no parallel has been preserved for the beginning of the column in 4QS<sup>g</sup> or
4QS<sup>e</sup>).[34]

1QS VIII,1-IX,26a: The text of columns 1QS VIII-IX has been highly
debated among scholars. Some commentators suppose section 1QS VIII-IX
to refer to the time of the founding of the community and consider that it
represents a kind of 'Manifesto' or 'programme of the community.'[35]
Stegemann, on the other hand, argues that the whole of columns VIII and

---

[32] Josephus, Bell. Iud. II,137-142, has also illustrated the Essene ways of admitting new
members, and his account differs to some extent from 1QS VI,13b-23. The two different
versions have been analysed e.g. by Leaney 1966,191-192 and Knibb 1987,120-121.

[33] In 1QS VII,9 and VII,15 the offender is referred to with a participle.

[34] For details, see pp. 51-52, 60.

[35] Sutcliffe 1959, 134-138, Leaney 1966, 112,115,211, Murphy-O'Connor 1969, 529,
Pouilly 1976, 15, Dohmen 1982, 81-86, Knibb 1987, 129. For recent discussion on the
passage, see Brooke 1994, 117-132, Charlesworth 1994, 279-281 ("Morphological and
Philological Observations...") and Glessmer 1996, 125-164.

IX consist of secondary additions.[36] In my view, the manuscripts 4QS[d] and 4QS[e], together with the internal evidence of 1QS, shed new light on the problem.

Particularly difficult to interpret has been the material preceding the sections addressed to the wise leader (1QS IX,12-26). Introductory formulas outline the structure of this part of the text. The formula בהיות אלה בישראל appears threefold in 1QS VIII,4b,12b and IX,3. The passage 1QS VIII,10b-12a starts with the formula בהכין אלה ביסוד היחד, and the section VIII,20-IX,2 with the formula ואלה המשפטים אשר ילכו בם. The section 1QS VIII,16b-19 has no introductory formula, but as a penal code it clearly differs from the preceding material.

The passage parallel to 1QS VIII,15b-IX,11 is completely lacking in the manuscript 4QS[e] and, as indicated in the previous chapter, there are good grounds for thinking that the passage is a secondary insertion consisting of three smaller interpolations. Two of them (1QS VIII,16b-19 and VIII,20-IX,2) provide a code of discipline, the third one (IX,3-11) is a duplicate based on 1QS VIII,1-15a.[37] In the light of 4QS[e] it seems that the section parallel to 1QS VIII,1-15a formed an introductory passage for the following sections addressed to the wise leader. Although these regulations for the wise leader may be of early origin,[38] I no longer think it appropriate to speak of a Manifesto, but simply of an introduction which is comparable with two other introductions in 1QS, namely with those at the beginning of columns I and V.

A comparison between manuscripts 4QS[d] and 4QS[e] indicates that the most original form of the introduction of column VIII did not include the passage of 1QS VIII,13b-14 with the citation of Isa 40:3. The passage was inserted later, presumably in order to provide a motive for the community's withdrawal into the desert. The addition was most likely made by the same redactor who was responsible for the work of editing in columns 1QS V-VII (cf. 4QS[b,d]). The earliest form of the introduction of 1QS column VIII thus consisted of 1QS VIII,1-13a+15a.

The section 1QS IX,12-26a addressed to the wise leader (למשכיל) is divided into two halves by a *vacat* and a new heading (ואלה תכוני הדרך למשכיל), which is very similar to the one in 1QS IX,12. Since the passages IX,12-21aα and IX,21aβ-26a are stylistically coherent, it is very difficult to assume any redactional joins between them.[39] Other sections addressed to the wise leader in the Community Rule are the introduction 1QS I,1 ff.,

---

[36] Stegemann 1993, 158-159.
[37] See pp. 71-73.
[38] The question will be more thoroughly dealt with on pp. 124 and 125.
[39] So also Murphy-O'Connor 1969,529-530 and Knibb 1987,142-143.

the doctrine of the two spirits 1QS III,13-IV,26 and the parallel to 1QS V in manuscripts 4QS[b],[d]. It cannot, however, be assumed that there is a common source behind the material of these sections.

1QS IX,26b-XI,22: The final psalm containing a calendaric section at the beginning had an independent existence before its insertion in the composition. This can be demonstrated with the aid of the material reconstruction of the manuscript 4QS[e], where the psalm was replaced by the calendrical text 4QOtot. The manuscript 4QS[e] shows, in addition, that the calendar of prayer times in 1QS IX,26b-X,8a did not belong with the sections addressed to the wise leader (1QS IX,12-26a),[40] but it was attached to the psalm when introduced into the composition. The first sentence at the beginning of the calendric section (1QS IX,26b-X,1a) functions as a link, and it was presumably created by the compiler.[41]

### 3. Comparison of Thematically Parallel Passages

On the basis of the analysis of the contents and the internal structure of the Community Rule the sections included in the document can be divided into six categories:

3.1. Introductions
  - 1QS I,1-15; V,1-7a; VIII,1-13a + 15a [+ VIII,15b-16a + IX,3-11]
  - 4QS[a] 1 (1QS I,1-5); 4QS[b] 5 (1QS V,1-20); 4QS[c] 1 I (1QS I,2); 4QS[d] 1 I (1QS V,1-19); 2 I (1QS VIII,6-21); 2 II (1QS VIII,24-XI,10); 4QS[e] 1 III (1QS VIII,11-15 + IX,12-20)
3.2. Penal codes
  - 1QS VI,24-VII,25; VIII,16b-19; VIII,20-IX,2
  - 4QS[b] 9 (1QS VII,7); 4QS[d] 2 II (1QS VIII,24-IX,10); 4QS[e] 1 I (1QS VII,8-15); 1 II (1QS VII,20-VIII,10); 4QS[g] 2 (1QS VI,22-25); 3 (1QS VII,9-13); 4 (1QS VII,16-18?)
3.3. Procedures for the admission of new members
  - 1QS V,7b-20a; V,20b-VI,1a; VI,13b-23
  - 4QS[b] 5 (1QS V,1-20); 7 (1QS VI,10-13); 8 (1QS VI,16-18); 4QS[d] 1 I (1QS V,1-19); 1 II (1QS V,21-VI,7); 4QS[g] 1 (1QS V,22-24); 2 (1QS VI,22-25)

---

[40] Cf. Murphy-O'Connor 1969, 529-532.
[41] Following the view of Knibb (1987, 144). Weise (1961, 68) suggests that the transitional passage (Übergangsabschnitt) was longer and consisted of IX,24bβ-X,1aα.

3.4. Rules for the organization of the community
  - 1QS VI,1b-8a; VI,8b-13a
  - 4QS^d 1 II (1QS V,21-VI,7); 1 III (1QS VI,9-12); 4QS^i 1 (1QS VI,1-4)
3.5. Sections addressed to the wise leader
  - 1QS III,13-IV,26; IX,12-21a; 21b-26a
  - 4QS^a 3 (1QS III,20-25?); 4QS^b 5 (1QS V,1-20); 10 I (1QS IX,18-22);
    4QS^c 2 (1QS IV,4-10); 3 (1QS IV,13-15); 4QS^d 1 I (1QS V,1-19); 2
    III (1QS IX,15-X,3); 4QS^e 1 III (1QS VIII,11-15 + IX,12-20); 2 (1QS
    IX,20-24); 4QS^f 1 V (IX,23-24)
3.6. Sections concerning the cult of the community
  - 1QS I,16-III,12; IX,26b-XI,22
  - 4QS^a 2 (1QS III,7-12); 4QS^b 1 (1QS I,16-19); 2 (1QS I,21-23); 3
    (1QS II,4-5); 4 (1QS II,7-11); 10 II (1QS X,3-7); 11 (1QS X,14-18);
    12 (1QS XI,22-?), 4QS^c 1 II (1QS II,4-11); 1 III (1QS II,26-III,10),
    4QS^d 2 III (1QS IX,15-X,3); 2 IV (1QS X,4-12); 2 V (1QS X,12-18),
    3 (XI,7); 4QS^f 1 II (1QS X,1-5); 1 III (1QS X,9-11); 1 IV (1QS X,15-
    20); 1 V (1QS X,20-24); 4QS^h 1 (1QS III,4-5); 4QS^j 1 (1QS XI,14-
    22), 5Q11 1 I (1QS II,4-7); 1 II (1QS II 12-14?)

*3.1. Introductions*

The manuscript 1QS includes three introductory passages, the first of which
is at the beginning of the whole manuscript (1QS I,1-15) before the liturgy
for entering the covenant. The second introduction (V,1-7a) is to be found
at the beginning of column V commencing a series of rules regulating the
internal life of the community. The third one (VIII,1-13a+15a)[42] is at the
beginning of column VIII. It has been supposed to form a part of the so-
called programme of the community, but the material from Cave 4
indicates that originally it preceded the regulations addressed to the wise
leader.[43] Although the introductions are placed in very different parts of the
Rule, they share a grammatical structure which is clearly distinguishable.
The headings of the texts that follow are naturally presented in the
introductions. The passages also deal with several common themes, which
makes the comparison of the passages possible.

  All the introductory sections set forth the general principles of
community life in series of infinitives with *lamed* (20x in 1QS I,1-15; 9x
in1QS V,1-7a; 10x in 1QS VIII,1-13a+15a). They are to be understood in
a predicative sense, denoting commands (e.g. 1QS I,1-2 "They *shall seek*
God"). Except for participles, the introductions have very few occurrences of

---

[42] 1QS VIII,13b-14 forms an interpolation with the citation of Isa 40:3.
[43] See pp. 118.

other verbal forms (1QS I,11; V,3,4; VIII,8,10,13,14,15). In 1QS VIII,1-13a+15a the infinitive structure can clearly be seen at the beginning of the section (VIII,1-4), but it shows signs of breaking down in the passages starting with בהיות אלה בישראל.

The comparison of headings reveals both differences and similarities. The heading in 1QS I,1, which is preserved only in fragmentary form, was supposedly something like ל[משכיל ללמד את אנ]שים לחיו ספר סרך היחד.[44] The word ספר, which can be restored with 4QSᵃ, does not appear in any other of the introductions. Apparently the writer or compiler intended it to designate the whole of the composition of 1QS I-XI, which he named "The book of the order of the community."[45] The term סרך, when appearing alone, denotes a smaller set of regulations. This can be seen in the title of 1QS V,1, וזה הסרך לאנשי היחד, but also elsewhere (1QS VI,8; 1QSa I,1). In the more original version of 1QS V,1-7 from cave 4 the text has been entitled מדרש למשכיל על אנשי התורה (4QSᵇ 5,1/4QSᵈ 1 I,1). The reason for choosing another word in 1QS was perhaps that מדרש never signifies a written text in 1QS (cf. VI,24; VIII,15 and 26). In 1QS V,1 the text is addressed to the men of the community (לאנשי היחד) but in 4QSᵇ 5,1/4QSᵈ 1 I,1 and presumably also in 1QS I,1, to the wise leader (למשכיל). It is difficult to say why the addressee in 1QS V,1 was changed. The position of the wise leader in the hierarchy of the community is extremely puzzling, for the term never appears in the same context with other community functionaries. It is not clear, for instance, whether the office of the wise leader was held by only one person at a time, or whether there were several wise leaders in the community. The section 1QS VIII,1-13a+15a does not provide any title, but it is clear that VIII,1 introduces a different text from the preceding material of column VII.

Listing the themes which appear in the introductions and examining how they are treated in the passages, or whether a certain theme is handled at all, sheds further light on the history of the sections and the relationships between them. The following themes can be discerned: the commitment to seek God, the ethical obligation of the community, the relation to the Law, the question of property, the polarization between love and hatred and between light and darkness, the separation from evil, the theme of the covenant, admitting members into the covenant, the appointed times (calendar), the question of authority in the community, the laying of a foundation for Aaron and Israel, the condemnation of the wicked, the

---

[44] See pp. 111-112.
[45] See also Murphy-O'Connor 1969, 538.

bringing of expiation, separation from the wicked, and the preparation of the way for God.

The expression לדרוש אל, "to seek God," is unique in 1QS I,1-2, but the community's commitment to Torah is brought to the fore in slightly different wordings in all the introductions (cf. 1QS I,2-3; 1QS V,1; 4QS[b] 5,1/4QS[d] 1 I,1; 1QS VIII,1-2). The ethical obligation of the members of the community is expressed in a very similar way in all the passages (cf. 1QS I,5-6, V,3-4; 4QS[b] 5,3-4/4QS[d] 1 I,3; VIII,2). Two themes occur in 1QS I,1-15 which do not occur in other introductions: the polarization between light and darkness and between love and hatred (I,3-4, 9-10), and admitting members into the covenant (I,7). The former theme has its background in the doctrine of the two spirits (1QS III,13-IV,26), the latter in the liturgy for entering the covenant (1QS I,16-III,12). The themes of atonement and condemnation of the men of injustice, which are central in the introduction of column 1QS VIII, do not occur in 1QS I,1-15. Nor is the question of the authority in the community dealt with; this is considered in 1QS V,2-3 and 4QS[b] 5,3/4QS[d] 1 I,2. However, 1QS I,1-15 does refer to subjects which are more thoroughly dealt with from column V onwards, such as property (1QS I,13; cf. VI,18-21) and the calendar (1QS I,9 and 13-14; cf. X,1-8). This provides further support for the assumption that the introduction of 1QS I,1-15 was written for the whole of the composition, not for columns 1QS I-IV only.

Besides the changes made in the titles of 1QS V,1 and 4QS[b] 5,1/4QS[d] 1 I,1, there are other differences between the two versions of the introduction preceding the legislative material (1QS V-VII). Whereas 4QS[b] 5,3/4QS[d] 1 I,2 mentions the *rabbim* as the authority, 1QS V,2-3 speaks of "the sons of Zadok, the priests who keep the covenant" and "the multitude of the men of the community who hold fast to the covenant." There cannot be any decisive difference in the denotation of the two expressions, for the *rabbim* includes both priests and (lay)men. It is interesting, however, that the term ברית has been introduced into the text. The very same term is also added in 1QS V,5 but it is missing in 4QS[b] 5,5/4QS[d] 1 I,4. The themes of atonement (לכפר) and judgement (להרשיע) have also been added to the text of 1QS V,6-7, for in 4QS[b] 5,6/4QS[d] 1 I,4 they are missing. All the themes mentioned above (covenant, atonement, judgement) play a prominent rôle in the introduction of 1QS VIII (cf. VIII,10 להקם ברית לחוקות עולם (see also VIII,3); VIII,10 לכפר בעד הארץ; VIII,10 ולחרוץ משפט רשעה (see also VIII,6-7)). The comparison between the passages leads one to suspect that the introduction in 4QS[b] 5,1-6/4QS[d] 1 I,1-5 was originally written for the legislative material (i.e. the material parallel to 1QS V-VII) only, and that the redaction, which can be seen in 1QS V,1-7, was carried out after the material of columns 1QS V-VII and VIII-IX were linked together. The purpose of the revision was to make the introduction of 1QS V,1-7 cover the material of columns 1QS VIII-IX, too, and thus combine columns V-VII and VIII-IX more closely. The joining of the two corpora can also explain the missing heading at the beginning of 1QS VIII. It may have been omitted secondarily.

Since the passages 1QS VIII,14-15 and VIII,15b-IX,11 have above proven to be insertions,[46] it is apparent that sections 1QS VIII,1-13a+15a originally formed an introduction to the rules for the *maskil* (1QS IX,12-26a). They should not be seen as part of the so-called programme of the community soon to be established. The idea of Sutcliffe and Murphy-O'Connor that 'the programme' covers most of the material of columns VIII and IX is thus no longer valid. One may still ask, however, whether there are elements in the remaining text which might indicate that it was written before the founding of the Qumran community.

The group of twelve men and three priests described as עצת היחד occurs in 1QS VIII,1 only.[47] It has been argued that the council of twelve plus three in 1QS VIII,1 might signify a smaller, inner council of the community.[48] Nowhere else in the Rule does this kind of leading group appear, however, but עצת היחד denotes all full members of the community (see e.g. 1QS III,2; V,7; VI,10,13,16; VII,2,22-24). The manuscript 4QpIs[d] provides an important parallel to 1QS VIII,1, for it speaks of "the priests and the people" as those who founded the council of the community (יסדו את עצת היחד, cf. 1QS VIII,5-6). I do not consider it impossible that the men and priests mentioned in 1QS VIII,1 could symbolically[49] signify the group which actually moved to Qumran. The section VIII,12b-15a is the only one in the Rule describing the separation from the "men of injustice" as going into the wilderness. It is difficult to interpret the saying otherwise than literally in this context.[50] The temporal phrase בהיות אלה בישראל could

---

[46] See above p. 71-73, 118.

[47] Regarding the other introductions, the *rabbim* are mentioned in 4QS[b] 5,3/4QS[d] 1 I,2, and synonymously also in 1QS V,2-3, for it speaks about "the priests and the multitude of the men of the community." In 1QS I,1-15, no governing body of the community is mentioned.

[48] E.g. Baumgarten 1976, 63; Stegemann 1993, 158: "Der Urteilsfindung im Straffall dient schliesslich ein Gerichtshof, dem stets drei Priester und zwölf Laien angehören müssen."

[49] The twelve tribes of Israel and three priestly families. See Milik 1957, 64f.

[50] See e.g. Stegemann 1993, 81-82. Although he assumes that the Qumran settlement was not founded before 100 B.C., he holds that 1QS VIII,13 should be understood as denoting the desert withdrawal literally. Cf. Wernberg-Moeller 1969, 69: "Is XL,3 is interpreted in a spiritualizing manner." Note esp. Brooke 1994, 132: "4QS[d] may partially vindicate the view by Golb by suggesting that there was some, possibly continuing, section of the community, which did not subscribe to the view that a literal journey to the wilderness was a necessary part of the movement's self-understanding. However, the form of the *Manual of Discipline* as represented in 4QS[e] and 1QS shows an explicit use of Isa 40:3 which... is best understood as

accordingly be understood as referring to the events connected with the founding the Qumran settlement.

It is not fully clear, however, whether 1QS VIII,1-13a+15a was written before the desert withdrawal. It may have been composed afterwards, when the community already existed, to describe the beginnings of the settlement. The theme of property typical of practical community life is missing in the introduction of column VIII (cf. I,11-12, V,2 and 3, 4QSᵇ 5,3/4QSᵈ 1 I,2 and 3). The question of authority is not thoroughly dealt with either (cf. 4QSᵇ 5,3/4QSᵈ 1 I,2, 1QS V,2-3), although the council of twelve men and three priests can be regarded as some kind of predecessor of the *rabbim*. But merely on the basis of these missing themes, it is hardly possible to draw the conclusion that the section must have originated before the desert withdrawal. The relation of the introduction to the following passages addressed to the *maskil* is a more crucial question. The qualities and responsibilities attributed to him seem rather to refer to actual, contemporary life than to events in the future. The material of 1QS VIII,1-13a+15a + IX,12-26 may be of an early origin, but it was not necessarily composed before the founding of the community. In any case, the question as to when the material was brought into the composition remains an open one.

## 3.2. The Penal Codes

Material consisting of penal codes is to be found in 1QS VI,24-VII,25 and VIII,16b-IX,2. Both sections include the formula ואלה המשפטים (VI,24, VIII,29), although in the latter one it does not appear at the beginning of the code, but in the middle commencing a new set of regulations. Both sections deal with judicial cases where the authority lies in the hands of the *rabbim* (see e.g. VII,21, VIII,19, IX,2). The very fact that sections belonging together thematically have been placed in different parts of the manuscript raises the suspicion that they do not form a uniform set of regulations but represent different stages in the development of the legislation.[51] The idea is confirmed by comparison of the passages, for there are both stylistical differences and tensions in content. Manuscripts 4QSᵉ and 4QSᵍ have preserved parallels to 1QS VI,22-25 (4QSᵍ), VII,8-15 (4QSᵉ, 4QSᵍ), VII,16-18? (4QSᵍ) and VII,20-25 (4QSᵉ). A small fragment of 4QSᵇ containing the word דרוש belongs most likely to a parallel of 1QS VII,7. In 4QSᵈ a text corresponding to 1QS VIII,16-IX,2 (frg. 2 I-II) has been preserved. The code of 1QS VIII,16b-IX,2 is included in the long passage of 1QS VIII,15b-IX,11, which is completely missing in 4QSᵉ.

---

being used both literally and metaphorically."
    [51] Hunzinger 1963, 242.

The way the cases have been described differs greatly between the two passages of 1QS VI,24-VII,25 and VIII,16b-IX,2. Even the ways of referring to a transgressor are unalike. In 1QS VIII,16b-IX,2 there are a great number of attributes attached: וכול איש מאנשי ברית היחד אשר (VIII,16), כול הבא בעצת הקודש ההולכים בתמים דרך כאשר צוה כול איש מהמה (VIII,21-22). In 1QS VI,24-VII,25 a transgressor is always referred to in very simple terms: ואשר (VI,25,27; VII,3,5,8,9,10,12,13,14), ואיש (VII,16), האיש אשר/איש אשר (VII,4,10-11,13,15,17,18), a participle (ולמדבר VII,9, והמוציא VII,15). Common to the two codes is, however, the fact that there is no distinction made between the novices and the full members of the community.

In 1QS VIII,16b-IX,2 violations are described in very general terms: "No man among the men of the covenant of the community, who presumptuously leaves unfulfilled any one of the commands shall touch the purity of the men of the holiness or know any of their commands" (VIII,16b-18a). How long the punishment should last, is not told in advance, but the transgression is seen to be atoned for, when "his deeds have been cleansed from all injustice, so that he walks in perfection of way" (VIII,18b). The criteria for being cleansed are not determined. There is merely a statement that the *rabbim* should make the decision of reversing the previous status of the member (VIII,19). The procedure described above is very different from the detailed cases of 1QS VI,24-VII,25. For example: "If a man is found among them who has knowingly lied about wealth, they shall exclude him from the purity of the *rabbim* for one year, and he shall do penance with respect to one quarter of his food (VI,24-25)."

There are twenty-six diverse cases listed in 1QS VI,24-VII,25. They seem to be arranged in a rather haphazard order: the offences of insulting and slandering another person, which are of a similar kind and both of which lead to exclusion and penance for a period of one year, are placed in two different parts (VII,4-5 and VII,15-16). The literary *Gattung* of the list is that of casuistic law which has its prototype in the Old Testament, especially in the Book of the Covenant (Exod 20:22 - 23:33). The introductory formula ואלה המשפטים (VI,24) is the same as in Ex 21:1, but while never starting with ואשר[52], the usual way of presenting a new case in Exod 21:1-22:19 is וכי/-אם. In 1QS VI,24-VII,25, the conjunction אם appears mainly[53] in additional clauses in regulations starting with ואשר:

---

[52] In Qumran Hebrew, אשר has in some contexts lost its character as a relative pronoun and has changed into a pronoun commencing a main clause, see also e.g. 1QM X,1. Even though this kind of use of אשר is not attested in the Book of the Covenant, which otherwise is to be compared with our passage, there exists, in fact, a case of a similar use of אשר elsewhere in the Pentateuch, namely in Deut 15:2. On the syntax of this verse, see Weinfeld 1990, 39-62 (esp. p. 50).

[53] With the exception of 1QS VI,24b.

"Whoever (ואשר) speaks deceitfully to his neighbour or knowingly acts deceitfully shall do penance for six months. If (ואם) he is negligent towards his neighbour, he shall do penance for three months. But if (ואם) he is negligent with regard to the wealth of the community so that he causes its loss, he shall restore it in full. If (ואם) he is unable to restore it, he shall do penance for sixty days (VII,5b-8)."[54] The adverb כ also appears linking regulations: "Whoever bears a grudge against his neighbour without cause shall do penance for six months/one year[55]. And likewise (וכן) for anyone who avenges anything himself" (VII,8b-9a).[56]

There are basically three different types of punishments mentioned in the penal codes of the Community Rule: exclusion (מובדל/הבדיל), penance (נענש) and expulsion (לוא ישוב עוד + הבדיל). In the case of losing communal property, there is also the possibility of compensation (שלם pi.). The exact meaning of the first two is not fully clear. Exclusion cancelled the member's right to "touch the purity (טהרה) of the *rabbim*." In rabbinic literature, the word טהרה is used to refer to ritually clean articles, and particularly to ritually clean food,[57] but it is likely that the word should be understood here in a broader cultic sense, including not only the common meals, but also the ritual baths of the community.[58] It would be natural to think that the session of the *rabbim* also had a cultic connotation and that the offender was also excluded from attending the decision-making of the community, but in VIII,17-18 'the purity' and 'the counsel' are mentioned separately (אל ינע בטהרת אנשי הקודש ואל ידע בכול עצתם). The content of penance is clear only in its first occurrence in the text (VI,25): cutting the food ration by one quarter. Whether the meaning of נענש is the same later in the text when the term appears alone without any further definitions, remains questionable. There are no other explanations available, however.

A new question arises while reading the latter part, VIII,20-IX,2, of the section 1QS VIII,16b-IX,2. According to VIII,21b-23a "Every man of them who transgresses a word from the law of Moses presumptuously or negligently shall be sent away from the council of the community and shall never return." This is in contradiction with the first part, VIII,16b-19, where the consequence of a transgression is said to be only exclusion from

---

[54] See also VI,27 (ואשר) - VII,1 (ואם) - VII,2 (ואם) - VII,3 (ואם); VII,17 (והאיש אשר) - VII,17 (ואם).

[55] "One year" is corrected above the line by the second scribe.

[56] See also 1QS VII,10. The adverb (ו)כן is used similarly e.g. in Deut 15:17; 20:15; 22:3,26.

[57] t. Berakot 19ᵃ; t. Demai II, 20 and III,1; t. Giṭṭin 62ᵃ; b. Šabbat 13ᵃ; b. Ḥagiga II,7; b. Baba Meṣiʿa 59. E.g. Lieberman (1952, 203) and Vermes (1987, 7-8) interpret the term טהרה in the Qumran texts in a similar way to the rabbinic tradition.

[58] Cf. 1QS III,4-7.

the purity of the men of holiness: "No man among the men of the covenant of the community, who presumptuously leaves unfulfilled any one of the commands shall touch the purity of the men of the holiness or know any of their commands." The difference in punishments in VIII,16b-19 and VIII,21b-23a has led some scholars to think that the first part involved the breaches of the community's own law (כול המצוה ?), the latter breaches of Mosaic law (תורת מושה).[59] This kind of separation between the community's own law and the law of Moses, however, does not occur anywhere else in the penal codes of the Community Rule. Undoubtedly the community considered its own halakhic rules to be in accordance with the Torah. Only in 1QS VI,14, where the *paqid* is commanded to teach the candidate the regulations of the community, is a term differentiated from the law of Moses employed, but the term is משפט היחד, not מצוה.[60] It has also been suggested that the latter regulation is directed to the inner, more seriously committed council of the community. The term אנשי התמים קודש (VIII,20) would be a sign of this.[61] Yet again it is to be noted, that nowhere else does תמים refer to the existence of such a group. Since section VIII,20-IX,2 starts with a new heading (ואלה המשפטים), and since there is a mark in the margin and the passages appear to be separate, it is more likely that they belong to different stages of development and reflect a change of practice at a certain period.[62] Hunzinger considers section VIII,20-IX,2 to be older than

---

[59] E.g. Dupont-Sommer 1959, 102 and Leaney 1966, 224. Stegemann (personal consultation) holds the view that 1QS VIII,16-19 deals with transgressions of the community's own law, but he nevertheless denies that VI,24-VII,25 and VIII,16-19 are duplicate passages: He argues that VIII,16-19 considers more fundamental violations against the community than those of VI,24-VII,25. Stegemann has overlooked VII,18b-25a, where a violation against the fundamental principles of the community is regulated explicitly.

[60] In 1QS the word מצוה appears in VIII,17 only, but CD uses the term very frequently. In twelve occurrences out of fourteen, it is clear that מצוה refers to the Torah (CD II,8,21; III,2,6,8,12; V,12; VIII,19; IX,7; XIX,2,5,32). Only in CD VII,2 (כמצוה) and X,3 מן דבר (המצוה) is it not stated explicitly whether it is the Torah that is referred to. I find it most plausible. So also Levine 1984, 1095: "Zwei Belege verdienen besondere Aufmerksamkeit: 1) CD 7,2 sagt, dass man seinen Bruder "nach dem Gebot" zurechtweisen soll. Dies bezieht sich deutlich auf Lev 19,17, wo es heisst, dass man den Nächsten zurechtweisen soll, wenn er das Gesetz übertritt. Wichtig ist hier der Gebrauch der bestimmten Form *hammiṣwah* mit Bezug auf die Torah als Ganzes. In späterem rabbinischem Sprachgebrauch würde es heissen *kakkātûb*, "wie geschrieben ist", d.h. in der Torah. 2) CD 10,2f. sagt, dass ein Zeuge nicht als zuverlässig betrachtet werden kann, der "etwas ('ein Wort') vom Gebot übertritt (*'ôḇer dāḇār min hammiṣwah*)". Ein ähnlicher Ausdruck findet sich 1QS 8,17: "der überhaupt von etwas im Gebot abweicht (*'ᵃsae'r jāsûr mikkol hammiṣwah dāḇār*)". *hammiṣwāh* ist hier mit *hattôrāh* gleichbedeutend; in rabbinischer Sprache findet sich sogar der Ausdruck *dāḇār min hattôrāh*. Die Qumranhandschriften repräsentieren also einen Übergang von der at.lichen zu der späteren jüdischen Auffassung der *miṣwāh* als Gesetz, das durch Dtr. und P vorgebildet ist."

[61] The idea was put forward by Hunzinger (1963,243), although he himself rejected it in the same connection.

[62] Hunzinger 1963, 243, Knibb 1987, 136.

VIII,16b-19, but his argumentation at this point is not fully clear.[63] I think it more probable that in proportion as the community grew and the number of judicial cases increased, it became necessary to create more detailed lists of regulations. Therefore, section 1QS VIII,20-IX,2 with an additional clause about inadvertently committed transgressions should represent a later stage than VIII,16b-19 in the development of legislation. For the same reason, I consider section 1QS VI,24-VII,25 to be the latest of the penal codes of the Community Rule.[64] When the redactor added the material of 1QS VIII,15b-IX,11 - which in 4QS[e] was still lacking - to the composition, he did not compose the sections 1QS VIII,16b-19 and VIII,20-IX,2 himself, but borrowed from a source older than 1QS VI,24-VII,25.[65]

The way the penal legislation in the community developed can also be traced in changes made to the punishments. In VII,8, the second scribe has written above the line "one year" and substituted for a punishment of six months a more severe one. Apparently, in judging cases of bearing a grudge against one's neighbour there had been a change of practice in the community. An example contrary to this can be detected between 1QS VII,14 and 4QS[e] 1 I,10. In the more original version of 4QS[e], the punishment for display one's nakedness lasts sixty days, but in 1QS VII,14 it is said to last only thirty days. The punishment had become more lenient over a period of time. On the basis of S-material only, it is impossible to conclude whether there was a general tendency in one direction or another, either towards more lenient or more severe punishments. A comparison with other penal codes found at Qumran might shed more light on the matter.

---

[63] Hunzinger (1963, 243-244) bases his view on supposed parallels between section 20 f. with IX,7 which is in clear contradiction with what is stated elsewhere in the Community Rule (V,2-3). Scholars have generally seen IX,7 as older than V,2-3. The article of Hunzinger gives the impression that just because IX,7 is older than V,2-3, VIII,20 ff. is older than section VIII,16b-19. The questions of the community's authority and the nature of punishments cannot be linked in this way. In doing so, Hunzinger should at least note that in section VIII,20b-IX,2 the *rabbim* (i.e. priests and laymen together) are also mentioned (IX,2 and presumably also VIII,26).

[64] Although Hunzinger (1963, 243) considers VIII,20-IX,2 older than VIII,16-19, he nevertheless thinks that VI,24-VII,25 is the latest of the sections. See also Murphy-O'Connor 1969, 532-543 and Knibb 1987, 137.

[65] E.g. Schürer (1986, 383) also reckons with the possibility of 1QS containing material that earlier on had an independent existence: "...it can safely be argued that the Community Rule incorporates pre-existing literary materials..."

## 3.3. Procedures for the Admission of New Members

Three passages in 1QS need to be taken into consideration when discussing the passages which describe the procedures for the admission of new members. The first such section speaks about the oath taken by the member of the community (1QS V,7-20a), the second and the third describe the examinations a candidate must pass before becoming accepted as a full member (1QS V,20b-23[-VI,1a?]) and VI,13b-23. All the three sections contain the formula בוא בברית (see V,8, V,20, VI,14-15). Moreover, the opening sentences of all these sections express the fact that the text deals with joining the community (V,7b בהאספם ליחד, V,20 להוחד לעדת קודש, VI,13b להוסיף על עצת היחד). Manuscripts 4QS[b], 4QS[d], and 4QS[g] have preserved material parallel to all these sections (4QS[b]: 1QS V,7-20, VI,13, VI,16-18; 4QS[d]: 1QS V,7-19, V,21-VI,1; 4QS[g]: 1QS V,22-24, VI,22-23). In some parts, and in V,7-20a in particular, they demonstrate that the text has undergone a thorough redaction. There is no indication in the reconstructions, however, that any of these passages were missing in any of the manuscripts. In the following I shall commence with the sections dealing with the examinations of new members.

There has been some divergence of opinion as to how the relationship between V,20b-VI,1a and VI,13b-23 is to be viewed. Van der Ploeg holds the sections to be duplicates, i.e. to concern the same procedure where one passage gives a more detailed description than does the other.[66] Murphy-O'Connor argues that the sections speak about two different subjects: VI,13-23 involves the admission of new members, whereas V,24-V,25 describes the annual examination of the status of members. The *Sitz im Leben* of V,20-23 is more difficult, according to Murphy-O'Connor, but it is related to the registration of members.[67] The view of Becker differs from both of these. He considers that the theme in both sections is the same and that the passages do not overlap but are independent. This leads to the conclusion, he argues, that the sections witness to two different stages in the history of the community.[68] As for the question which of the sections represent earlier practice, he does not provide an answer, however.

---

[66] Van der Ploeg 1951, 114.

[67] Murphy-O'Connor 1969, 536: "Le *Sitz im Leben* de V,20-23 est moins clair, mais le fait qu'il traite de l'inscription des membres selon leur ordre montre qu'il doit être associé au second, plutôt qu'au premier. Il n'y est pas question d'acceptation ou rejet, comme c'est explicitement le cas en VI,18-23."

[68] Becker 1964, 42: "Ferner sind 5,20-25 und 6,13-23 wohl zwei Texte zum gleichen Sachverhalt, die aber je selbstständig sind und auch in den Aussagen sich nicht decken, so dass man vermuten kann, dass hier verschiedene Stadien innerhalb der Entwicklung der Sekte ihren Niederschlag gefunden haben."

In my opinion, both V,20-23 and VI,13-23 do speak about the admission of new members. The formula בוא בברית common to both passages is the same as in the ceremony for entry into the covenant (I,16). This is sufficient for us to reject Murphy-O'Connor's claim of a different *Sitz im Leben* for V,20-23. Murpy-O'Connor is correct, however, in arguing that V,24-25 deals with the annual inspection of members' ranks. Strictly speaking, then, the thematic parallel to VI,13-23 is included in V,20-23a only[69] (the sentences in V,24b-VI,1 belong together with V,24a, for they explain the words לפי שכלו ותום דרכו and כנעויתו of 24a). But sections V,20-23a and VI,13-23 are not duplicates in the sense that one passage gives a more detailed description of the same procedure as does the other one, since the pictures of the procedure of admission given by the two sections differ. The first of the sections gives the impression that full admission takes place during the first stage of examination (V,20-23), whereas the second presupposes a period of probation that lasts for over two years, with gradual consecration to the practices of the community (VI,13-23). Section V,20-23a does not mention the examination by the *paqid* at all, nor the restrictions with respect to touching the purity or drink of the *rabbim*, or the pooling of wealth. In the first section registration happens immediately after the approval by "the sons of Aaron and the multitude of Israel," in the latter section the candidate is approved only after a period of over two years' testing. The procedure described in VI,13-23 is more complicated and more precisely regulated. Although it is difficult to find any decisive evidence as to which of the sections represents earlier practice, I think it more probable that the direction of the development advanced from a simpler procedure towards a more regulated one than *vice versa*.

Section 1QS VI,13-23 has close affinities with the report of Josephus about the admission of new members among the Essenes. The passage Bell.Iud.II.8.7/137-9 reads as follows:[70]

> A candidate anxious to join their sect is not immediately admitted. For one year, during which he remains outside the fraternity, they prescribe for him their own rule of life, presenting him with a small hatchet, the loin-cloth already mentioned, and white raiment. Having given proof of his temperance during this probationary period, he is brought into closer touch with the rule and is allowed to share the purer kind of holy water, but is not yet received into the meetings of the community. For after this exhibition of endurance, his character is tested for two years more, and only then, if found worthy, is he enrolled in the society.

---

[69] Also Stegemann (1993, 157) thinks that 1QS V,20-24 contains a rule for the examination of entry (die Aufnahmeprüfung) and for the annual inspection of the ranking of the members (die jährlich erneuerte Festsetzung der internen Rangordnung).

[70] The translation follows that by Colson 1989, 374-377.

But, before he may touch the common food, he is made to swear tremendous oaths.

Both 1QS VI,13-23 and Josephus' report declare that joining the community is a voluntary decision (ζηλοῦσιν/המתנדבים).[71] Common to both passages is also the statement that admission should happen in stages. But whereas Josephus speaks of an initial period of probation lasting one year spent outside the sect, in 1QS VI,13-23 the amount of time in the initial period is unspecified and the candidate appears to be in some sense within the community from the very beginning of the period of probation. Both passages mention the novice's closer contact with the community after the initial period (πρόσεισιν μὲν ἔγγιον τῇ διαίτῃ/בקרב),[72] and both Josephus and 1QS VI,13-23 report a two-year period of further testing. According to Josephus, after the initial period the candidate is admitted to participate in the purificatory baths, though he is still excluded from the "communal life" i.e. from the common meals. Having passed the two-year period of testing the candidate could be listed as a member of the community. Before participating in the common meal he was required to swear tremendous oaths, however. In 1QS VI,13-23 the privileges of the candidate after the initial period are not specified, but VI,16-17 states that the candidate was not permitted to "touch the purity of the *rabbim*", i.e. join in the common meal,[73] nor permitted to share in the wealth of the *rabbim*, before he had passed one year of further testing.[74] After the second year the candidate was allowed to "touch the drink of the *rabbim*," and the final examination gave him the rights of a full member: the participation in "law, judgement, purity and wealth." The oath of the candidate mentioned by Josephus does not occur in 1QS VI,13-23, but occurs in V,7-20. The hatchet, the loin cloth, and the white garments are, however, not mentioned in 1QS at all. It is nevertheless clear that the description by Josephus, written about 70-75 A.D., follows the procedure reported in 1QS VI,13-23 rather than the practise described in 1QS V,20-23.

Manuscripts 4QS[b] and 4QS[d] reveal signs of redaction in all sections of 1QS dealing with the admission of new members. Especially 1QS V,7-20 concerning the oath of the candidate has undergone a deep moulding

---

[71] The terminological affinity has been noted by Beall 1988, 74.

[72] The similarity in the terminology was first noted by Michel and Bauernfeind 1959, 434-435 n. 59.

[73] See the discussion on p. 126.

[74] 1QS VI,17b-18a is missing in 4QS[b,d]. Omitting the two sentences does not substantially change the content of the text, however, for it is mentioned in VI,19-20, too, that the candidate's property was not to be combined with that of the community before a probation period of one year.

process. In the following translation of this passage the text which is not
included in the more original version of 4QS$^{b,d}$ is printed in italics:[75]

> (V,7) *These are their rules of conduct, according to all these statutes, when
> they are admitted to the community.* Everyone who joins the council of the
> community (8) *shall enter into the covenant of God in the presence of those
> who willingly offer themselves.* He shall undertake by a *binding* oath to return
> to the law of Moses with all his (9) heart and soul, *following all that he has
> commanded,* and in accordance with all that has been revealed from it *to the
> sons of Zadok, the priests who keep the covenant and seek his will, and to the
> multitude of the men of their covenant* (10) *who together willingly offer
> themselves for his truth and to walk according to his will. He shall undertake
> by the covenant*[76] to separate himself from all the men of injustice *who walk*
> (11) *in the way of wickedness. For they are not counted in his covenant
> because they have not sought or consulted him about his statutes in order to
> know the hidden things in which they have guiltily gone astray,* (12) *whereas
> with regard to the things revealed they have acted presumptuously, arousing
> anger for judgement and for taking vengeance by the curses of the covenant to
> bring upon themselves mighty acts of judgement* (13) *leading to eternal
> destruction without a remnant. He shall not enter the waters in order to*[77]
> touch the purity of the men of holiness, *for men are not purified* (14) *unless
> they turn from the evil; for he remains unclean amongst all the transgressors
> of his word. No one shall join with him with regard to his work or his
> wealth lest he burden him* (15) *with iniquity and guilt. But he shall keep away
> from him in everything, for thus it is written, 'You shall keep away from
> everything false.'*[78] No one of the men of the community shall answer (16) to
> their authority with regard to any law or decision.[79] No one shall eat *or drink
> anything of their property, or take anything at all from their hand,* (17) *except
> for payment, as it is written, 'Have no more to do with man in whose nostrils
> is breath, for what is he worth?' For* (18) *all those who are not counted in
> his covenant, they and everything that belongs to them are to be kept separate.*
> No man of holiness shall rely on any deeds (19) of vanity, for vanity are all
> those who spurn his word; all their deeds are impure (20) before him, and all
> their wealth unclean.

---

[75] Except for the italics and the footnotes, the translation follows that by Knibb 1987, 104-
108.

[76] Instead of "to the sons of Zadok, the priests who keep the covenant and seek his will,
and to the multitude of the men of their covenant who together willingly offer themselves for
his truth and to walk according to his will. He shall undertake by the covenant" the version of
4QS$^{b,d}$ reads "to the multitude of the council of the men of the community".

[77] Instead of "They shall not enter the waters in order to" the version of 4QS$^{b,d}$ reads:
"They shall not".

[78] Instead of the passage "for men are not purified (14) unless they turn from the evil; for
he remains unclean amongst all the transgressors of his word. No one shall join with him
with regard to his work or his wealth lest he burden him (15) with iniquity and guilt. But he
shall keep away from him in everything, for thus it is written, 'You shall keep away from
everything false" 4QS$^{b,d}$ read: "He shall not eat with him in the community".

[79] 4QS$^{b,d}$ has space for about three more words here, which are not preserved.

The character of the additions to the text indicates that it was not a change of practice in the community which motivated the editorial work but the need theologically to justify the practice which already prevailed. By the oath the member bound himself to the law of Moses as it was understood and interpreted in the community, as well as to committing separate from the "men of injustice", i.e. from outsiders. According to Josephus, the oath of the candidate consisted of ten stipulations. Michel and Bauernfeind have correctly pointed out that the list of Josephus corresponds closest to the passage 1QS I,1-15.[80]

## 3.4. Rules for the Organization of the Community

Two sections dealing with the meetings of the Essenes have been linked in the first half of column 1QS VI. Section 1QS VI,1c-7a concerns the meetings in the places of מגורים, 1QS VI,8b-13a is a rule for the sessions of the *rabbim*. The sentence in between, i.e. in VI,7b-8a (והרבים ישקודו ביחד את שלישית כול לילות השנה לקרוא בספר ולדרוש משפט ולברך ביחד), was composed by the redactor in order to combine the passages.[81] He used the words דורש (דורש בתורה VI,6b/ולדרוש משפט VI,7b) and הרבים (VI,7b/VI,8b) as bridges in his sentence, which has no real logical connection with either of the passages. Essential questions for the understanding of these passages are (1) whether the sections describe meetings at the same or at a different organizational level, and (2) whether the context of sections 1QS VI,1c-7a and VI,8b-13a is the same, i.e. the Qumran community, or whether the first section describes a practice observed outside Qumran as has been suggested by some scholars.[82] There is only one variant of some significance for these sections in the fragments from cave 4. Instead of ולממון (1QS VI,2) 4QS[i] reads ולה[ו]ן, which is somewhat synonymous, however.[83] The text preserved in 4QS[i] covers 1QS VI,1-3. In 4QS[d] there are preserved fragments parallel to 1QS VI,1-7 and 9-12.

The impression that sections 1QS VI,1c-7a and VI,8b-13a are related to each other arises foremost from similarities in the vocabulary. Both sections use the word תכון in denoting the rank of members. The preposition connected with this word is different in the passages, however: איש כתכונו (VI,4)/איש בתכונו (VI,9). Ordinal numbers, לרשונה - בשנית, occur in both passages designating the order of the members (VI,5; VI,8). The ways of

---

[80] Michel-Bauernfeind 1959, 435 n. 60.
[81] Leaney (1966, 185) noted already that the regulation in VI,7b-8a "serves as a link." It remains unclear, however, whether he attributes it to the same writer as the rules before and/or after.
[82] Guilbert 1961, 44 n. 72, Leaney 1966, 180, Knibb 1987, 115, Stegemann 1993, 157.
[83] See p. 94 n. 91.

prescribing the regulations for decision-making are almost identical: וכן
וכן ישאלו למשפט ולכול עצה ודבר אשר יהיה לרבים/(VI,4) ישאלו לעצתם לכול דבר
(VI,9). The council of the community, עצת היחד, is mentioned in both
passages (VI,3; VI,10). The purpose of both sections is to regulate how the
members should behave toward each other, איש את רעהו (VI,2; VI,10). A
clear terminological difference, one could argue, lies in the manner the
members are grouped in the passages. In VI,1c-7a the members are divided
simply into priests and laymen, whereas in VI,8b-13a the groups
mentioned are priests, elders and the rest of the people. The division of the
members into two groups is not exceptional in the Rule, however, since it
also appears in V,2 and 9, VI,9 and VIII,1. So far, there is nothing to
indicate that one of the  passages would not fit in the context of the texts
written for the members of the Qumran community.

Yet there are dissimilarities between VI,1c-7a and VI,8b-13a, which can
be perceived by studying the *Sitz im Leben* of the passages. According to
VI,8b, the rule in the following is meant for the general assembly of the
community (למושב הרבים), the head officer of which is named the *mebaqqer*
(האיש המבקר על הרבים). The picture in the section VI,1c-7a is different. The
words "In every place where there are ten men from the council of the
community (מעצת היחד)" indicate that the meetings in question belonged to
a lower level of decision-making than those of the general assembly. Since
the comparison between VI,8 and 10 shows that there is no difference in
meaning between the terms הרבים and עצת היחד, the sentence in VI,3 could
also be read "where there are ten men from the *rabbim*." Any priest was
permitted to function as head of the counsel at this kind of minor meetings.
Unlike VI,8b-13a, the rule in VI,1c-7a involves not only the decision-
making (the counsel), but various kinds of communal gatherings, prayer,
the meal and the study of the law, and the member's obligation to obey his
superior is also said to cover the matters of work and property. At the
common meal, as in the counsel, the priest takes precedence.

Several arguments can be put forward in favour of the view that 1QS
VI,1c-7a concerns meetings held outside Qumran: The word מגורים
designates a more or less temporary lodgement,[84] and the settlement at
Qumran cannot be characterized as such. Also the idea of meeting someone
else is most appropriate somewhere else than Qumran where the members
were permanently in contact with one another. The injunction to act
together (VI,2-3), as has been pointed out by Leaney, was surely

---

[84] The word מגורים is always in the plural in the Old Testament and often has the
connotation of exiles, see e.g. Gen 17,8; Ex 6,4; Ezek 20,38. The root גור, however, means
simply 'to dwell as a client'. Most commentators have understood the noun here neutrally as
'a dwelling.'

superfluous at Qumran.[85] One could also think it self-evident that there were more than ten attendants and priests present at the meetings in Qumran. Therefore at the site of Qumran the regulation in VI,3-4 seems also to be somewhat superfluous. The scholars who think 1QS VI,1b-7a was intended for the Essene members living outside Qumran refer to Philo's and Josephus' statements about the Essenes in towns and villages.[86] Indeed, the passage is well suited in the same context. There remains the question, however, why the text in 1QS VI,1c-7a was introduced into the composition of the Community Rule, which seems to mirror the circumstances of a larger Essene settlement rather than those of the small local communities of towns and villages. The close affinities with the vocabulary of VI,8b-13a can be seen as one reason. One might also consider the possibility that the purpose of the section was perhaps to serve as a rule for the members while they were visiting areas outside large settlements such as Qumran, and were in contact with the Essenes living in towns and villages amongst other Jews.

## 3.5. Sections Addressed to the Wise Leader

The title למשכיל appears at the beginning of five sections in the Community Rule. The first occurrence of the title is based on a conjectural reading in 1QS I,1. The second section addressed to the *maskil* is the doctrine of the two spirits (1QS III,13-IV,26). In the manuscripts 4QS[b] and 4QS[d] the parallel to 1QS V,1 ff. begins with למשכיל. The fourth and the fifth occurrences of the title are to be found in column 1QS IX commencing two sections (IX,12-21a and 21b-26) concerned with the *maskil*'s duties and the qualities required of him. In what follows I shall mainly concentrate on passages which stress the teaching responsibility of the *maskil*, namely on 1QS III,13-IV,26, IX,12-21a and 21b-26[87] (the other two sections have been more thoroughly dealt with in connection with the introductions). In the manuscripts 4QS[d] and 4QS[e], which contain a more original text than 1QS, the doctrine of the two spirits was not included at all. Manuscript 4QS[c], however, has preserved a parallel to 1QS IV,4-10, and 4QS[a] contains a fragment which has no direct parallel in 1QS but which forms a part of the doctrine. The reconstructed 4QS[b] points in the direction that the doctrine was included in this manuscript, which otherwise shows similarities to

[85] Leaney 1966, 180, Knibb 1987, 115.

[86] Philo, Omn. prob. lib. XII.76, Apol.Iud. II.1; Josephus, Bell.Iud. II.8.4/124.

[87] The passages IX,12-21a and 21b-26a are stylistically very coherent and there are affinities in the vocabulary (see e.g. רצון אל IX,13; IX,23,24, כאשר צוה IX,15; IX,24, אהבתו עם שנאתו IX,16; IX,21, אנשי השחת IX,16; IX,22). A new heading in IX,21b similar to IX,12 may indicate, however, that the passages did not originally belong together.

4QS<sup>d.</sup> In 4QS<sup>b</sup> and 4QS<sup>d</sup> there are parallels preserved for 1QS IX,18-22 (4QS<sup>b</sup>) and 1QS IX,15-26 (4QS<sup>d</sup>).

The term משכיל appears in the Qumran texts some twenty times; in addition to the Community Rule it is also used in the Rule of the Congregation, the Damascus Document, the War Rule, Hymns, the Songs of the Sabbath Sacrifice, and in the manuscripts 4Q510-4Q511. Some commentators have parallelled the term with its occurrences in the Book of Daniel (11:33; 12:3) and understood it in a general way, translating it 'wise man.'[88] Most scholars, however, consider that the term designates a particular office or functionary in the community,[89] and on the basis of 1QS IX,12 III,13 and 1QSb I,1, III,22, V,20 it is difficult to come to any other conclusion. Hempel, Knibb and Koenen have argued that the *maskil* was a lay member in a leading position,[90] but the responsibility of the *maskil* to bless the God-fearing, the priests and the prince of the congregation leads rather in the direction that the *maskil* was either a priest or a Levite[91] (see 1QSb I,1, III,22, V,20).[92]

---

[88] Wernberg-Moeller 1957, 66 n. 39: "Both in Daniel and and in Pseudepigraphal literature the designation 'wise' is used in a general sense about a member of the pious community, and this is probably the meaning in which the word is used also in 1QS and CD..."; Newsom (1985, 3) also writes that "in certain occurrences of the word at Qumran it may... have a non-technical meaning, "person of understanding" (e.g. 1QH xii 11; 4Q510 I 4)," but she continues that "in most of its occurrences in QL, however, משכיל is used as a technical term to designate a particular office or functionary in the Qumran community."

[89] E.g. Dupont-Sommer 1952, 12, Newsom 1985, 3, Lohse 1986, 283 n. 23, Koenen 1993, 794.

[90] J. Hempel 1963, 197, Knibb 1987, 96, Koenen 1993, 794.

[91] Cf. 2 Chron 30,22 כל־הלוים המשכילים. In 1QS I,16-II,18 only priests and Levites, never laymen, act as those who pronounce blessings and curses. In 4Q510 and 4Q511 the *maskil* has the function of reciting protective hymns against evil spirits.

[92] The term משכיל can be compared with two other offices appearing in the Community Rule, namely *paqid* and *mebaqqer*, which occur in column VI of 1QS. The *paqid* is named as being a person at the head of the *rabbim* whose task it is to examine persons wishing to become members of the community and to teach them the rules of community life (1QS VI,14-15). Also the *mebaqqer* appears at the head of the *rabbim* (VI,12). His special responsibility is to administer the property of the candidates during their second year of probation (VI,20). The similarity of the duties of the *mebaqqer* and *paqid* leads us to ask the question whether they signify one and the same person. Most scholars, e.g. Brownlee (1951, 25 n. 27), Wernberg-Moeller (1957, 107), Cross (1958, 176), Delcor (1979, 855) and Knibb (1987, 118), have answered in the affirmative, though with slight reserve, having compared the occurrences with those in the Damascus Document. In CD XV,8 the *mebaqqer* of the *rabbim* (המבקר אשר לרבים) is mentioned (cf. 1QS VI,12). According to CD XIII,7-11 the *mebaqqer* is the head of the camp, whose duty it is to teach the *rabbim*. He is the one to examine the candidates, and the verb used in this context is פקד (cf. 1QS VI,14). On the basis of this comparison it seems likely that *mebaqqer* and *paqid* are synonymous terms used of the same office. Milik (1957, 99-100) has argued, that the *paqid* was a priestly leader, but the *mebaqqer* a layman. Priest (1962, 55-61) came to the same conclusion having investigated the question together with the messianic ideas of the community. Vermes (1962, 19-25), on the other hand, has argued that the *mebaqqer* (whom he identifies with the *paqid*) and the

Although it is clear that there cannot be any literary dependence between 1QS III,13-IV,26 and IX,12-26, the former being of a theological and doctrinal nature, the latter being halakhic, there are interesting thematic affinities between the sections: as indicated above, in both sections teaching is mentioned as the duty of the *maskil* (III,13; IX,13). According to IX,14, the *maskil* "shall separate and weigh the sons of righteousness according to their spirit"; the qualities of the spirits of truth and injustice are listed in IV,2-14. In IX,14 it is stated that the *maskil* "shall keep firm hold of the chosen ones of the time"; IV,22 also speaks of those "whom God has chosen". Sections III,13-IV,26 and IX,12-26 share a common terminology: שכל (IV,3; IX,13,15), דעת (IV,4,6,22; IX,17), משפט (III,17, IV,2,4,18,20; IX,17,25), רז (IV,6,18; IX,18), דעה (III,15; IX,18), אמה (III,19,24, IV,2,5,6,17,19,20,21,23,24,25; IX,18), צדק (IV,2,4,9,24, צדק בני III,20,22; IX,5,17; בני הצדק[93] IX,14), שחת (IV,12; אנשי השחת IX,16, שחת אנשי IX,22).

In 1958 J.Licht put forward a theory concerning the structure of the section 1QS III,13-IV,26 that the writer of the doctrine of the two spirits modelled his text in a chiastic form.[94] This view has subsequently been accepted by e.g. Guilbert, Leaney and Dimant.[95] The theory includes the premise that the section forms a literary unity, but this has to be rejected on the basis of the evidence of 4QS^a. Fragment 3 indicates that the text has undergone redaction.[96] The manuscript of 4QS^a represents a crude cursive script and may be even older than 1QS.[97] It is very questionable whether the version in 1QS is the original one. Yet, the scribe of 4QS^a is hardly likely to have created the doctrine himself. Allison's theory that the doctrine originated with the Teacher of Righteousness also remains hypothetical.[98] The text may very well have its beginnings outside

*maskil* were one and the same person. This is hardly the right conclusion, for in the Community Rule the *maskil* appears as the spiritual teacher and leader of the community rather than as an administrative officer. The responsibility of the *maskil* is to lead new members into the secrets of the interpretation of the Law (1QS IX,14,17-18) and to ensure that the secrets remain within the community, hidden from outsiders (IX,16-20). A special duty of the *maskil* is to teach the doctrine of the two spirits (1QS III,13-IV,26).

[93] 1QS reads הצדוק, while 4QS^c 1 III,10 has הצדק. Editors have usually considered the form of 1QS as erroneous and corrected it on the basis of 4QS^c. R. Kugler, however, argues in his forthcoming (DSD 3/3) article "A Note on 1QS 9:14: The Sons of Righteousness or the Sons of Zadok" that the change was deliberate and that "1QS typifies a later recension of the Rule that on the whole introduced the Zadokites as prominent and authoritative community members..." I should like to thank Robert Kugler for making his article available to me before its publication.

[94] Licht 1958, 88-89.

[95] Guilbert 1959, 328, Leaney 1966, 145-146, Dimant 1984, 501.

[96] The vocabulary of 4QS^a 3 is similar to the doctrine of the two spirits, although 4QS^a has no direct parallel in 1QS. There is a slight possibility that 4QS^a represents a shorter and perhaps more original form of 1QS III,20-25. See pp. 90-91.

[97] For the dating of 4QS^a, see p. 18-19.

[98] Allison 1980, 257-268.

Qumran.[99] In spite of some affinities with the War Scroll and the Hymns, the section in 1QS III,13-IV,26 remains rather unique among the texts of Qumran.

Von der Osten-Sacken questioned the view that 1QS III,13-IV,26 forms a literary unity even without having access to the evidence of 4QSᵃ. He compared the two halves of the section, 1QS III,13-IV,14 and IV,15-26, and I find his analysis to be still of value.[100] Von der Osten-Sacken observed that some terms, such as נגיע, מחשבה, הלך, סוד, מלאך, חושך, אור, שלום and ברא occur in III,13-IV,14 only. Accordingly, some terms can only be found in IV,15-26: מפלג, בד בבד, נחלה, נזל, חרץ (niph.), נלל (hith.), נבר,

---

[99] One of the most interesting exegetical questions in 1QS III,13-IV,26 involves the background to the dualistic ideas in the section. Can the doctrine be explained through its affinities with the Old Testament, on the one hand, and with the other Qumranic writings, on the other hand? Should it be seen as a reflection of the beliefs of some Jewish and pre-Christian circles? Has the doctrine been affected by Zoroastrianism? It is not a simple task to create a synthesis. One can legitimately ask, however, whether it is ultimately necessary to look for explanatory factors in Zoroastrianism, when significant parallels can be found in writings geographically and historically much closer to the Qumran texts than the Gathas of Avesta. See Wernberg-Moeller 1961, 417. The same kind of criticism was put forward even earlier by Nötscher 1960, 343. - In the Old Testament, see e.g. Gen 1-3, Num 27:16, 1 Sam 10:10; 16:14-16, 1 Kings 22:21-23, 2 Kings 19:7. - The affinities between the War Scroll and 1QS III,13-IV,26 have been widely discussed. Both of the texts are strongly dualistic, and there are similarities in terminology, see von der Osten-Sacken 1969, 116-123. Stegemann (1988, 126-127) acknowledges the terminological likeness, but the similarities on the side of dualism, he says, are rather formal: In the War Scroll the kingdoms of light and darkness are described as quite independent entities; in the final battle the kingdom of light defeats the kingdom of darkness. In the Community Rule both light and darkness are assigned to serve godly purposes, and the same kind of final battle does not occur. In the War Scroll the kingdom of light is identified with Israel (or with the remnant of Israel), and the kingdom of darkness with the pagan world and wrongdoing Israelites. In the Community Rule light and darkness range over all mankind. No particular Israel aspect occurs, although Israel is mentioned once in connection with the name of God (III,24). 1QS III,13-IV,26 also has affinities with some of the psalms of 1QH. In addition, there frequently appears the idea that in the beginning God determined the destiny of all creation, and a man merely carries out the plan which God has disposed. The terminology of these sayings is in part similar to 1QS III,13-IV,26, see e.g. 1QH I,1-20. No actual doctrine of the two spirits, or conception of man being a mixture of good and evil, does occurs in the Hymns, however. - Significant parallels to the doctrine of the two spirits can be found e.g. in the Book of Jubilees (e.g. 7-12), Ben Sira and 1 Enoch (Sir 33 and 42; 1 En 2-5 and 41-48), and in the Testaments of the Twelve Patriarchs (T. Judah 20:1-4, T. Asher 1:3 ff.; 3-6, T. Benjamin 4:1 ff.). In the early Christian writings interesting parallels are Didache 1-6, the Epistle of Barnabas 18-21 and Hermas 6. - It cannot be denied that the doctrine does contain elements alien to the Old Testament which are surprisingly similar to the dualistic ideas in the Gathas of Avesta (esp. Yasna). K.-G. Kuhn already paid attention to these similarities in 1950 (pp. 192, 211; see also 1952, 296-316). A more detailed analysis has been provided by Dupont-Sommer 1952, 5-35.

[100] Von der Osten-Sacken 1969, 17-26. Duhaime (1977, 566-594) has developed the theory of Osten-Sacken further and sees the text as having been constructed in the following way: 1) 1QS III,13*-18a.25b-IV,14 with the additions III,18b-23a.23b-25a.13**, 2) 1QS IV,15-23a.23b-26, 3) 1QS IV,23b-26. His analysis, especially as regards additions, has been recently criticised by Puech 1993, 430 n. 16.

הלך (hith.), פעולה מעשים. The word עולה occurs just once in III,13-IV,14, but seven times in the latter part. The word צדק appears five times in III,13-IV,14, but only once in IV,15-26. In the first part the members of the community and the outsiders are distinguished by using the terms בני אור, בני צדק, בני עול and בני אמת.[101] The separation does not occur in the latter part, but people are referred to in a general way: גבר or בני איש. The observations on the level of vocabulary are supported by differences in syntax: causal clauses expressed through the conjunction כיא are common in IV,25-26. They have no parallels in III,13-IV,26.[102]

When analyzing the contents of the text von der Osten-Sacken paid attention to the fact that in the first part III,13-IV,14 dualism is presented in a cosmological framework (a man belongs either to the domain of the spirit of truth or of the spirit of injustice), but in the latter part anthropologically (the battle between the two spirits takes place in the heart of a man).[103] Von der Osten-Sacken also sees it as possible that the latter part, IV,15-26, was originally more concise. IV,23b-26 speaks about the same theme as IV,15-18a (in between there is a passage, 18b-23a, dealing with the eschatological judgement), and on these grounds it is possible to think that IV,23b-26 was later created as an interpretative addition to 15-18a.[104] Delcor has argued against this view by saying that the introduction of the doctrine indicates that the text consists of three parts: III,15-IV,14, IV,15-23a, and IV,23b-26.[105] The supposition of von der Osten-Sacken can be correct only if the introduction (III,13-15a) was also composed afterwards, and this, indeed, seems entirely probable to me. The stylistic differences and far-reaching theological reflection indicate that the doctrine did not originally belong to the group of texts addressed to the *maskil*, which rather consisted of rules.[106] The doctrine may have been later addressed to the

---

[101] Von der Osten-Sacken (1969, 17) leaves out of consideration the singular forms אנוש (III,17), איש (IV,2) and also the term כול בני איש in the introductory sentence (III,13).

[102] Von der Osten-Sacken 1969, 17-18.

[103] Von der Osten-Sacken 1969, 17-18,24. K.-G. Kuhn already noted the tension between IV,23 and III,12 in 1952 (p. 301 n. 4) but he did not yet draw similar conclusions.

[104] Von der Osten-Sacken 1969, 22-26.

[105] Delcor 1979, 963. In his article Delcor has actually delimited the first section III,14-IV,14, but III,14 must be a typing error and should be corrected to III,15b. The introduction covers III,13-15a.

[106] I consider it possible that the sections addressed to the *maskil* in the Community Rule (including 1QS I,1 ff. and par. 1QS V,1 in 4QS[b,d] but excluding 1QS III,13-IV,26) were originally part of one early source. When evaluating sections 1QS IX,12-21a and 21b-26 Leaney (1966, 162) argued that the birth of a community would be an appropriate time for creating halachic sets of regulations for its leader or leaders. When the community grew and became organized, the regulations which were originally meant to function as a manual for the wise leader (or wise leaders?) may have gradually become common property of the community and thus found their way into the composition of the Community Rule.

*maskil* simply because of the sayings in the Community Rule which stress his duties as a teacher (1QS IX,13, 18-21). Addressing the section to him made it easier to connect the text of the doctrine into the composition of legislative or halachic texts. The reason for bringing the doctrine into the composition was probably to provide an explanation as to why in the community of the התמים even lists of punishments were needed.[107] During its independent existence the text of the doctrine presumably served as a cosmology in a more general sense.

## 3.6. *Sections Concerning the Cult of the Community*

In the composition of the Community Rule, the passage concerning the liturgy for the covenant ceremony (1QS I,16-III,12) and the final psalm containing a calendaric part at the beginning (1QS IX,26b-XI,22) are relatively late. The manuscripts of 4QS[d] and 4QS[e], which have preserved older versions of the Rule than has 1QS, do not include the material of 1QS I-IV at all. Instead of the final psalm, 4QS[e] has the calendaric text 4QOtot appended. Several manuscripts have preserved parallels to sections 1QS I,16-III,12 and 1QS IX,26b-XI,22, however: 4QS[a] (1QS III,7-12), 4QS[b] (1QS I,16-19; 21-23; II,4-5; 7-11; X,3-7; 14-18; XI,22), 4QS[c] (1QS II,4-11; II,26-III,10), 4QS[d] (IX,26b-X,3; X,4-12; 12-18; XI,7), 4QS[f] (1QS X,1-5; 9-11; 15-20; 20-24), 4QS[h] (1QS III,4-5), and 4QS[j] (XI,14-22), and 5Q11 (1QS II,4-7; 12-14(?)). The variants from Cave 4 involve mainly orthographical and grammatical differences. The fragment of 5Q11 has been preserved in a very fragmentary form and the original text can no longer be traced, but there appears to have been omissions and additions compared to the form in 1QS.

The liturgical passage in 1QS I,16-III,12 can be divided into three parts: 1QS I,16-II,18 describes the ceremony of entry into the covenant, II,19-25a provides a rite for the annual renewal of the covenant, II,25b-III,12 condemns those who refuse to enter the covenant. The sentence in 1QS I,16-18a serves as a transitional passage between the introduction (1QS I,1-15) and the ceremony of entry; the actual account of the liturgy begins in I,18b ff.[108] Wernberg-Moeller has argued that 1QS II,19-25 forms a cultic ceremony separate from that of I,18b-II,18,[109] but Weise has pointed out

---

[107] See the qualities of the members of the community of the חמים in 1QS II,24, cf. IV,2-9. Schiffman (1983, 4) is correct in stating that "... the structure of this document points up the importance of seeing the theological and doctrinal aspects in the light of the legal, and the legal in the light of the doctrinal. The redactor has certainly intended us to understand the two as a unity, inseparable in meaning."
[108] See Weise 1961, 64.
[109] Wernberg-Moeller 1957, 55.

that in 1QS the formula עבר בברית occurs in the transitional sentence (I,16-18a), in the account of the liturgy (I,18b-II,18) and in the passage II,19-25a only. The formula עבר בברית goes back to Deut 29:11, where it denotes the concrete act of the whole congregation submitting itself to the covenant with God. It is most probable that in all of its occurrences in 1QS the formula has a specific reference to one cultic act as well, and it should be interpreted in the sense of the more complete formula of 1QS I,16.[110] New members were formally admitted in the annual renewal of the covenant.

According to Deut 31:9-13, the renewal of the covenant was to take place every seven years at the Feast of *Sukkoth*. At Qumran this happened annually, presumably during the Feast of *Shabu'ot*, for 4QD (4Q270 11 I,16-18) speaks about gathering of people yearly in the third month, and in Jub 6:17-19 the Feast of *Shabu'ot* together with the renewal of covenant is told to have been celebrated on the fifteenth day of the third month.[111] The confession of sins in 1QS I,24-26, on the other hand, is connected in the Old Testament with the Feast of *Sukkoth* and goes back to Lev 16:21.[112] This shows - not that the ceremony took place at the Feast of *Sukkoth*, as has been suggested by Wernberg-Moeller[113] - but that 1QS I,18b-II,18 has assimilated several ancient Old Testament liturgical patterns.[114] Among other obvious examples can be mentioned the blessing in II,2b-4 based on Lev 6:24-26, and the curse in II,4b-10, which has its background in Deut 27:14-26.[115] A similar kind of ritual as in 1QS I,18b-II,18 has been described in 1QM XIII,1-6.

Recognizing redactional joins in a liturgical text is a rather difficult task. I consider it possible that the statement in 1QS II,19a (ככה יעשו שנה בשנה כול יומי ממשלת בליעל) was created secondarily by the compiler. The sentence does not form part of the account of a dialogue between the liturgical groups, but functions rather as a summarizing comment and as a bridge to the next section II,19b-25a. It is strange, moreover, that the order of entering into the covenant comes only after the description of the ceremony and not before it. A more careful reading of the last section II,25b-III,12 suggests that it belongs to a different genre than the two

---

[110] Weise 1961, 69-70.

[111] Cf. 2 Chron 15,10-13.

[112] Weise 1961, 79-80, see esp. the parallel in m. Yoma 6:2. In the Old Testament further examples of confession of sins: Ps 106:6, 1 Kgs 8:47, Jer 3:25, Dan 9:5.

[113] Wernberg-Moeller 1957, 50.

[114] The words of Dimant (1984, 497), originally written as referring to apocalyptic works also suit, in my opinion, in the context of this liturgy: "... they use complex forms, embracing various smaller forms, often modelled after biblical precedents. Such works may and do use various sources of distinct forms and periods, but they work them out into one overall framework which expresses the intention of the author."

[115] For further affinities, see e.g. Baumgärtel 1953, 263-265 and Leaney 1966, 105-107.

previous passages. While I,18b-II,18 and II,19b-25a provide for conduct in a cultic ceremony, II,25b-III,12 serves a catechetical purpose.[116] It is unlikely, though not impossible, that the text would have played any rôle as a text recited during the ceremony.

On the whole, it is unclear how accurately the text in 1QS corresponded to the actual course of the liturgy. Stegemann considers the passage I,16-II,18 to be agenda-like in the strictest sense,[117] but I somewhat prefer the alternative view put forward by Weise: "Fraglich bleibt allerdings, ob die jeweiligen Stücke in der einmaligen Abfolge vorge tragen wurden, oder ob man nicht lieber daran denken sollte, dass ein mehrmaliger Wechsel zwischen Priester- und Levitenverkündigung stattfand. Sollte das letztere zutreffen, so bieten sich aus der at.lichen Psalmen- und Gebetsliteratur genügend Beispiele dafür, wie etwa Ps. 77, 78, 105, 106 und Dt. 32."[118]

Several scholars have seen a close connection between the passages 1QS I,16-III,12 and IX,26-XI,22 and assumed the final psalm to have formed part of the covenant liturgy.[119] Linking the passages 1QS I,16-III,12 and IX,26-XI,22 seems to me to be overhasty. If the hymn was meant to be recited in the ceremony of covenant renewal, why did the compiler not place it together with other passages belonging to the covenant ceremony? Moreover, in 4QS[d] the final psalm was included, whereas the material of 1QS I-IV was not. Although Kuhn may be correct in assuming that the original *Sitz im Leben* of the communal psalms[120] was in the ceremony of the covenant renewal, he himself reckons with the possibility that the psalms were taken over into the practice of daily prayer.[121] Indeed, the calendaric part at the beginning of the final hymn describes the daily, monthly and yearly times of prayer,[122] but says nothing of the annual festivals. The reason for inserting the calendar into the composition of the Rule seems rather to have been in the sayings which stress the *maskil*'s responsibility for keeping appointed times (cf. 1QS IX,12,14,18,23).

---

[116] Murphy-O'Connor (1969, 539) attributes only the text in I,16-II,25a to the liturgy. The observation that II,25b-III,12 has a catechetical purpose is Murphy-O'Connor's, p. 540.

[117] Stegemann 1993, 153.

[118] Weise 1961, 74. Cf. also Baltzer 1971, 49: "It is therefore striking to observe that 1QS presents blessings and curses immediately after the confession of sins, without saying a word about forgiveness and renewal of the covenant. I am unable to explain the fact."

[119] Weise's observations (1961, 79 n. 2, 85, 89 n. 2) were utilized e.g. by Murphy-O'Connor (1969, 544) and Pouilly (1976, 81). Note Leaney's (1966, 237) critical remark on Weise's view of the connection between these passages.

[120] Leaney 1966, 115 suggests that the author of the final psalm of the Rule was the Teacher of Righteousness himself. The analysis by Jeremias (1963, 169-173) indicates, however, that 1QS IX,26b-XI,22 belongs to the group of the hymns of the community.

[121] Kuhn 1966, 31-32.

[122] See Weise 1961, 2.

It is to be noted that instead of the final psalm the calendaric text 4QOtot, which lists the rota of the weekly service of the priestly families in the temple, was included in 4QS[e]. The calendar in 1QS IX,26b-X,8a has very little in common with the text of 4QOtot; they speak of two different things.[123] The reason for replacing one calendaric text with another was presumably that in a community which existed outside Jerusalem and which had rejected the cult in Jerusalem as impure, the temple practices were less relevant. In the community, the life of prayer had taken the place of the cult in the temple (cf. 1QS IX,4-5).[124]

### 4. Redaction of the Community Rule[125]

No copy of the Community Rule has been preserved where the material parallel to 1QS V-VII and VIII-IX existed separately, but the differences in style and vocabulary between 1QS VII and the beginning of 1QS VIII indicate that sections 1QS V-VII and VIII-IX did not originally belong together. It is difficult to judge which of the sections, V-VII or VIII-IX, formed the nucleus of the text, but I am inclined to think that it was the material of 1QS V-VII, even though complete certainty in the matter cannot be achieved. It is to be noted, however, that the text of 1QS V-VII was originally much shorter. A more original version of the section has been preserved in manuscripts 4QS[b] and 4QS[d], and they address the text to the wise leader (למשכיל).

A considerable amount of the material of 1QS VIII-IX was also lacking in the first phases of redaction. The passage 1QS VIII,15b-IX,11 is absent in the manuscript 4QS[e], which has a form of the text earlier than that of 1QS. Section 1QS VIII,15b-IX,11 consists of two penal codes (1QS VIII,16-19 and VIII,20-IX,2) and a duplicate based on 1QS VIII,1-15. The comparison between the penal codes included in 1QS indicates that the penal regulations in 1QS VIII,16-IX,2 were borrowed from a source older than the one behind the code of 1QS VI,24-VII,25. The impetus for inserting the material of 1QS VIII,16-IX,2 in its present place was presumably provided by the theme of the Mosaic law which occurs in the text shortly before. A tendency towards modernization, on the other hand,

---

[123] For 4QOtot, see Glessmer 1991, 386-398 (the present siglum for 4QS[b] in the inventory lists of the Rockefeller Museum is 4QS[e]).

[124] Cf. Stegemann 1993, 159.

[125] My article "The Textual Traditions of the Qumran Community Rule," forthcoming in *Legal Texts and Legal Issues: Second Meeting of the IOQS, Cambridge 1995* (eds. M.J.Bernstein and J.Campen), summarizes the main results of my thesis and overlaps with some of the passages presented in this chapter.

may be perceived through the comparison of 1QS VIII,14-15 and IX,9-10: 1QS VIII,14-15, which is attested in both versions, speaks about the study of Law as "preparing the way," but IX,9-10, which is present only in the text of 1QS, warns about departing from it and emphasizes the importance of observing "the first rules."

In the text of 4QS$^e$ the parallel to 1QS VIII-IX consists of sections 1QS VIII,1-15a and IX,12-26. The passage VIII,1-15a thus originally formed an introductory passage for the sections dealing with the duties and responsibilitites of the *maskil* (1QS IX,12-26). Some sayings in the introduction of 1QS VIII,1-15a may refer to the actual desert withdrawal and the founding of the settlement, but we can no longer speak of a 'Manifesto' in the sense intended by Sutcliffe and Murphy-O'Connor.[126] The material in 1QS VIII,1-15a may have an early, even pre-Qumranic origin, but at least the passages addressed to the *maskil* in IX,12-26 can easily be interpreted as referring to an already existing communal life.

The final psalm parallel to 1QS IX,26b-XI,22 was also lacking in the earliest version(s) of the Community Rule. In 4QS$^e$ the regulations addressed to the Maskil (1QS IX,12-26a) are directly followed by the calendrical text 4QOtot. The text of Otot was only later replaced by the psalm containing a calendrical section at the beginning (1QS IX,26b-XI,22). The text of Otot, which provides a list of the weekly service of the priestly families in the temple was presumably no longer considered relevant in the community, which had rejected the temple because they regarded it as defiled. The reason for linking any calendric text with the passages addressed to the *maskil* may have been the sayings which stress his responsibility to observe the appointed times (cf. IX,12,14,18).

The manuscripts 4QS$^b$ and 4QS$^d$ have transmitted a more original version of the Community Rule than has 1QS; the introductory text parallel to 1QS V,1-7a and the rule of the oath of the candidate (par. 1QS V,7b-20) underwent a particularly profound process of editing. The purpose of this redaction, which is to be detected through the comparison of 4QS$^{b,d}$ and 1QS, was to strengthen the self-understanding of the community, and with the aid of Scriptural proof-texts to to provide a theological justification of the regulations already in force in the community. Unfortunately, hardly any fragments parallel to the penal code in 1QS VI,24-VII,25 have been preserved; the contents of the section appears to be most heterogeneous.

---

[126] To begin with, the section which supposedly formed the Manifesto did not originally contain all of the three occurrences of the formula בהיות אלה בישראל, which has been described as characteristic of the nucleus of the text.

It may be asked whether the sections addressed to the *maskil* in 4QS<sup>b</sup> 5,1 ff./4QS<sup>d</sup> 1 I,1 ff. (par. 1QS V,1 ff.) and in 1QS IX,12-26 originate from a common source, from some kind of handbook addressed to the leaders of the Essene communities. The existence of such a source is not inconceivable, even though a clear dissimilarity between the sections in 4QS<sup>b</sup> 5,1 ff./4QS<sup>d</sup> 1 I,1 ff. (par. 1QS V,1 ff.) and IX,12-26a is to be perceived: Whereas the regulations in par. 1QS V-VII concern all members of the community, the passages in 1QS IX,12-26 deal merely with the duties of the *maskil* and the qualities expected of him.

The doctrine of the two spirits in 1QS III,13-IV,26 has also been addressed to the *maskil*. It is doubtful, however, whether it ever belonged to the same group of texts as 4QS<sup>b</sup> 5,1 ff./4QS<sup>d</sup> 1 I,1 ff. and 1QS IX,12-26. It is more likely that the doctrine originally had an independent existence, and that it was later addressed to the *maskil* only in order to provide a better context for the insertion of the passage.

The conjectural reading in 1QS I,1 assumes that the title at the beginning of the manuscript commenced with the word למשכיל (the title is not preserved in full in any of the fragments). As in the case of the doctrine of the two spirits, the title may only have been created for editorial purposes, since the introduction in 1QS I,1-15 appears to have been brought into the composition only at a stage when the composition had already reached more or less the form which it has in 1QS.

The material parallel to 1QS I-IV was brought into the composition at a very late stage; it is lacking in 4QS<sup>d</sup> and likely to have been absent also in 4QS<sup>e</sup>.[127] The manuscript 5Q11 and two fragments from 4QS<sup>a</sup> and 4QS<sup>h</sup> indicate, however, that the liturgical section and the doctrine of the two spirits also underwent redaction. The manuscript 5Q11 provides loose parallels to 1QS II,4-5 and 12-14(?). The fragments from 4QS<sup>a</sup> and 4QS<sup>h</sup> have no direct parallel in 1QS, but they probably form part of the doctrine of the two spirits.

The biblical citations, which are missing in the version of 4QS<sup>b,d</sup>, seem to have been included in the version of 4QS<sup>e</sup>.[128] Since section 1QS VIII,15b-IX,11, which is missing in 4QS<sup>e</sup>, is nevertheless included in the version of 4QS<sup>d</sup>, it is clear that neither 4QS<sup>b,d</sup> nor 4QS<sup>e</sup> represent the most original text of the Community Rule. Yet another version of the Community Rule can be traced behind all the preserved copies of the document.

---

[127] On the reconstruction of 4QS<sup>e</sup>, see 49-51.

[128] To be precise, the parallel to 1QS VIII,13-15 is preserved in 4QS<sup>d</sup> only. It is most probable, however, that the citation was also missing in 4QS<sup>b</sup>, for the texts of 4QS<sup>b</sup> and 4QS<sup>d</sup> belong to the same line of tradition and are almost identical.

The original version (O) of the Community Rule, which thus can be traced through a comparison of the manuscripts 1QS and 4QS$^{a-j}$, but which is not attested in any of the preserved manuscripts, had characteristics which can be described as follows: the document did not include the material of 1QS I-IV at all, but commenced with par. 1QS V. The text was addressed to the *maskil*, and it was shorter than the text of 1QS. The section parallel to 1QS VIII,15b-IX,11 was completely missing. The version did not include the hymn parallel to 1QS IX,26b-XI,22 either, but might have contained a calendric text of 4QOtot instead, attached to the parallel to IX,26a.

One line of tradition (A), which departed from this early version and which represents the first stage of redaction, has been preserved in 4QS$^e$. At this stage, the scriptural proof-texts and the additions strengthening the self-understanding of the community were brought into the text. The material parallel to 1QS I-IV and the section parallel to 1QS VIII,15b-IX,11 were not yet included. In its composition this line of tradition transmitted the text of 4QOtot.

Another line of tradition (B) which also departed from the earliest form of the Rule, is represented by 4QS$^d$. In this line the text parallel to 1QS V ff. follows the early, concise form without biblical citations, but the section providing a loose parallel to 1QS VIII,15b-IX,11 was inserted into the composition. The text following 1QS IX,26a is a hymn containing a calendric section at the beginning (1QS IX,26b-XI,22) but not the text of Otot. The evidence provided by manuscript 4QS$^d$ may presuppose that the text parallel to columns 1QS I-IV was not included in the earliest stage of this tradition, but manuscript 4QS$^b$ demonstrates that later on the B tradition combined the material parallel to 1QS I-IV with that parallel to 1QS V-XI.

The redactor of 1QS (or of its predecessor) may be described as a compiler (C). He knew both lines of tradition, both that of 4QS$^e$ and that of 4QS$^{b,d,}$ since in the version of 1QS the biblical proof-texts, the material of 1QS I-IV and X-XI, and section 1QS VIII,15b-IX,11 are attested. Unfortunately it is not possible to provide a complete reconstruction of all the manuscripts of the Community Rule in order to find out whether, for example, manuscripts 4QS$^{f,g,i,j}$, which in their preserved parts seem to follow 1QS fairly closely, contained all the sections of the version of 1QS.

Yet another phase of redaction (D) may be detected in the corrections and additions made by a second copyist in columns VII-VIII of 1QS. In some places the second scribe seems to have followed another manuscript while revising the text. This *Vorlage* was apparently a combination of both traditions of 4QS$^{b,d}$ and 4QS$^e$, for in some places the corrections seem to follow the text of 4QS$^{b,d}$, while in other places they seem to follow that of

4QS^e. The nature of the additions and corrections in some places and their absence in all the known manuscripts of the Community Rule indicate, however, that the second scribe also independently supplemented and clarified the text. There cannot be a very long interval between the work of the first and second scribes of 1QS, but they manifest changes and developments in the practices of the community.

To sum up, the mutual relationships of the primary versions of the Community Rule may be described with the aid of the following stemma:

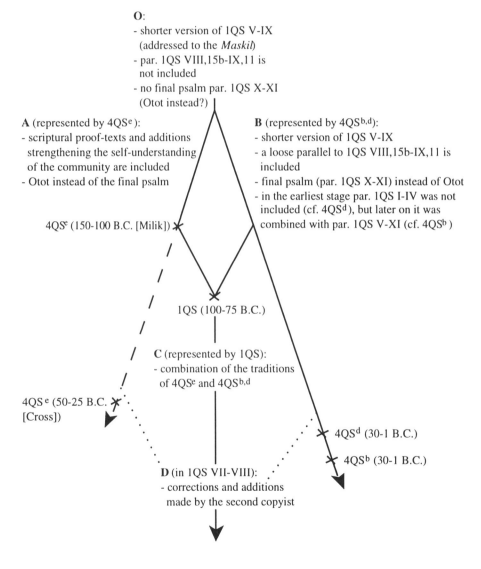

**O**:
- shorter version of 1QS V-IX (addressed to the *Maskil*)
- par. 1QS VIII,15b-IX,11 is not included
- no final psalm par. 1QS X-XI (Otot instead?)

**A** (represented by 4QS^e ):
- scriptural proof-texts and additions strengthening the self-understanding of the community are included
- Otot instead of the final psalm

**B** (represented by 4QS^b,d):
- shorter version of 1QS V-IX
- a loose parallel to 1QS VIII,15b-IX,11 is included
- final psalm (par. 1QS X-XI) instead of Otot
- in the earliest stage par. 1QS I-IV was not included (cf. 4QS^d), but later on it was combined with par. 1QS V-XI (cf. 4QS^b )

4QS^e (150-100 B.C. [Milik])

1QS (100-75 B.C.)

**C** (represented by 1QS):
- combination of the traditions of 4QS^e and 4QS^b,d

4QS^e (50-25 B.C. [Cross])

4QS^d (30-1 B.C.)

4QS^b (30-1 B.C.)

**D** (in 1QS VII-VIII):
- corrections and additions made by the second copyist

The view of scholars who see the Community Rule as a collection of different texts originating at different times and from different sources is strengthened by the analysis of the 4QS manuscripts. The theory of a three-stage development from the Manifesto proposed by Jerome Murphy-O'Connor does not fully apply in the case of the evidence from Cave 4. Similarly problematical is the way he combines the redactional stages with the alleged historical phases of the community.[129] The evidence of manuscripts 4QS<sup>b,d</sup> indicates that the community continued to copy an earlier version of the text even though a more extensive version of 1QS was already available.

Also, the hypothesis of Devorah Dimant that the various parts of the Rule were arranged in chiastic form is to be rejected.[130] There was no ready-made scheme in the minds of the redactors which they would have followed when arranging the material and editing the text. A vague association prompted by a key-word was sufficient to provide the impetus for composing a new sentence or including a new passage. The material from Cave 4 indicates stages in the redactional process where no chiastic parallel to the instructions for the *Maskil* (1QS IX,12-26), for example, or to the final psalm (1QS IX,26-XI,22), was included in the composition.

Influenced by Weise's investigation,[131] several scholars have seen a close redactional connection between the liturgical material of the beginning of the document and the final psalm of columns 1QS X-XI. The theory put forward by Puech, that the first phase of redaction consisted of columns 1QS VIII-IX, the second phase of columns V-VII except for some interpolations, and the third phase of columns I-IV and X-XI,[132] points in the right direction in the sense that the major units have been correctly determined, but in the light of the material from Cave 4 it is clear that there was no connection between sections 1QS I-IV and X-XI; they were brought into the composition at different stages, the final psalm being the earlier.

Considering the heterogeneity of the material of the Community Rule and the discrepancy between the different versions of the text, the question as to the reality behind the text needs to be reconsidered. It seems to me

---

[129] Murphy-O'Connor 1969, 528-549. The theory of Murphy-O'Connor was further developed by Pouilly (1976). See also Puech's recension of Pouillly's investigation (1979, 103 111). Dohmen 1982, 81 96.

[130] Dimant 1984, 501-502. In a personal consultation Prof. Dimant pointed out that in discussing the chiastic pattern of the Community Rule she dealt with the latest level of redaction, i.e. with that of 1QS, but I consider it worthy of note that the material from Cave 4 indicates stages in the redactional process where no chiastic parallel is to be detected.

[131] Weise 1961.

[132] Puech 1993, 421-422.

that the relation between a written document (the Community Rule) and actual life in an Essene community has so far been conceived in too direct and simplistic a manner.

# SUMMARY

Material reconstruction has proved itself to be a useful method for the literary- and redaction-critical study of the Qumran manuscripts. This method enables us to determine the original measurements of a deteriorated scroll and to estimate the extent of the text which was once included in the parts of the scroll that have not been preserved. In order to reconstruct a manuscript, the preserved fragments must be sizeable and sufficient enough, however, so that the places where the fragments show signs of similar damage, indicating that they were located one on top of the other in the original scroll, can be recognized. After determining the direction in which the scroll was rolled, the amount of text in the unpreserved (inner) parts of the scroll can be calculated. Of the ten copies of the Community Rule from Cave 4 four manuscripts - 4QS[c], 4QS[d], 4QS[e] and 4QS[f] - can be fully reconstructed, and one - 4QS[b] - can be partly reconstructed. The manuscripts 4QS[a], 4QS[h], 4QS[i] and 4QS[j], as well as manuscript 5Q11, are so poorly preserved that no reconstruction is possible.

On the basis of the reconstructed manuscripts, it is clear that no standard collection of texts ever existed. There is no indication, for example, that the Rule of the Congregation (1QSa) and the Words of Blessings (1QSb) were ever copied together with the text of the Community Rule. Even the sections included in the Community Rule varied to some extent: The manuscripts 4QS[d] and 4QS[e] seem not to have contained any of the text parallel to 1QS I-IV, but to have commenced with the parallel to 1QS V,1 onwards. The final psalm parallel to 1QS IX,26b-XI,22 was lacking in 4QS[e]. Instead, the calendrical text Otot was directly attached to the regulations addressed to the wise leader (1QS IX,12-26a). The final psalm may also have been absent in the papyrus 4QS[c]. The manuscript 4QS[b] appears to be the only copy of the Community Rule from Cave 4 of which it can be stated with certainty that it included all the same sections of the Community Rule as does 1QS. The form of the text in 4QS[b] was much shorter than that of 1QS, however.

The literary- and redaction-critical analysis of a certain document cannot be limited solely to the external characteristics of the manuscripts. Therefore, transcriptions of the preserved fragments of 4QS[a-j], 5Q11, as well as of a fragment of 5Q13 containing a citation from the Community Rule, have been included in this work. The work has been carried out independently; only in the last stages of the work have I included a discussion concerning the recent edition of the Community Rule by Qimron and Charlesworth (1994). The discussion involves all manuscripts of the Community Rule from Caves 1, 4 and 5, and suggests a number of alternative readings to those provided by Qimron and Charlesworth. As is not the case with Qimron and Charlesworth, I have attempted to transcribe all fragments included in the copies of the Community Rule, including the ones which have no direct parallels in 1QS. Only the smallest fragments of 4QSᵍ, some of which are less than 1 sq.cm. in size, have remained untranscribed. Moreover, the edition of Qimron and Charlesworth provides no infirmation as to the overall structure and contents of the manuscripts from Cave 4.

The manuscripts from Cave 4 contain a large number of variants in comparison with 1QS. Most of them involve orthography, as one would anticipate. The manuscript 1QS appears to have transmitted the features of the Qumranic orthography most consistently; in general the manuscripts from Cave 4 prefer the defective spelling more often than 1QS. The number of linguistic variants is also very high, particularly in manuscripts 4QS b,d and 4QS e. The greatest differences in the contents are also to be found in manuscripts 4QS b,d and 4QS e. The shorter version in 4QS b,d reveals that the text of 1QS V-VII underwent a thoroughgoing redaction, which involved both the language and the contents. The major differences in 4QS e concern the missing passages 1QS VIII,15b-IX,11 and IX,26b-XI,22. The other manuscripts from Cave 4 also show differences in content as compared with 1QS, but these differences are of lesser extent. A separate group, however, is formed by the two fragments from 4QS a and 4QS h, which have no direct parallels in 1QS.

Compared to 1QS, the manuscript 5Q11 contains omissions and additions, but so little has been preserved from the manuscript that not much can be said about the redaction there. The fragment of 5Q13, which quotes a phrase from the Community Rule does not shed any new light on the literary development of the Rule, either. Interestingly enough, however, the only fragment of 4QS h (frg. 1) which provides a parallel to 1QS, quotes the very same phrase (1QS III,4-5) as does 5Q13. The other preserved fragment of 4QS h (frg. 2) has no direct parallel in 1QS, but it may come from the section on the doctrine of the two spirits. There is a small possibility that 4QS h is not a copy of the Community Rule at all, but some other manuscript citing a phrase from the Rule.

Two different lines of tradition, both of which are older than that of 1QS, are represented by the manuscripts 4QS b,d and 4QS e. In the manuscripts 4QS b,d the additions strengthening the self-understanding of the community (the terms הברית and היחד, for example, occur in 1QS more often than in 4QS b,d), as well as the direct Old Testament quotations, the purpose of which was to provide a Scriptural legitimation for the regulations already prevailing in the community, as attested in 1QS, are absent. The line of 4QS e does not contain the modernizing changes which are to be detected through a comparison with 1QS. The text of Otot, which provides a list of the weekly service of the priestly families in the temple, is included in 4QS$^e$, but it was no longer relevant in a community which had rejected the temple as defiled. In 1QS the text of Otot is replaced by a final psalm containing a calendrical section at the beginning. The tendency towards modernization is also apparent, when 1QS VIII,14-15, which is attested in both 4QS$^e$ and 1QS, speaks about the study of the Law as "preparing the way", while 1QS IX,9-10, which is included only in 1QS, warns about departing from it, and emphasizes the importance of keeping "the first rules".

Of the further copies of the Community Rule the manuscripts 4QS$^a$ and 5Q11 call for mention. The papyrus 4QS$^a$ has preserved a fragment (frg. 3) which displays vocabulary similar to that of the doctrine of the two spirits, but which has no direct parallel in 1QS (the other preserved fragments of this manuscript have direct parallels in 1QS). The manuscript 5Q11 has preserved loose parallels to parts of the liturgical section (1QS II,4-5 and 12-14(?)). The material from Cave 4 thus indicates that each of the main sections of the Community Rule, even the liturgical passage and the doctrine of the two spirits, underwent redactional activity. The redaction of the document not only involved joining passages together but also entailed more radical editing of the passages.

The corrections and additions made by the second scribe in columns 1QS VII and VIII most likely represent the latest stage of redaction to be seen in the preserved copies of the Community Rule. A comparison between these corrections and the manuscripts from Cave 4 indicates that at least in some places the second scribe possessed another manuscript, which he used to revise the text of the first scribe. This manuscript was not identical with any of the copies of the Community Rule found in Cave 4, however, for in some places the corrections follow the text of 4QS$^{b,d}$, but in other places that of 4QS$^e$. Some of the corrections and additions made by the second scribe are of such a character that they may have been made independently, without the aid of any other manuscript. Chronologically, interval between the work of the first and the second scribes cannot have been very long, but it may be seen that during this time changes occurred in community practice.

The oldest version of the Community Rule (O) can be traced through a comparison of manuscripts 4QS$^e$ and 4QS$^{b,d}$. In addition, four stages of redaction are to be detected in the manuscripts from Cave 4. One line of textual tradition (A), which departed from this early version, is represented by 4QS$^e$, another line (B), which also departed from this early version, is to be seen in manuscripts 4QS$^{b,d}$. The next stage of redaction (C) is present in 1QS, which is a combination of the traditions of 4QS$^e$ and 4QS$^{b,d}$. The last stage of redaction (D) is to be seen in the corrections and additions of the second scribe in columns 1QS VII-VIII. (The stages in the textual development have been more thoroughly dealt with in the chapter *Redaction of the Community Rule*) The manuscripts 1QS, 4QSªⁱ and 5Q11 were transmitted over a period of more than one hundred years. Remarkably, however, the major changes in the process of redaction had already taken place in c. 100 B.C.

Even though earlier theories regarding the overall redaction of the Community Rule, such as the one proposed by Murphy-O'Connor, do not fully apply in the case of the material from Cave 4, several analyses regarding the smaller sections of the document have proven to be correct. Several interpolations in column 1QS V, for example, were recognized even before the material from Cave 4 was available. The analysis of the preserved copies of the Community Rule provides further support for the applicability of the conventional exegetical methods developed for the exegesis of the Old and New testament; the picture evolving from the use of these methods corresponds to the one to be obtained through a comparison of the manuscripts. Since only some of the copies of the Community Rule have been preserved, it is quite obvious that not all stages in the redaction can be detected through their comparison. Some of the stages are to be found only with the aid of the internal indicators contained in the text. Very little has been preserved of the large penal code parallel to 1QS VI,24-VII,25, for example, and this section appears to be one of the most heterogeneous in the passages of the Rule.

On the basis of the comparison between the manuscripts of the Community Rule found in Caves 1, 4 and 5 it is clear that there never existed a single, legitimate and up-to-date version of the Community Rule. The community continued copying the older and shorter form of the text even when a more extensive version was already available. The idea of a sole legitimate version is not supported by the internal indicators in the text, either: the earlier regulations were not omitted from the composition in proportion as new rules were created. Therefore, the Community Rule, for example, contains two different sections describing the procedure of the admission of the new members originating at different times and three different penal codes. The question as to whether the various redactional stages also provide differing pictures of the organization of the community cannot fully be answered in this study. It is to be noted, however, that the *mebaqqer* and the *paqid* do not occur in columns 1QS I-IV at all, and that at one stage of redaction the term *ha-rabbim* was replaced by a reference to the sons of Zadok and the men of the community. The position of the *maskil* in relation to the other community officials is not completely clear, either.

It is evident that the picture given by the document and the historical reality behind it do not dovetail. The manuscripts attest to the existence of contradictory practices, and it is not always clear which practice was followed at any particular time. Literary- and redaction-critical analysis can provide some indication as to the comparative age of each practice, but linking one with an actual historical period or time is rather a hazardous undertaking. For us to reconstruct the history of the Essene community, we need to extend our study to include a larger number of documents, and they would require extremely thorough analysis. The texts belonging to a same literary genre need first to be considered, so that the position and the *Sitz im Leben* of a particular document within the Essene movement can be determined. The crucial question as to the relationship between the Community Rule and the Damascus Document, for example, can be solved only after an analysis of the 4QD material. (It is to be hoped that such a study is already under preparation). The present writer is confident - and trusts that she has succeeded in demonstrating - that new methods, such as material reconstruction, can provide a fruitful contribution to expanding the more conventional exegetical approaches of literary and redaction criticism in the study of the Dead Sea Scrolls.

# BIBLIOGRAPHY

*1. Sources and Reference Works*

ALLEGRO, J.M., *Qumrân Cave 4, I (4Q158-4Q186)*. DJDJ V. Oxford 1968.
BAILLET, M., *Qumran Grotte 4, III (4Q482-4Q520)*. DJD VII. Oxford 1982.
BARDTKE, H., *Hebräische Konsonantentexte*. Leipzig 1954, 37-48.
BARTHÉLEMY, D. and MILIK, J.T., *Qumran Cave 1*. DJD I. Oxford 1955.
BAUER, H. und LEANDER, P., *Historische Grammatik der hebräischen Sprache des Alten Testaments*. Erster Band: Einleitung, Schriftlehre, Laut- und Formenlehre. Halle a/S 1922.
BAUMGARTEN, J.M. and DAVIS, M.T. (eds.), "Cave IV, V, VI Fragments Related to the Damascus Document (4Q266-273 = 4QDa-h, 5Q12 = 5QD, 6Q15 = 6QD)." *The Dead Sea Scrolls. Hebrew, Aramaic and Greek Texts with English Translation*. Vol. 2: Damascus Document, War Scroll, and Related Documents, ed. J.H.Charlesworth with J.M. Baumgarten, M.T. Davis, J. Duhaime, Y. Ofer, H.W.L. Rietz, J.J.M. Roberts, D. Schwartz, B.A. Strawn, and R.E. Whitaker. Tübingen, Louisville 1995, 59-79.
BAUMGARTNER, W., *Hebräisches und aramäisches Lexikon zum Alten Testament von Ludwig Koehler und Walter Baumgartner*. Dritte Auflage neu bearbeitet von W. Baumgartner, u.a., Bd. I-IV. Leiden 1967-90.
BROCKELMANN, C., *Grundriss der vergleichenden Grammatik der semitischen Sprachen*. Bd. I-II. Berlin 1908-13.
BROWN, R.E., FITZMYER, J., OXTOBY, W.G. and TEIXIDON, J. (prepared), *A Preliminary Concordance to the Hebrew and Aramaic Fragments from Qumran Caves II-X, including especially the unpublished material from cave IV*. Printed from a card index. Prepared and arranged for printing by Hans-Peter Richter (distributed by H.Stegemann). Vols. I-V. Privately printed in Göttingen 1988.
BURROWS, M. with TREVER, J.C., BROWNLEE, W.H., *The Dead Sea Scrolls of St. Marks's Monastery*. Vol. I. The Isaiah Manuscript and the Habakkuk Commentary. New Haven 1950.
——, *The Dead Sea Scrolls of St. Mark's Monastery*. Vol. II, Fasc. 2. Plates and Transcription of the Manual of Discipline. New Haven 1951.
CHARLES, R.H. (ed.), *The Apocrypha and Pseudepigrapha of the Old Testament in English. With introductions and critical and explanatory notes to the several books*. Vol. I. Apocrypha. First published 1913. Repr. Oxford 1963.
CHARLESWORTH, J.C. (ed.), *The Old Testament Pseudepigrapha*. Vols. I-II. London 1983-85.
CHARLESWORTH, J.H., "Possible Fragment of the Rule of the Community (5Q11)." *The Dead Sea Scrolls. Hebrew, Aramaic, and Greek Texts with English Translations*. Vol. 1: Rule of the Community and Related Documents, ed. James H. Charlesworth with F.M. Cross, J. Milgrom, E. Qimron, L.H. Schiffman, L.T. Stuckenbruck and R.E. Whitaker. Tübingen, Louisville 1994, 105-107.
CHARLESWORTH J.H. with WHITAKER, R.E., HICKERSON, L.G., STARBUCK, S.R.A, STUCKENBRUCK, L.T., *Graphic Concordance to the Dead Sea Scrolls*. The Princeton Theological Seminary Dead Sea Scrolls Project. Tübingen, Louisville 1991.
COLSON, F.H. (ed.), *Philo in ten Volumes (and two supplementary volumes) with an English Translation*. Vol. IX. First printed 1941. Repr. Cambridge, Massachusetts, London, England 1985.
CROSS, F.M. et al. (eds.), *Scrolls from Qumran Cave I: The Great Isaiah Scroll, The Order of the Community, the Pesher to Habakkuk*. Jerusalem 1972, 127-147.
ELLIGER, K., RUDOLPH, W. (eds.), *Biblia Hebraica Stuttgartensia*. Stuttgart 1977.
GELDNER, K.F. (ed.), *Avesta. The sacred books of the Parsis*. Part I: Yasna. Stuttgart 1886. Repr. Delhi 1982.

GESENIUS, H.W.F., *Gesenius' Hebrew Grammar*. Edited and Enlarged by E. Kautzsch. Second English Edition by A.E. Cowley. Oxford 1988 [19].
GESENIUS, W., KAUTZSCH, E., *Hebräische Grammatik*. Darmstadt 1985 [28].
GOLDSCHMIDT, L., *Der babylonische Talmud*. Bd. I-XII. 3. Aufl. Königstein 1980-81.
HABERMANN, A.M., *'Edah we'eduth. Three Scrolls from the Judaean Desert. The Legacy of a Community*. Edited with Vocalization, Introduction, Notes and Indices (Hebr.). Jerusalem 1952.
——, *Megilloth Midbar Yehuda. The Scrolls from the Judaean Desert*. Ed. with Vocalization, Introduction, Notes and Concordance. Jerusalem 1959.
JASTROW, M., *A Dictionary of the Targumim, The Talmud Babli and Jerushalmi, and the Midrashic Literature*. Vols. I-II. London, New York 1903.
KASOWSKI, H.J., *Thesaurus Thosephtae. Concordantiae Verborum quae in Sex Thosephtae ordinibus reperiuntur*. Vols. I-VI (vols. V-VI ed. M. Kasowski). Hierosolymis 1932-61.
KASOVSKY, Ch.Y., *Thesaurus Mishnae. Concordantiae verborum quae in sex Mishnae ordinibus reperiuntur*. Vols. I-IV. Hierosolymis 1957-61.
KOEHLER, L., BAUMGARTNER, W., Lexicon in Veteris Testamenti libros. Leiden 1953. Repr. Leiden 1985.
KUHN, K.G. unter Mitarbeit von STEGEMANN, H. und KLINZING, G., *Rückläufiges hebräisches Wörterbuch*. Göttingen 1958.
KUHN, K.G. (Hg.), *Konkordanz zu den Qumrantexten*. Göttingen 1960.
LICHT, J., *Megillat has-Serakim: The Rule Scroll: A Scroll from the Wilderness of Judaea: 1QS, 1QSa, 1QSb: Text, Introduction and Commentary*. Jerusalem 1965.
LIDDELL, H.G., SCOTT, R., *A Greek-English Lexicon*. Revised by Henry Stuart Jones with the assistance of Roderick McKenzie. With a Supplement, ed. by E.A. Barber. Repr. London 1973 [9].
LOHSE, E. (Hg.), *Die Texte aus Qumran. Hebräisch und Deutsch. Mit Masoretischer Punktation. Übersetzung, Einführung und Anmerkungen*. München 1986 [4].
MARTONE, C., *La "Regola della Comunità". Edizione critica*. Quaderni di Henoch 8. Torino 1995.
MICHEL, O., BAUERNFEIND, O. (Hgg.), *Flavius Josephus. De Bello Judaico. Der jüdische Krieg. Griechisch und Deutsch*. Band I, Buch I-III. München 1959.
MILIK, J.T., "Annexes à la Règle de la Communauté." *Qumran Cave I* by D. Barthelemy and J.T. Milik. DJD I. Oxford 1955, 107-130, pls. XXII-XXIX.
——, *Textes de la Grotte 5Q. Les 'Petites Grottes' de Qumran. Textes*. DJDJ III par de Vaux. Oxford 1962, 167-197.
——, *The Books of Enoch. Aramaic Fragments of Qumran Cave 4*. Oxford 1976.
NESTLE-ALAND, *Novum Testamentum Graece*. 27. revidierte Auflage. Stuttgart.
NEUSNER, J., *The Tosefta*. Translated from the Hebrew, vols. I-VI (vol. I eds. J. Neusner and R.S. Sarason). New York 1977-86.
——, *The Mishnah. A New Translation*. New Haven 1988.
NEWSOM, C., *Songs of the Sabbath Sacrifice: A Critical Edition*. HSS 27. Atlanta, Georgia 1985.
QIMRON, E., *The Community Rule*. The Dead Sea Scrolls. Supervised by M. Sekine. Tokyo 1979, 112-132.
——, *The Hebrew of the Dead Sea Scrolls*. HSS 29. Atlanta, Georgia 1986.
QIMRON, E., CHARLESWORTH, J.H., "Rule of the Community (1QS)." *The Dead Sea Scrolls. Hebrew, Aramaic, and Greek Texts with English Translations*. Vol. 1: Rule of the Community and Related Documents, ed. James H. Charlesworth with F.M. Cross, J. Milgrom, E. Qimron, L.H. Schiffman, L.T. Stuckenbruck, and R.E. Whitaker. Tübingen, Louisville 1994, 1-51.
QIMRON, E., CHARLESWORTH, J.H., with an Appendix by CROSS, F.M., "Cave IV Fragments (4Q255-264 = 4QS MSS A-J)." *The Dead Sea Scrolls. Hebrew, Aramaic, and Greek Texts with English Translations*. Vol. 1: Rule of the Community and Related Documents, ed. James H. Charlesworth with F.M. Cross, J. Milgrom, E. Qimron, L.H. Schiffman, L.T. Stuckenbruck, and R.E. Whitaker. Tübingen, Louisville 1994, 53-103.

RABIN, C., The Zadokite Documents. Oxford 1958².
RAHLFS, A., *Septuaginta. Id est Vetus Testamentum Graece iuxta LXX interprets*. Vols. I-II. Stuttgart.
SCHIFFMAN, L.H., "Sectarian Rule (5Q13)." *The Dead Sea Scrolls. Hebrew, Aramaic, and Greek Texts with English Translations*. Vol. 1: Rule of the Community and Related Documents, ed. James H. Charlesworth with F.M. Cross, J. Milgrom, E. Qimron, L.H. Schiffman, L.T. Stuckenbruck, and R.E. Whitaker. Tübingen, Louisville 1994, 132-143.
SUKENIK, E.L., *The Dead Sea Scrolls of the Hebrew University* (Hebr.). Jerusalem 1954.
THACKERAY, H.St.J., *Josephus in nine Volumes with an English Translation*. Vol. II. The Jewish War, Books I-III. Cambridge, Massachusetts, London, England 1989.
TOV, E. (ed.), *The Dead Sea Scrolls on Microfiche. A Comprehensive Facsimile Edition of the Texts from the Judaean Desert*. I Photographs (ed. by E. Tov with the collaboration of S.J. Pfann), II Companion Volume (ed. by E. Tov with the collaboration of S.J. Pfann), III Inventory List of Photographs (compiled by S.A. Reed, ed. by M.J. Lundberg). Leiden, New York, Köln 1993.
ZEITLIN, S., *The Zadokite Documents. Facsimile of the Manuscripts in the Cairo Genizah Collection in the Possession of the University Library, Cambridge, England*. JQRM 1. Philadelphia 1952.


## 2. Literature

ALLISON, D.C., "The Authorship of 1QS III,13 - IV,26." *RevQ* 10 (1980), 257-268.
ARATA MANTOVANI, P., "La stratificazione letteraria della *Regola della Communita'*: A propositio di uno studio recente." *Henoch* 5 (1983), 69-91.
AVIGAD, N., "The Palaeography of the Dead Sea Scrolls and Related Documents. Aspects of the Dead Sea Wcrolls." Eds. C. Rabin and Y. Yadin. *Scripta Hierosolymitana* 4. Jerusalem 1958, 56-87.
BALZER, K., *The Covenant Formulary in Old Testament, Jewish, and Early Christian Writings*. (Das Bundesformular. Wissenschaftliche Monographien zum Alten und Neuen Testament, No. 4. Second rev. edition, with a bibliographical appendix. Neukirchen-Vluyn 1960. Transl. by D.E. Green.) Oxford 1971.
BARDTKE, H., *Die Handscriftenfunde am Toten Meer. Mit einer kurzen Einführung in die Text- und Kanongesichte des Alten Testaments*. Berlin 1952.
——, "Literaturbericht über Qumran. VII Teil." *TRu* 38 (1974), 256-291.
BAUMGÄRTEL, F., "Zur Liturgie in der "Sektenrolle" vom Toten Meer." *ZAW* 65 (1953), 263-265.
BAUMGARTEN, J.M., "The Duodecimal Courts of Qumran, Revelation, and the Sanhedrin." *JBL* 95 (1976), 59-78.
——, *Studies in Qumran Law*. SJLA 24. Leiden 1977.
——, "The Cave 4 Versions of the Qumran Penal Code." *JJS* 43 (1992), 268-276.
——, "Purification after Childbirth and the Sacred Garden in 4Q265 and Jubilees," *New Qumran Texts and Studies*, ed. G.J. Brooke. Leiden 1994, 3-10.
BEALL, T.S., *Josephus' Description of the Essenes Illustrated by the Dead Sea Scrolls*. SNTSMS 58. Cambridge, New York, New Rochelle, Melbourne, Sydney 1988.
BECKER, H., *Das Heil Gottes: Heil- und Sündenbegriffe in den Qumrantexten und im Neuen Testament*. SUNT 3. Göttingen 1964.
BIRNBAUM, S.A., *The Qumran (Dead Sea Scrolls) and Palaeography*. BASOR, Supplementary Studies 13-14. New Haven, Connecticut 1952.
BONANI, G., BROSHI, M., CARMI, I., IVY, S., STRUGNELL, J., WÖLFLI, W., "Radiocarbon Dating of the Dead Sea Scrolls." *Atiqot* 20 (1991), 27-32.
BROOKE, G.J., "Isaiah 40:3 and the Wilderness Community." *New Qumran Texts and Studies. Proceedings of the First Meeting of the International Organization for Qumran Studies, Paris 1992*, eds. G.J. Brooke and F. García Martínez. Leiden, New York, Köln 1994, 117-132.

BROWNLEE, W.H., *The Dead Sea Manual of Discipline* . BASOR, Supplementary Studies, Nos 10-12. New Haven, Connecticut 1951.

BURROWS, M., *The Discipline Manual of the Judaean Covenanters*. Old Testament Studies 8 (1950), 156-192.

——, *The Dead Sea Scrolls*. New York 1955.

CAMPBELL, J.G., "Scripture in the Damascus Document 1:1 - 2:1." *JJS* 44 (1993), 83-99.

CARMIGNAC, J., "Conjecture sur la première ligne de la Règle de la Communauté." *RevQ* 2 (1959), 85-87.

——, "HRBYM: les Nombreux ou les Notables?" *RevQ* 7 (1971), 575-586.

CHARLESWORTH, J.H., "Morphological and Philological Observations: Preparing the Critical Text and Translation of the Serek Ha-Yaḥad." *Methods of Investigation of the Dead Sea Scrolls and the Khirbet Qumran Site. Present Realities and Future Prospects*, eds. M.O. Wise, N. Golb, J.J. Collins, and D.G. Pardee. Annals of the New York Academy of Sciences 722. New York, New York 1994, 271-283.

COX, M.G., "Augustine, Jerome, Tyconius and the *Lingua Punica*." *StudOr* 64 (1988), 83-105.

CROSS, F.M., *The Ancient Library of Qumran and Modern Biblical Studies. The Haskell Lectures*. Garden City, New York 1958, 1961 2. Repr. 1980.

——, "The Development of the Jewish Scripts." *The Bible and the Ancient Near East*, ed. G.E. Wright. Garden City, New York 1961, 170-264.

——, "The Paleographical Dates of the Manuscripts." *The Dead Sea Scrolls. Hebrew, Aramaic, and Greek Texts with English Translations*. Vol. 1: Rule of the Community and Related Documents, ed. James H. Charlesworth with F.M. Cross, J. Milgrom, E. Qimron, L.H. Schiffman, L.T. Stuckenbruck and R.E. Whitaker. Tübingen, Louisville 1994, 57.

DAVIES, P.R., "Communities at Qumran and the Case of the Missing 'Teacher'." *RevQ* 15 (1991), 273-286.

——, "Redaction and Sectarianism in the Qumran Scrolls." *The Scriptures and the Scrolls. Studies in honour of A.S.van der Woude on the occasion of his 65 th birthday*, eds. F. García Martínez, A. Holhorst and C.J. Labuschagne. VTSup 49. Leiden, New York, Köln 1992, 152-163.

DELCOR, M., "Contribution à l'étude de la législation des sectaires de Damas et de Qumrân." *RB* 61 (1954), 533-553. *RB* 62 (1955), 60-75.

——, "Qumran. La Règle de la Communauté. Doctrines des Esséniens. I. L'Instruction des deux esprits." *DBSup* 9. Paris 1979, 851-857, 960-970.

DEL MEDICO, H.E., *Deux manuscrits hébreux de la Mer Morte*. Paris 1951.

——, *L'énigme des manuscrits de la Mer Morte*. Paris 1957.

DENIS, A-M., "Evolution de structures dans le secte de Qumran." *Aux origines de l'Eglise*. RechBib 7. Bruges 1964, 23-49.

DIMANT, D., "Qumran Sectarian Literature." *Jewish Writings of the Second Temple Period. Apocrypha, Pseudepigrapha, Qumran Sectarian Writings, Philo*. Compendia Rerum Iudaicarum ad Novum Testamentum 2, ed. M. Stone. Assen, Philadelphia 1984, 483-550.

DOHMEN, C., "Zur Gründung der Gemeinde von Qumran (1QS VIII-IX)." *RevQ* 11 (1982), 81-96.

DOMBROWSKI, B.W., "דחד in 1QS and τὸ κοινόν. An Instance of Early Greek and Jewish Synthesis." *HTR* 59 (1966), 293-307.

DUHAIME, J., "L'instruction sur les deux esprits et les interpolations dualistes à Qumran." *RB* 84 (1977), 566-594.

DUPONT-SOMMER, A., "L'instruction sur les deux Esprits dans le 'Manuel de Discipline'." *RHR* 142 (1952), 5-35.

——, Nouveaux apercus sur les manuscrits de la mer Morte. Paris 1953.

——, "Le rouleau de la Règle. Les Esséniens (IV)." *Evidences* 57 (1956), 9-23.

——, *Les écrits esséniens découverts près de la Mer Morte*. Paris 1959.

ESHEL, E., "4Q477: The Rebukes by the Overseer," *JJS* 45 (1994), 111-122.

FITZMYER, J.A., "The Use of Explicit Old Testament Quotations in Qumran Literature and in the New Testament." *NTS* 7 (1961), 297-333.

FRAADE, S.D., "Interpretative Authority in the Studying Community at Qumran." *JJS* 44 (1993), 46-69.

GARCÍA MARTÍNEZ, F., "Review of Vermes, Preliminary Remarks on Unpublished Fragments of the Community Rule from Qumran Cave 4." *JSJ* 23 (1992), 159.

——, *Textos de Qumrán. Introducción y editión de Florentino García Martínez*. Madrid 1993².

——, *The Dead Sea Scrolls Translated. The Qumran Texts in English*. Transl. by W.G.E. Watson (Textos de Qumrán. Introducción y editión de Florentino García Martínez. Madrid 1992). Leiden, New York, Cologne 1994.

——, "Nouveaux livres sur les manuscrits de la Mer Morte." *JSJ* 27 (1996), 46-74.

GLESSMER, U., "Der 364-Tage-Kalender und die Sabbatstruktur seiner Schaltungen in ihrer Bedeutung für den Kult." *Ernten, was man sät. Festscrift für Klaus Koch zu seinem 65. Geburtstag*, hgg. D.R. Daniels, U. Glessmer und M. Rösel. Neukirchen-Vluyn 1991, 379-398.

——, "The Otot-Texts (4Q319) and the Problem of Intercalations in the Context of the 364-Day Calendar." Qumranstudien. Vorträge and Beiträge auf dem Internationalen Treffen der Society of Biblical Literature. Schriften des Institutum Judaicum Delitzschianum 4. Göttingen 1996, 125-164.

GUILBERT, P., "Deux écritures dans les colonnes VII et VIII de la Règle de la Communauté." *RevQ* 1 (1958), 199-212.

——, "Le plan de la Régle de la Comminauté." *RevQ* 3 (1959), 323-324.

——, "La Règle de la Communauté." *Les Textes de Qumran traduits et annotés* I, par J.Carmignac et P.Guilbert. Paris 1961, 9-80.

HAUCK, F., "μαμωνᾶς". *TWNT* IV, Hg. G. Kittel. Stuttgart 1942, 390-392.

HEMPEL, C., "Comments on the Translation of 4QSᵈ I,1." *JJS* 44 (1993), 127-128.

HEMPEL, J., "Die Stellung des Laien in Qumran." *Qumran-Probleme. Vorträge des leipziger Symposions über Qumran-Probleme vom 9. bis 14. Oktober 1961*, Hg. H. Bardtke. Berlin 1963, 193-215.

HERR, M.D., "Midrash." *EncJud* 11. Jerusalem 1972, 1507-1514.

HUNZINGER, C-H., "Beobachtungen zur Entwicklung der Disziplinarordnung der Gemeinde von Qumran." *Qumran-Probleme. Vorträge des Leipziger Symposions über Qumran-Probleme vom 9. bis 14. Oktober 1961*, Hg. H. Bardtke. Berlin 1963, 231-247.

HUPPENBAUER, H., "דב, דוב, רבים in den Sektenregel." *TZ* 13 (1957), 136-137.

ILG, N., "Überlegungen zum Verständnis von ברית in den Qumrantexten." *Qumran. Sa piété, sa théologie et son milieu*, ed. M.Delcor. BETL 46. Paris, Leuven 1978.

JEREMIAS, G., *Der Lehrer der Gerechtigkeit*. SUNT 2. Göttingen 1963.

JULL, A.J.T., DONAHUE, D.J., BROSHI, M. and TOV, E., "Radiocarbon Dating of Scrolls and Linen Fragments from the Judean Desert." *Radiocarbon* 37 (1995), 11-19.

KLINZING, G., *Die Umdeutung des Kultus in der Qumrangemeinde und im Neuen Testament*. SUNT 7. Göttingen 1971.

KNIBB, M.A., *The Qumran Community*. Cambridge commentaries on writings of the Jewish and Christian world 200 BC to AD 200. Volume 2. Cambridge 1987.

KOENEN, K., "שָׁכַל." *TWAT* 7, hgg. H.J.Fabry und H.Ringgren. Stuttgart, Berlin, Köln 1993, 782-795.

KRUSE, C.G., "Community Functionaries in the Rule of the Community and the Damascus Document. A test of chronological relationships." *RevQ* 10 (1981), 543-551.

KUGLER, R., "A Note on 1QS 9:14: The Sons of Righteousness or the Sons of Zadok." *DSD* 3/3 [forthcoming].

KUHN, H.-W., *Enderwartung und gegenwärtiges Heil*. Göttingen 1966.

KUHN, K.-G., "Die in Palästina gefundenen hebräischen Texte und das Neue Testament." *ZTK* 47 (1950), 192-211.

——, "Die Sektenschrift und die iranische Religion." *ZTK* 49 (1952), 296-316.

——, "Der gegenwärtige Stand der Erforschung der in Palästina neu gefundenen hebräischen Handschriften." *TLZ* 85 (1960), 649-658.

LAMBERT, G., "Le Manuel de Discipline de la grotte de Qumrân: Traduction intégrale du 'Manuel de Discipline'." *NRT* 73 (1951), 938-975.

LEAHY, T., "Studies in the Syntax of 1QS." *Bib* 41 (1960), 135-157.

LEANEY, A.R.C., *The Rule of Qumran and Its Meaning. Introduction, translation and commentary.* London 1966.

LEVINE, B., "מצה." *TWAT* 4, hgg. G.J. Botterweck, H. Ringgren und H.-J. Fabry. Stuttgart, Berlin, Köln, Mainz 1984, 1086-1095.

LICHT, J., "An Analysis of the Treatise on the two Spirits in DSD." *Scripta Hierosolymitana* 4 (1958), 88-99.

LIEBERMAN, S., "The Discipline in the so-called Dead Sea Manual of Discipline." *JBL* 71 (1952), 199-206.

MAIER, J., *Die Texte vom Toten Meer*, I-II. München, Basel 1960.

——, *Die Qumran-Essener. Die Texte vom Toten Meer*, I-II. München -Basel 1995.

MARCUS, R., "Mebaqqer and *Rabbim* in the Manual of Discipline vi.11-13." *JBL* 75 (1956), 298-302.

MARTIN, M., *The Scribal Character of the Dead Sea Scrolls*, I-II. Louvain 1958.

METSO, S., "The Primary Results of the Reconstruction of 4QS$^e$." *JJS* 44 (1993), 303-308.

——, "The Use of Old Testament Quotations in the Qumran Community Rule." *Qumran Between the Old and the New Testament*, eds. N.P. Lemche and T.L. Thompson. Copenhagen International Seminar. Sheffield Academic Press [forthcoming].

——, "The Textual Traditions of the Qumran Community Rule." *Legal Texts and Legal Issues: Second Meeting of the IOQS, Cambridge 1995*, eds. M.J. Bernstein and J. Campen [forthcoming].

——, "In Search of the *Sitz im Leben* of the Community Rule," *Proceedings of the 1996 International DSS Conference, 15-17 July, 1996, Provo, Utah*, eds. D. Parry and E. Ulrich [forthcoming].

MILIK, J.T., "Manuale Disciplinae." *VD* 29 (1951), 129-158.

——, "Le travail d'édition des fragments manuscrits de Qumran." *RB* 63 (1956), 60-62.

——, *Dix ans de découvertes dans le Désert de Juda.* Paris 1957.

——, *Ten Years of Discovery in the Wilderness of Judaea.* Transl. by J. Strugnell (Dix ans de découvertes dans le Désert de Juda. Paris 1957). SBT 26. London 1959.

——, "Texte des variantes des dix manuscrits de la Règle de la Communauté trouves dans la Grotte 4. Recension de P.Wernberg-Moeller, The Manual of Discipline." *RB* 67 (1960), 410-416.

——, "Milkî-ṣedeq et Milkî-reša dans les anciens écrits juifs et chrétiens." *JJS* 22 (1972), 95-144.

——, *The Books of Enoch. Aramaic Fragments of Qumran Cave 4.* Oxford 1976.

——, "Numérotation des feuilles des rouleaux dans le scriptorium de Qumran (Planches X et XI)." *Sem* 27 (1977), 75-81.

MURPHY-O'CONNOR, J., "La genèse littéraire de la Règle de la Communauté." *RB* 76 (1969), 528-549.

——, "Recension: G.Klinzing, Die Umdeutung des Kultus in der Qumrangemeinde und im Neuen Testament." *RB* 79 (1972), 435-440.

——, "The Judaean Desert." *Early Judaism and Its Modern Interpreters*, eds. R.A. Kraft and G.W.E. Nickelsburg. Atlanta, Georgia 1986, 119-156.

NÖTSCHER, F., "Heiligkeit in den Qumranschriften." *RevQ* 2 (1960), 315-344.

VON DER OSTEN-SACKEN, P., *Gott und Belial. Traditionsgeschichtliche Untersuchungen zum Dualismus in den Texten aus Qumran.* SUNT 6. Göttingen 1969.

PARISIUS, L., "Studie zur Form des 1. Abschnitts des DSD und zu Brownlees Ergänzungen zur Zeile 1 und 2." *ZAW* 67 (1955), 103-106.

VAN DER PLOEG, J., "Le 'Manuel de Discipline' des rouleaux de la Mer Morte." *BO* 8 (1951), 113-126.

POUILLY, J., *La Règle de la Communauté. Son evolution littéraire.* Cahiers de la Revue Biblique 17. Paris 1976.

PRIEST, J.F., "Mebaqqer, Paqid, and the Messiah." *JBL* 81 (1962), 55-61.

PUECH, E., "Recension: J. Pouillly, La Règle de la Communauté de Qumran. Son evolution littéraire." *RevQ* 10 (1979), 103-111.
——, "Remarques sur l'écriture de 1QS VII-VIII." *RevQ* 10 (1979), 35-43.
——, *La croyance des Esséniens en la vie Future: Immortalité, résurrection, vie éternelle? Histoire d'une croyance dans le judaïsme ancien.* Vol. II: Les donnés qumraniennes et classiques. Paris 1993.
QIMRON, E., "The Need for a Comprehensive Critical Edition of the Dead Sea Scrolls." *Archaeology and History in the Dead Sea Scrolls. The New York University Conference in Memory of Yigael Yadin.* JSPSup 8. Sheffield 1990, 121-131.
——, "Manuscript D of the Rule of the Community from Qumran Cave IV: Preliminary Publication of Columns 7-8" (Hebr.). *Tarbiz* 60 (1991), 434-443.
RABINOWITZ, I., "Sequence and Dates of the Extra-Biblical Dead Sea Scrolls Texts and 'Damascus' Fragments." *VT* 3 (1953), 175-185.
REICKE, B., *Handskrifterna fran Qumran (eller 'Ain Feshcha) I-IV.* SymBU 14. Uppsala 1952.
SANDERS, E.P., *Paul and Palestinian Judaism. A Comparison of Patterns of Religion.* London 1977.
SCHIFFMAN, L.H., *The Halakhah at Qumran.* SJLA 16. Leiden 1975.
——, *Sectarian Law in the Dead Sea Scrolls. Courts, Testimony and the Penal Code.* Brown Judaic Studies 33. Chico, California 1983.
SCHÜRER, E., *The History of the Jewish People in the Age of Jesus Christ (175 B.C. - A.D. 135).* A new English Version revised and edited by Geza Vermes, Fergus Millar, Martin Goodman. Vol. III, Part I. Edinburgh 1986.
STEGEMANN, H., "Zu Textbestand und Grundgedanken von 1QS III,13-IV,26." *RevQ* 13 (1988), 95-131.
——, "Das Gesetzeskorpus der 'Damaskusschrift' (CD IX-XVI)." *RevQ* 14 (1990), 409-434.
——, "Methods for the Reconstruction of Scrolls from Scattered Fragments." *Archaeology and History in the Dead Sea Scrolls. The New York University Conference in Memory of Yigael Yadin,* ed. L.H. Schiffman. JSP Supplement Series 8. Sheffield 1990, 189-220.
——, *Die Essener, Qumran, Johannes der Täufer und Jesus. Ein Sachbuch.* Freiburg, Basel, Wien 1993.
STEUDEL, A., *Der Midrasch zur Eschatologie aus der Qumrangemeinde (4QMidrEschat$^{a.b}$). Materielle Rekonstruktion, Textbestand, Gattung und traditionsgeschichtliche Einordnung des durch 4Q174 ("Florilegium") und 4Q177 (Catena$^a$) repräsentierten Werkes aus den Qumranfunden.* STDJ 13. Leiden, New York, Köln 1994.
STOLL, D., "Die Scriftrollen vom Toten Meer - mathematisch: oder Wie kann man einer Rekonstruktion Gestalt verleihen. Qumranstudien." *Vorträge und Beiträge auf dem internationalem Treffen der Society of Biblical Literature; Münster, 25.-26. Juli 1993,* hgg. H.-J. Fabry, A. Lange und H. Lichtenberger. Schriften des Institutum Judaicum Delitzschianum 4. Göttingen 1996, 205-218.
STRUGNELL, J., "Notes en marge du volume V des 'Discoveries in the Judaean Desert of Jordan'." *RevQ* 7 (1970), 163-276.
SUTCLIFFE, E.F., "The First fifteen Members of the Qumran Community. A Note on 1QS 8:1 ff." *JSS* 4 (1959), 134-138.
TALMON, S., "The Qumran יחד - a Biblical Noun." *The World of Qumran from within. Collected Studies.* Jerusalem, Leiden 1989, 53-60.
TOV, E., "The Orthography and Language of the Hebrew Scrolls Found at Qumran and the Origin of these Scrolls." *Textus* 13 (1986), 31-49.
——, "Letters of the Cryptic A Script and Paleo-Hebrew Letters Used as Scribal Marks in Some Qumran Scrolls." *DSD* 2 (1995), 330-339.
VERMES, G., *The Dead Sea Scrolls in English.* Harmondsworth 1962.
——, *The Dead Sea Scrolls in English.* London 1987³.
——, "Biblical Proof-Texts in Qumran Literature." *JSS* 34 (1989), 493-508.
——, "Preliminary Remarks on Unpublished Fragments of the Community Rule from Qumran Cave 4." *JJS* 42 (1991), 250-255.

WEINFELD, M., *The Organizational Pattern and the Penal Code of the Qumran Sect. A Comparison with Guilds and Religious Associations of the Hellenistic-Roman Period.* NTOA 2. Göttingen 1986.

——, "Sabbatical Year and Jubilee in the Pentateuchal Laws and their Ancient Near Eastern Background." *The Law in the Bible and in its Environment*, ed. T.Veijola. Publications of the Finnish Exegetical Society 51. Göttingen 1990.

WEISE, M., *Kultzeiten und kultischer Bundesschluss in der Ordensregel vom Toten Meer.* SPB 3. Leiden 1961.

WERNBERG-MOELLER, P., "Some Reflections on the Biblical Material in the Manual of Discipline." *ST* 9 (1956), 40-66.

——, *The Manual of Discipline Translated and Annotated with an Introduction.* STDJ 1. Leiden 1957.

——, "*Waw* and *Yod* in the Rule of the Community (1QS)." *RevQ* 2 (1960), 223-236.

——, "A Reconsideration of the Two Spirits in the Rule of the Community (I Q Serek III,13 - IV,26)." *RevQ* 3 (1961), 413-441.

——, "The Nature of the YAḤAD according to the Manual of Discipline and Related Documents." *ALUOS* 6 (1969). 56-81.

# INDEX OF ANCIENT SOURCES

## OLD TESTAMENT

# APPENDICES

## 1. Plates of Photographs

| | | |
|---|---|---|
| I | 4QS<sup>a</sup> (4Q255) | PAM 43.254 |
| II | 4QS<sup>b</sup> (4Q256) | PAM 43.250 |
| III | 4QS<sup>b</sup> (4Q256) | PAM 43.240 |
| IV | 4QS<sup>c</sup> (4Q257) | PAM 42.374 |
| V | 4QS<sup>c</sup> (4Q257) | PAM 43.256 |
| VI | 4QS<sup>d</sup> (4Q258) | PAM 43.244 |
| VII | 4QS<sup>d</sup> (4Q258) | PAM 43.246 |
| VIII | 4QS<sup>e</sup> (4Q259) | PAM 43.264 |
| IX | 4QS<sup>e</sup> (4Q259) | PAM 43.263 |
| X | 4QS<sup>e</sup> (4Q259) | PAM 43.283 |
| XI | 4QS<sup>f</sup> (4Q260) | PAM 43.265 |
| XII | 4QS<sup>g</sup> (4Q261) | PAM 43.266 |
| XIII | 4QS<sup>h</sup> (4Q262) | PAM 43.267 |
| | 4QS<sup>i</sup> (4Q263) | |
| | 4QS<sup>j</sup> (4Q264) | |

## 2. Charts of Reconstructions

A. Material Reconstruction of 4QS$^c$

B. Material Reconstruction of 4QS$^d$

C. Material Reconstruction of 4QS$^e$ - 4QOtot

D. Material Reconstruction of 4QS$^f$

PLATES

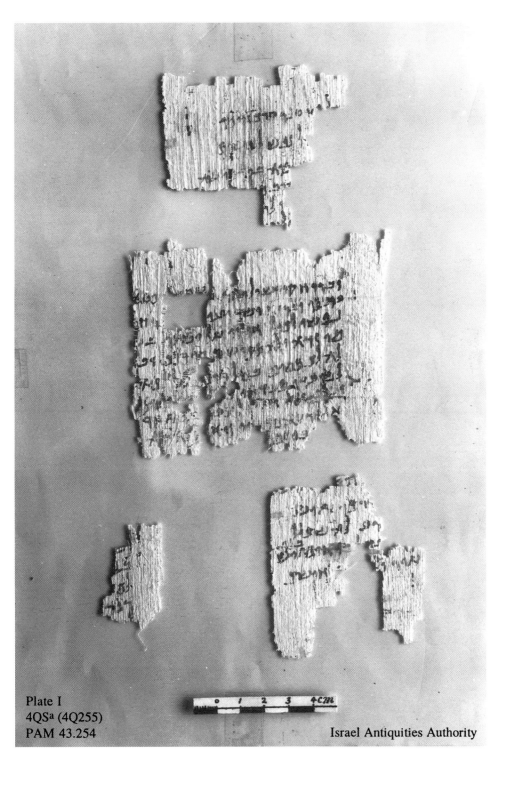

Plate I
4QS<sup>a</sup> (4Q255)
PAM 43.254

Israel Antiquities Authority

Plate II
4QS^b (4Q256)
PAM 43.250

Israel Antiquities Authority

Plate III
4QSᵇ (4Q256)
PAM 43.240

Israel Antiquities Authority

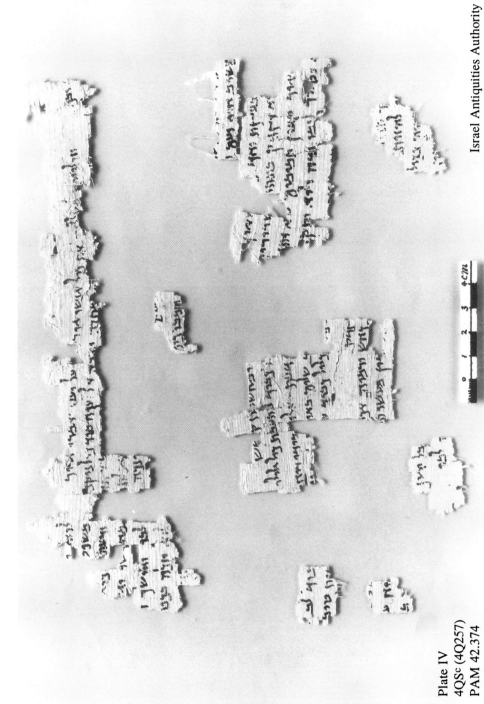

Plate IV
4QSᶜ (4Q257)
PAM 42.374

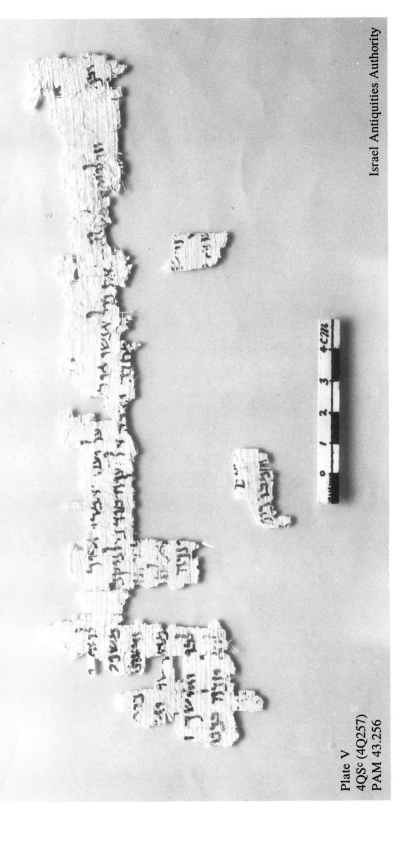

Plate V
4QSᶜ (4Q257)
PAM 43.256

Israel Antiquities Authority

Plate VI
4QS<sup>d</sup> (4Q258)
PAM 43.244

Israel Antiquities Authority

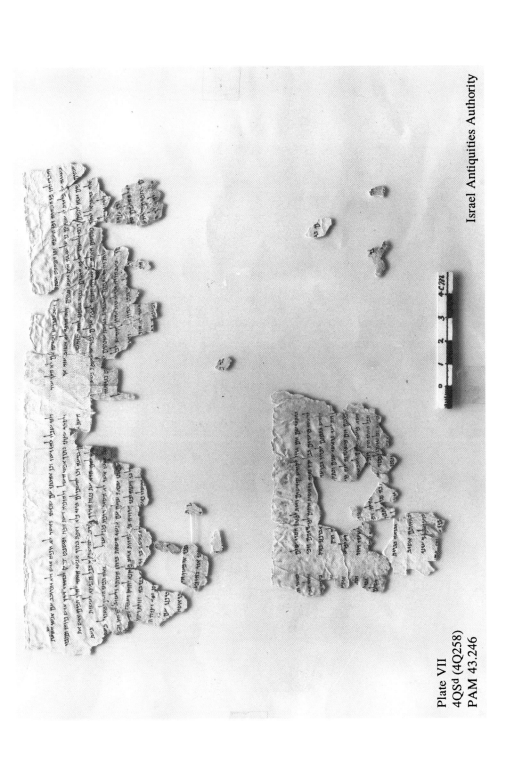

Plate VII
4QS<sup>d</sup> (4Q258)
PAM 43.246

Plate IX
4QSᵉ (4Q259)
PAM 43.263

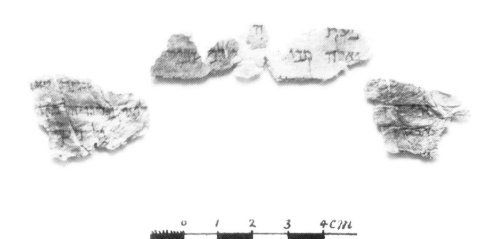

Plate X
4QSᵉ (4Q259)
PAM 43.283

Israel Antiquities Authority

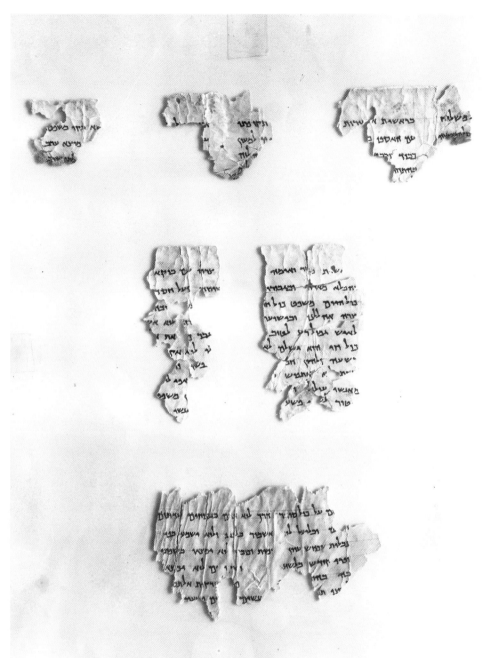

Plate XI
4QS^f (4Q260)
PAM 43.265

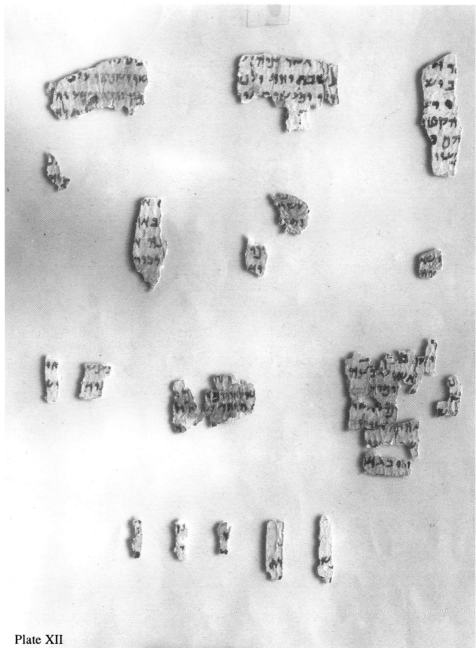

Plate XII
4QSg (4Q261)
PAM 43.266

Israel Antiquities Authority

Plate XIII
4QS<sup>h</sup>, 4QS<sup>i</sup>, 4QS<sup>j</sup>
(4Q262, 4Q263, 4Q264)
PAM 43.267

Israel Antiquities Authority

# STUDIES ON THE TEXTS
# OF THE DESERT OF JUDAH

1. WERNBERG MØLLER, P. *The Manual of Discipline*. Translated and Annotated, with an Introduction. 1957. ISBN 90 04 02195 7
2. PLOEG, J. VAN DER. *Le rouleau de la guerre*. Traduit et annoté, avec une introduction. 1959. ISBN 90 04 02196 5
3. MANSOOR, M. *The Thanksgiving Hymns*. Translated and Annotated with an Introduction. 1961. ISBN 90 04 02197 3
5. KOFFMANN, E. *Die Doppelurkunden aus der Wüste Juda*. Recht und Praxis der jüdischen Papyri des 1. und 2. Jahrhunderts n. Chr. samt Übertragung der Texte und Deutscher Übersetzung. 1968. ISBN 90 04 03148 0
6. KUTSCHER, E.Y. *The Language and Linguistic Background of the Isaiah Scroll (1 QIsa$^a$)*. Transl. from the first (1959) Hebrew ed. With an obituary by H.B. ROSÉN. 1974. ISBN 90 04 04019 6
6a. KUTSCHER, E.Y. *The Language and Linguistic Background of the Isaiah Scroll (1 QIsa$^a$)*. Indices and Corrections by E. QIMRON. Introduction by S. MORAG. 1979. ISBN 90 04 05974 1
7. JONGELING, B. *A Classified Bibliography of the Finds in the Desert of Judah, 1958-1969*. 1971. ISBN 90 04 02200 7
8. MERRILL, E.H. *Qumran and Predestination*. A Theological Study of the Thanksgiving Hymns. 1975. ISBN 90 04 042652
9. GARCÍA MARTÍNEZ, F. *Qumran and Apocalyptic*. Studies on the Aramaic Texts from Qumran. 1992. ISBN 90 04 09586 1
10. DIMANT, D. & U. RAPPAPORT (eds.). *The Dead Sea Scrolls*. Forty Years of research. 1992. ISBN 90 04 09679 5
11. TREBOLLE BARRERA, J. & L. VEGAS MONTANER (eds.). *The Madrid Qumran Congress*. Proceedings of the International Congress on the Dead Sea Scrolls, Madrid 18-21 March 1991. 2 vols. 1993. ISBN 90 04 09771 6 *set*
12. NITZAN, B. *Qumran Prayer and Religious Poetry* 1994. ISBN 90 04 09658 2
13. STEUDEL, A. *Der Midrasch zur Eschatologie aus der Qumrangemeinde (4QMidrEschat$^{a,b}$)*. Materielle Rekonstruktion, Textbestand, Gattung und traditionsgeschichtliche Einordnung des durch 4Q174 („Florilegium") und 4Q177 („Catena A") repräsentierten Werkes aus den Qumranfunden. 1994. ISBN 90 04 09763 5
14. SWANSON, D.D. *The Temple Scroll and the Bible*. The Methodology of 11QT. ISBN 90 04 09849 6
15. BROOKE, G.J. (ed.). *New Qumran Texts and Studies*. Proceedings of the First Meeting of the International Organization for Qumran Studies, Paris 1992. With F. García Martínez. 1994. ISBN 90 04 10093 8
16. DIMANT, D. & L.H. SCHIFFMAN. *Time to Prepare the Way in the Wilderness*. Papers on the Qumran Scrolls by Fellows of the Institute for Advanced Studies of the Hebrew University, Jerusalem, 1989-1990. 1995. ISBN 90 04 10225 6
17. FLINT, P.W. *The Dead Sea Psalms Scrolls and the Book of Psalms*. 1995. ISBN 90 04 10341 4

18. LANGE, A. *Weisheit und Prädestination*. Weisheitliche Urordnung und Prädestination in den Textfunden von Qumran. 1995. ISBN 90 04 10432 1
19. GARCÍA MARTÍNEZ, F. & D.W. PARRY. *A Bibliography of the Finds in the Desert of Judah 1970-95*. Arranged by Author with Citation and Subject Indexes. 1996. ISBN 90 04 10588 3
20. PARRY, D.W. & S.D. RICKS (eds.). *Current Research and Technological Developments on the Dead Sea Scrolls*. Conference on the Texts from the Judean Desert, Jerusalem, 30 April 1995. 1996. ISBN 90 04 10662 6
21. METSO, S. *The Textual Development of the Qumran Community Rule*. 1997. ISBN 90 04 10683 9

BM 488 .M3 M48 1997

Metso, Sarianna.

The textual development of
the Qumran Community rule